OUTBACK NEVADA

JOHN M. GLIONNA

OUTBACK NEVADA

Real Stories from the Silver State

UNIVERSITY OF NEVADA PRESS | *Reno & Las Vegas*

University of Nevada Press | Reno, Nevada 89557 USA
www.unpress.nevada.edu
Copyright © 2022 by John M. Glionna
All rights reserved
Cover photographs © Randi Lynn Beach, except for "Flash and Mr. Cool" © David Becker
Book design by Jinni Fontana

Library of Congress Cataloging-in-Publication Data
Names: Glionna, John M., author.
Title: Outback Nevada : real stories from the Silver State / John M. Glionna.
Description: Reno ; Las Vegas : University of Nevada Press, [2022]
Identifiers: LCCN 2021041565| ISBN 9781647790448 (paperback) | ISBN 9781647790455 (ebook)
Subjects: LCSH: Nevada—Description and travel. | Nevada—Social life and customs—21st century. |
Nevada—Social life and customs—20th century.
Classification: LCC F841 .G685 2022 | DDC 917.93—dc23
LC record available at https://lccn.loc.gov/2021041565

The paper used in this book meets the requirements of American National Standard for Information
Sciences—Permanence of Paper for Printed Library Materials, ANSI/NISO 39.48-1992 (R2002).

First Printing

Manufactured in the United States of America

*This book is dedicated to all those people
who go their own way.*

CONTENTS

The East

The West

ACKNOWLEDGMENTS

The collected stories in this book were a decade in the making and written for various publications, so there are a lot of people to thank—all of them top-of-the-line professionals whose guidance and generosity helped make this all happen.

First, at the *Los Angeles Times,* where I worked as a staff reporter for 26 years, I'd like to thank longtime editor Steve Padilla, who quickly got to know my writer's voice (literally) because for years he listened patiently as I read my stories aloud to him over the phone. When I was done, before making his cogent and pithy suggestions, he would often pause and say, "Read it again." A gift from the editing gods, that one.

At the *Las Vegas Review-Journal,* where I have been a freelance contributor since 2016, my guardian angel has been editor Marian Green, always a quiet, supportive presence with a wild imagination, who knows a good story when she sees one. We began as colleagues but quickly became friends.

At Southern Nevada's *Desert Companion* magazine, it has always been the dynamic duo of editors Andrew Kiraly and Scott Dickensheets. Both have been decidedly open to even the most off-based stories I have pitched their way. Andrew is hipster-smart, and Scott is the name you want to hear when you're told who's going to edit your story. Scott has since moved on to another publication, but I hope my relationship with both of these mentors continues for years to come.

But good stories take more than good editing; the work requires good visual storytelling, and nobody does it better than Randi Lynn Beach. For years, over numerous publications, Randi and I have teamed up to kick ass first and get the names later. She's funny and generous and kooky, but a woman-to-be-reckoned-with when she raises that camera to her eye. We're a team, Randi and I. And this book would not have been possible without her.

I have also worked with freelance photographer David Becker, probably the most fearless photojournalist I've had the pleasure to know. On any story, David is indefatigable, works dawn until dusk, and then late into the night. He's quiet, driven and never fails to get the job done. And more. He keeps me on my toes.

And a big shout-out to my buddy Ed Komenda, an old soul inhabiting a young writer's body. For years, Ed has kept me honest, breaking down the writing, helping me choose which words and phrases work, and which I must part with.

And hearty thanks to Kyle Roerink, a journalist-turned-environmental-activist who knows rural Nevada as well as anyone and has led me to good stories, like a horse to water, and drink I did.

I would also like to recognize two supportive voices from the book-publishing world: Clark Whitehorn formerly of the University of Nevada Press first encouraged this book; and Margaret Dalrymple, who has spent months helping me hone my ideas into publishable form.

I'd also like to thank my parents, John and Jean Glionna, who fostered my love of words and adventure. And to my wife, Lily, who each and every day provides the biggest adventure of them all.

Many people—mostly tourists, but also urban Nevadans—seem bewildered by the concept of taking that unheralded drive between Las Vegas and Reno, or exploring any of the state's hinterlands, like it was some crazy rocket launch into the void of outer space.

"What's out there?" they ask. "Just a bunch of nothingness?" The question has always baffled me. "It's not nothingness," I say. "But something-ness." Because out there is where the real Nevada lies.

Whenever I grow weary of the noise of my Las Vegas life, when my suburban neighbors begin to grate and I itch for infinite vistas and endless two-lane straightaways, I point my car north, toward Nevada's untamed outback. Toward Beatty and Goldfield, Tonopah, Pioche and the Big Smoky Valley, Austin, Middlegate Station and Gerlach, Carvers, Jackpot and countless points in between.

I drive when I want to see wild mustangs and burros graze on the leather-colored landscape just off the highway tarmac. I drive when I want to gaze up at night skies so profoundly black I can see the glowing Milky Way and imagine just how far away heaven might be. I drive when I want to follow the swirling dust clouds kicked up by a country boy in a pickup truck, gleefully barreling down some anonymous dirt road, carving out his own freewheeling rite of passage, a young man leaving a trail of smoke and grit to rival any jet engine, one that might be seen from the moon, for all I know.

When doing journalism or just for thrills, I drive when I want to see, hear and feel rural Nevada, the real Nevada, that country-hearted salve for my curious big-city soul.

■ ■ ■

I first launched my explorations into Nevada in 1994 as a reporter for the *Los Angeles Times*. I worked as a so-called "rover," a parachutist who dropped into places far outside city limits, on the lookout for hidden subcultures and offbeat tales.

On one of my first assignments, a profile of the controversial Yucca Mountain nuclear waste repository, one federal official sized up the bitter community resistance to the proposal. With most projects, he said, you have your NIMBYs—Not in My Backyard. "But when it came to nuclear waste, you had the NOPEs—Not on Planet Earth."

Nevada, I soon discovered, could be a land of scorching debate, with battles over such issues as horse-versus-cattle grazing rights and the preservation of such endangered species as the Mojave desert tortoise, Peregrine falcon and Lahontan cutthroat trout.

In 2012, I returned to Nevada full-time as a national correspondent. Early on, I asked my editor about the right mix of stories between big metropolises such as Vegas, Phoenix, Salt Lake City and Denver and the less-peopled high-desert wilderness. He said I'd figure that out, and I did: I preferred being somewhere out there. I put the city lights squarely in my rearview mirror whenever I could.

In 2015, I left the *Los Angeles Times* after 26 years, but remained in the Las Vegas suburb of Henderson to launch a freelance career. I wasn't done with Nevada, not by a long shot. I'd tell friends that while I could take or leave Las Vegas, the desert still beckoned. It kept me here. It rooted me.

I met with an editor at the *Las Vegas Review-Journal* and told him that while I believed his paper aggressively covered Las Vegas, its reporters rarely ventured out into state's wide-open spaces. I offered to wander Nevada's outback as a freelancer. And to my delight, he agreed.

I set out to tell real-life stories of hard-edged stubborn characters, both loners and fools, and chronicle small-town goings-on. For leads, I sought out judges, ranchers, shop owners and weekly newspaper editors, those shrewd tour guides to rural life.

Because the best ideas always come through word of mouth—somebody knows somebody else whose story will just plain amaze. Like the drug-user who got clean through Pahrump's supervisory drug court and then went on to run the program. Or the toolmaker in Tonopah who still fashioned mining implements on the same grease-blackened lathes and contraptions his grandfather once used. Or the ghost town innkeeper who barely suffered his guests. Or the two young mayors with personal résumés that would seem hard sells in the conservative hinterlands: They're both gay.

Out there, I soon learned, the people just seemed more genuine. Their politics are conservative, colored by a bit of leave-me-alone libertarianism and plainspoken country values. Residents tend to favor less government and more freedom to live unfettered—to take their guns to church and their God into the voting booth.

They live in enclaves with far-fetched names derived from the state's history of mining and railroad development, where pioneers pounded wooden stakes with speculative place-names that somehow stuck. Many withered into ghost towns, with the stories behind those names sometimes now resembling more fiction than fact.

Drive across Nevada and you'll pass through towns named Jiggs, Puckerbrush, Gabbs, Scotty's Junction, Carp and Duckwater. Or how about Fatty Martin Lake, Toe Jam Mountain and Winnemucca, named after a Native American warrior and chief.

There's Stagecoach, Steamboat Hot Springs, Lovelock, Deeth (rhymes with teeth), Tunnel, Sulphur and Slim Creek. And don't forget the old mining town known as Dinner Table, or Adaven, which is Nevada spelled backward.

There are place-names borrowed from Native American tongues, such as the Paiute, Goshute, Mojave, Shoshone and Washoe. There's the town of Jarbidge, which allegedly means "devil" in Shoshone. The phrase "Pah," which means water in Paiute, appears in Pahrump, Tonopah and Mizpah.

Jeff Kintop, chairman of the Nevada State Board on Geographic Names, told me about the town of Beowawe, where a railroad speculator once scouted out prospective towns. "He supposedly weighed over 300 pounds," he said. After watching the outsider hammer in spikes, the Paiutes coined the name Beowawe. Said Kintop: "It means Great Posterior."

In many small towns, folks follow a frank rural credo: They don't care what you do, as long as they know you're doing it. As a rule, they get up before the rest of us, because there are endless chores—cows to milk, cattle to feed, small shops to run, horses to hay—and they go to bed earlier too, to rest up for the day ahead. In between, they savor the smaller moments of their isolated lives, meeting for coffee at the local diner or delving into that greasy daily special of chicken fried steak.

In many regards, Nevada's rural residents are a collection of contradictions. They're scattered among gossipy small towns and far-off ranches, but they form communities nonetheless. They're folks such as Jay Gunter who, when I profiled him in 2016, wore many hats in Nevada's sparsely settled high desert. He was a veteran funeral director, justice of the peace, volunteer firefighter and deputy registrar. Not only that, he was also Esmeralda County's deputy coroner, whose sleek white hearse responded day and night to death calls across hundreds of miles of high desert. When his phone rang, for whatever reason, Gunter just went.

There's wild-horse activist Laura Leigh, a tough-talking New Jersey native with long red hair, who dresses in cowboy boots and a tattered denim Carhartt jacket, a woman who speaks in a *Sopranos* accent but whose mission is decidedly Western. Driving her Ford F-250 with its chassis jacked up so high she must often tumble down from the driver's seat, she wanders the outback, contesting the federal Bureau of Land Management's removal of the wild mustangs from the Western range. Binoculars in hand, she observes roundups, takes telling photographs and files lawsuits, all to help protect the wild animals whose indomitable spirit she has come to cherish.

There's Serbian-born Victor Antic, who in 2016 took a hardline stand at Austin's International Cafe & Bar, plastering political placards outside his historic Civil War-era building in the heart of town. Antic's restaurant has become the unofficial and unapologetic rustic headquarters for all things Donald Trump. While locals might agree with his stand, many tourists who roll through town along U.S. Highway 50 choose to drive another 100 miles rather than support Antic's positions. And the owner offers them a throaty farewell from his café window. When we met, he sized me up and said, "What are you, some kind of liberal?"

Two hundred miles away, in the isolated Fish Lake Valley, Val Trucksa and Nancy Knighten are two advanced EMTs covering 3,500 square miles in Esmeralda County, whose population density is the nation's second lowest, equal to the lonely Australian Outback. At 69 and 73, the two said they were proud they've never lost a patient during their medical dashes to the nearest hospital, across the state line in California. When I interviewed them in 2017, the pair wanted to retire. But in a rural Nevada the young are deserting, they can't find replacements. "What will they do when we're not here," Trucksa lamented. "And there will be a time, and soon, when we're gone."

■ ■ ■

You need patience, strong coffee and a couple of tanks of gas to cover the entire length of Nevada, say, from Laughlin in the far south to the border town of Jackpot in the north. It's not the West's longest state drive, but definitely one of its most dramatic.

The name Nevada derives from the Spanish word *nieve*, for "snow-covered," a reference to the powdery peaks of the eastern Sierra. It's America's most mountainous state, its ranges running north to south, like knuckles, or backbones.

Driving the state's major north-south arteries, U.S. Routes 93 and 95, takes you through vast valleys of sagebrush and creosote bushes, Joshua trees and Mojave poppy wildflowers, all flanked by prodigious mountain peaks on either side. It's only when you travel along latitudinal U.S. Highways 50 and 6 do these ranges take you on their heady rollercoaster ride of elevation rise and fall. Tens of thousands of miles of paved roads (and countless more unpaved ones) cross a state that ranks as the nation's seventh largest in landmass, yet is among America's least-populated places. More than 80 percent of its three million residents live clustered around Las Vegas or Reno.

Why? Water, or the lack of it.

Nevada is America's most arid state, and that absence of water—and the fact that 80 percent of the land is managed by the federal government—has kept the rural population low, allowing the landscape to remain primeval and wild. Most of its outlanders—farmers, ranchers and townspeople—have settled near water, leaving the rest to four-legged inhabitants, including wolves, coyotes, foxes and mountain lions.

And those Nevada vistas can be breathtaking. One sunny winter morning in 2012, I drove west over the Spring Mountains and began the descent into the sprawling Pahrump Valley. I had just returned from four years in Asia and was dumbstruck at the raw beauty and sheer scope of the high desert terrain looming outside my windshield. I called my father, another aficionado of all things Western, including the novels of Louis L'Amour, and waxed about the spectacle that lay before my eyes. We hail from Upstate New York and just aren't used to vistas like this.

"Dad," I said. "The land, it just goes on forever!"

Still, for some reason, Nevada gets overshadowed by its yellow-haired sister to the west. California, the so-called "Golden State," gets all the historical buzz for its 1848 gold rush, while Nevada, with its Comstock Lode, a massive deposit that gave the 36th state its identity as the "Silver State," has, to my mind, often been relegated to a less-precious metal, as though awarded the second-place prize.

But those mines also gave Nevada its quirky, colorful history. The discovery of an active vein meant an influx of fortune seekers, men who labored below ground and spent their earnings freely. Towns sprang up from nothing, with names such as Rhyolite, Berlin and Gold Point, many replete with opera houses, bars, hotels, newspapers, courthouses to try lawbreakers and jails to house them, and, of course, brothels. Then when the mineral veins died, so did the towns, in many cases receding back to dirt and dust from which they came.

Mining remains a large part of rural economy. Today, Nevada produces more gold than any other U.S. state, including California.

And Nevada's frontier culture also holds up against California or any other Western state as a place that teemed with pioneers-turned-national celebrities. A young Jack Dempsey worked as a bartender and bouncer at the Mizpah Hotel in Tonopah, a gritty mining town where lawman Wyatt Earp once wore a badge. Samuel Clemens took the pen name "Mark Twain" while working for Virginia City's *Territorial Enterprise*.

Reno tailor Jacob W. Davis created the first denim jeans, the durable apparel that later outfitted miners, cowboys, lawmen and desperados across the American West. U.S. Highway 50 still follows the trail of the old Pony Express. In the early 1900s, the ornate Goldfield Hotel featured the only elevator west of the Mississippi River, its 154 rooms each containing a telephone, electric lights and heating—luxury that matched the main boulevards of Manhattan.

But rural Nevada is more than just long-shuttered grand hotels, ghost towns and museums to the past. People continue to scratch out a living here, with grit and humor, in places such as Dyer, in the agricultural Fish Lake Valley. One bar is The Boonies. A T-shirt sold there reads, "Where the hell is Dyer?" Another features a telling mileage sign: "End of the World: 9 mi. Dyer, Nev.: 12 mi."

Ralph Keyes, an alfalfa farmer and county commissioner, says living in rural Nevada takes common sense. "You have to have a hardy pioneering spirit," Keyes told me in 2017. "If you want street lights and curbs, stay in the city." He relishes every day spent in this blissful middle-of-nowhere and described his life with plainspoken images, like a rural poet.

"This morning, I was up at 4 a.m. I rode an open tractor and watched the sun rise. I smelled the hay and watched the coyotes trot out of the fields, with the cool air and sun on my face." He paused. "Just being part of that keeps me here. The smells, the sights, the taste of dirt in your mouth."

■ ■ ■

That's one reason I drive into Nevada's outback; out there, I can taste dirt in my mouth and get sand between my teeth.

Driving north from Las Vegas along U.S. Route 95, I don't feel I've really entered the outback until I'm well north of Indian Springs, when four-lanes narrow to two, at the turnoff toward mysterious Mercury and its tall tales of green men and secret government programs. Only then does my mind get right, do I stretch my emotional legs and begin to unwind. I see dirt roads that jettison from the blacktop, exploding like laser beams toward the far horizon, and fight the urge to drive every one of them.

During my countless trips out there, I've hiked atop Big Dune, the rippling waves of sand crossing the Amargosa Valley, and crawled deep into old mining shafts with a pair of modern prospectors, in search of—not gold or silver—but the abandoned denim bibs and trousers now worth a fortune.

I've sat at the tiny bar in the Happy Burro in Beatty, clutching a $2 bottle of beer and a bowl of the spicy house chili, and later stood outside with two native residents as they pointed at a sandstone mountain that towers over town, admiring it like it was one of the French Alps, saying, "This is why we live here."

In Tonopah, a town situated atop Nevada's Mason-Dixon Line, that separates north from south, I've drank morning coffee with a circuit judge in the Mizpah Hotel, after a night of quaffing craft beers with a horse activist at the brewery across the street. Rural Nevada, it seems, always seems to throw you a surprise: One of the state's best used-book stores is on the Tonopah's main drag, and you can spot a lot of cowboy hats perusing the aisles.

I've stepped into the general store in Dyer to revel in town gossip and attended Native American scholar Boyd Graham's class on spoken

Shoshone at White Pine High School in Ely. I've traveled with a retired Michigan cop to chronicle the long-ago graves of Nevada's early pioneers on the internet, to make sure history endures.

I've escorted two college-aged filmmakers on a tour of Nye County brothels, so they could talk to real working girls. I bought one of them his first bottle of beer at Miss Kathy's Short Branch Saloon in Crystal.

I've written about dreamers such as Kim Bozarth, who built a modern home in the Big Smoky Valley out of bales of straw, and walked the ruins of artist Frank Van Zant's rough-hewn 1960s paean to the Native American spirit, a Burning Man-like revelation envisioned long before that festival found a home in Nevada's high desert.

Still, there are always new stories to tell out there. They're not death knells for the rural life, but stories of ongoing life and enduring culture—from battles over water rights to celebrations of cowboy poets, fiddle-playing ranchers and the spoken word.

Whenever I hit the road, I leave behind big-city traffic and crime like a good hunting dog shakes water from its coat. And as soon as I return, I'm already anxiously anticipating my next adventure into that peerless panorama of somethingness.

In the meantime, I think of that teenager behind the wheel of his pickup, kicking up some backroad dust, as if to remind the world that he's out there, and that farmer-poet perched atop his open-air tractor at dawn, the wind and the sun on his face. They're celebrating the dirt in their mouths, both feeling very much alive.

— Henderson, December 2019

The North

Michael "Flash" Hopkins holds a photo of his late friend and fellow radio deejay Tommy Cash Cosman. Photo by David Becker.

Flash and Mr. Cool

■ **Gerlach, September 2019.** Most days, they were on the radio waves as the town woke up: Flash and Mr. Cool, Gerlach's morning duo for traffic, weather and, well, whatever else they wanted to talk about.

Michael Hopkins and Tommy Cash Cosman broadcast from the defunct Gerlach Hotel, a ramshackle hulk with dim lighting, leaky pipes and no heat or AC. They were the familiar voices of KLAP Radio, "89.5 on your FM dial, the Fine 89," exhorting listeners to tune in to a signal that beamed 50 miles out of town. Their whimsical on-air routine was a perfect fit for this high-desert hamlet north of Reno, population 36, home to an oddball cast of recalcitrant ranchers, miners, retirees and other big-city refugees, a place one resident described as "living among 100 angry cousins."

Their repartee was unrehearsed and wholly unpredictable.

"OK, now it's time for the traffic report," Hopkins started. "Mr. Cool?"

"Well, I can see there's a dog crossing the road," Cosman responded. "That's all the traffic for today."

The daily weather report was no less deadpan.

"Let's turn to our chief meteorologist, Mr. Cool."

"It's hot."

"Tommy, it's the middle of winter."

"Well, then it's cold. Cold as hell. Even colder."

Hopkins, now 68, was a pioneering San Francisco artist who co-founded the infamous Burning Man festival, held each summer just outside Gerlach. With his wild-hazel eyes, New England accent and exploding shock of white hair, he knew all about wacky free spirits and high-flying kites.

Cosman, in his early 60s, was a mercurial, disheveled man with thick glasses and a scruffy beard who worshiped the San Francisco Giants. He was the emotional pulse for the Fine 89. And he was intellectually disabled.

Around Gerlach, he was an impish town crier, everybody's pest of a little brother, who made his daily rounds to heckle passersby, tell a naughty joke or call people names, before moving on in search of his next audience.

Not everyone had the everyday patience to deal with Cosman, but most folks celebrated his eccentricities. "He was goofy and innocent and often annoying," said bar owner Lacey Holle. "He was just Tommy," a man who reminded the townspeople of Gerlach that it was OK to be different.

"Tommy changed this town because he defied everything you thought you knew about the disabled," said Brooke Covey, who used to invite Cosman for dinner and TV. "He was a comedian. He loved my fried chicken, but he'd always say, 'This is awful, just terrible.' That meant he was loving every bite."

■ ■ ■

A crazy sense of misadventure brought Michael Hopkins from his Rhode Island home to San Francisco in 1978. He plunged into the counterculture scene, worked as a bike messenger and repo man before opening a punk-rock club called the Farm.

In 1986, he joined a group of artists that launched the first Burning Man festival, huddling around a ritualistic bonfire on San Francisco's Baker Beach to mark the summer solstice. Eventually, he earned his nickname "Flash" as the intellectual visionary who fueled many of the zany creations birthed by the avant-garde festival.

In 1990, he helped move the Burning Man party to a dust-choked stretch of land outside Gerlach known as the Playa, and remains an integral part of the madness.

For years, Hopkins lived in Gerlach part time, helping run a few bars, serving as the president of the Chamber of Commerce for a year, doing what he could to convince ranchers and cowboys to accept the flaky new California crowd.

But the miners and cowboys never could comprehend the madcap violence favored by the Burner crowd, how Hopkins and his pals took their adrenaline-fueled trips into the high desert to play pickup-truck polo and another twisted game where they put a car in drive with remote control and hunted it down with an AK-47.

One year, Hopkins parked his trailer alongside the long-shuttered Gerlach Hotel. That's when he got to know the owner-resident, a woman named Lola Sweet, a say-anything barfly and town roustabout, who cared for her son, Tommy Cosman.

Like Hopkins, Sweet reveled in the outrageous. As a younger woman, she was a professional tag-team wrestler with her sister Helen, performing on the East Coast circuit under the name Boobs LaRue. Born in Long Beach, California, Sweet settled in Gerlach in the 1960s, when Tommy was a child. Somehow, she ended up running the Gerlach Hotel.

At first, Tommy attended school in Gerlach, and then Reno, before Sweet took him back for years of homeschooling. She'd always insisted that reading, or even writing his name, was beyond him. Keeping her son in his place, some say, allowed her to keep collecting his monthly disability checks. Hopkins quickly saw how Sweet undermined her son. "Lola was a broad," Hopkins said. "She was into cocktails. She wasn't meant to be a mother."

Everything changed when Sweet died in 2012, at 83. "She finally decided she'd had enough," Hopkins said. "She just went to sleep. Lola died from a hard life."

For Cosman, his mother's death was like a release from prison, allowing him to strike out on his own. A savant with an encyclopedic knowledge of music, he pored over the covers of his 2,000-album record collection and often beat friends at Trivial Pursuit, always ready with a witty reply. With Sweet gone, he began volunteering at the senior center and helping out at the Miners Club. He also began his epic daily rounds to insult people, with barbs modeled after his comedic hero, Don Rickles. But folks worried about Cosman, who was often left without supervision at the old hotel. So they stepped up.

Women cooked him meals, took him to the doctor, barber and dentist, clipped his fingernails and toenails. When she was younger, Diana Rios, whose mother babysat Cosman as a boy, used to block her bedroom door with a chalkboard so he couldn't bother her. Now she invited him home to play Yahtzee while she did his laundry.

But few did more than Hopkins, who petitioned the court to become Cosman's legal guardian, taught him how to shave, perfect his signature and keep a checking account. He took him on outings to see his beloved Giants, and made sure someone stayed with Cosman when he wasn't around. As part of the guardianship process, Hopkins took Cosman to a social worker, who asked, "What's wrong with Tommy?"

"He's mentally challenged," Hopkins said.

Then Cosman spoke up.

"No, I'm not," he said. "I'm retarded."

But Hopkins knew that Cosman was merely repeating the words his mother used to use. "Tommy didn't have many social skills," Hopkins said. "But the thing is, a lot of people in Gerlach don't have social skills. So, he fit right in."

Years ago, the local radio station owner was looking for a new home for KLAP Radio. And Hopkins jumped at the chance to house the station in the Gerlach Hotel. Gerlach's new radio duo interrupted the programmed music format anytime they wanted—to kibbutz, dissect the news or gossip about community goings-on.

That's when Cosman became Mr. Cool. He even printed up business cards to announce his new identity, especially for female listeners. Cosman had a soft spot for women. He'd phone his female friends. "Do you love me?" he'd say. "I love you." And then he'd hang up. "He never had a girlfriend," Hopkins said. "But he had every woman in town wrapped around his finger." Except his mother. He never forgave Sweet, Hopkins said. "He'd say, 'Did you like my mom? I didn't. I'm glad she's gone,'" Hopkins said.

He always said the two would end up on opposite sides of heaven. And then one day, Tommy Cosman was gone, too. Last summer, Cosman died of a heart attack at age 63, leaving the town without its quirky radio star and public pest.

Gerlach held a potluck dinner at the Miners Club to celebrate Mr. Cool. People dressed up in his collection of Hawaiian shirts. Hopkins paid for an open bar. "This is for our Tommy. What the hell?" he told the crowd. "It's for all the drinks he never bought you." On a dry-erase board, friends posted pictures and scribbled things. "Yes, Tommy, I know you love me," one woman wrote. "I love you, too." Covey told how you could never watch movies with him because he drove you crazy with the fast-forward and rewind button on the disc player. "I miss his daily calls, how he made me laugh," Covey said. "I miss him."

Hopkins paid for Cosman's cremation and does what he can to keep his friend's spirit alive. One day, Hopkins saw John Farmer on the street and yelled, "Turkey Farmer! Turkey Farmer!" Just like Cosman used to do.Farmer smiled. You hear a taunt long enough, you start to miss it when it's gone.

A year after Cosman's death, Gerlach is still taking stock of its loss. Nearly every day, Cosman's name comes up during dart and pool matches at the Miners Club, at the post office, just about everywhere. At the senior center, the staff tells newcomers about the quirky volunteer who loved bingo but hated No. 13. Melanie McClenahan still telephones Cosman's closest friends. "I keep in contact with people I didn't know before, who I saw Tommy accepted so I accepted," she said. "He was some kind of oracle. He brought this community together."

Many here say Cosman left behind a personal legacy: a new way for residents to look at the disabled and be more accepting of one another. "This town is a pretty tough crowd," Hopkins said. "But Tommy taught them all about diversity. You could ask anybody here if he was disabled, and they'd say, 'No, he's smarter than us. He doesn't have to work.' Tommy detested work."

He also did something few others in town could do: He made a personal fantasy come true. "We all have our dreams," Hopkins said. "Tommy's was so simple, but he got to live it all. He was on the radio. He was Mr. Cool."

The Rural Nevada Football Team That Rarely Scores

■ **McDermitt, October 2018.** Every so often, football coach Richard Egan encounters a rare teaching moment to help shape his teenage players into more than just better athletes, but better young men.

One came last year when he brought his team to Eureka to play the hometown Vandals in their lush new stadium in central Nevada, a gleaming sports temple complete with a state-of-the-art weight room, field lighting and synthetic playing surface—all built by local mining money.

The McDermitt Bulldogs hail from a tiny town that straddles the Nevada-Oregon border. The McDermitt Combined School has 200 students in kindergarten through 12th grade. Most are Native Americans from the nearby Paiute Shoshone reservation. The lonely high-desert outpost bears its American Indian heritage with pride, but economic opportunities are few and far between in this town where the last working mine gave out decades ago—a place bereft of wealthy benefactors.

In Eureka, the Bulldogs stepped off a less-than-reliable yellow school bus pressed into service for the 12-hour round-trip drive. By late fall, its faulty heater turns the old vehicle into a mobile icebox, forcing players to huddle under blankets to keep warm. For their part, the Vandals are whisked to away games in the comfort of a sophisticated tour bus with their team insignia emblazoned on the side.

That day, the McDermitt boys marveled at a far more privileged world than the one they knew back home. At home, the state line runs through the school grounds, and its football field technically lies in Oregon, amid an isolated spread of dirt and sagebrush. A band of domestic horses grazes in the distance.

Folks around McDermitt are used to hardship. Originally named Dugout, the unincorporated town of 500 residents was established in the late 1800s to protect the stagecoach route from Virginia City to Idaho Territory. Even today, most everything here speaks to what remains of the stubborn and untended rustic American West.

The school's $60,000 annual sports budget is nearly consumed by

$38,000 in fees to bus players from all sports to distant away games, not to mention $12,000 for referees, leaving only $10,000 for everything else. So the football players make do with mostly hand-me-down equipment, with shoulder pads and tackling equipment donated by other schools. They only got new game uniforms two years ago because of an unexpected donation by a foundation run by the NFL's Washington football team.

The school's bleachers are decrepit. For years, there was little money to provide on-field services until the shop class built a humble restroom. This summer, locusts descended, turning the grass brown, forcing officials to work overtime to green up the field before the start of football season. The McDermitt kids know few luxuries compared with players in places like Eureka. For them, playing a Friday night home game under the lights remains as unimaginable as an unbeaten season, or two wins strung together.

Still, nobody moved.

That's where Egan stepped in. At 53, he's a Paiute Shoshone who stands 6-foot-1, sporting the big-man athletic build of a one-time ranch cowboy. He played on McDermitt's undefeated 1982 team that won the state championship. Back then, the Bulldogs were known as the "heavy hitters," and players spoke their native Paiute on the field to confuse opponents. Egan played quarterback, tight end, running back, even kicker—anything it took to win.

Decades later, in addition to his job as the school's groundskeeper, he coaches a team that resides among the cellar dwellers in Division 1A, the state's smallest league, where a handful of rural schools field only eight players a game rather than the traditional 11, and their season is a short six contests.

Many years, the Bulldogs fail to win a single game. This season, they're ranked at the very bottom of the 22-team league. With one game to go next Saturday, their record stands at 0-5, including one forfeit because the team didn't have enough players. They had been outscored 282-87, including an away-game 78-0 drubbing. Every Bulldog touchdown is celebrated like it's Christmas morning.

The losses don't come from a lack of trying. Each year, the tiny school struggles to field even a diminished team. In 2013, the Bulldogs canceled their season because they lacked enough players. This summer, a new principal gave Egan a four-week deadline to find enough kids to avoid yet another lost campaign. He eventually assembled nine boys: two freshman, a sophomore, two juniors and four seniors, but one senior and a sophomore are first-time players. There are two white kids, two Latinos and a Pacific Islander joining four Native Americans.

Long after his playing days, Egan—a grandfather of three—remains a proud Bulldog. That day in Eureka, he would not stand to see his team's heart broken by another kid's birthright. Under Egan's watch, there would be no more damage to these teenagers' fragile egos. And so he rallied them together, like a coach and like a father. Nothing rah-rah, just humble encouragement. "Sure, these kids are lucky to have everything they have here," he said of the Vandals. "But they can only put eight players on that field, just like us. So once we step off that bus, we represent our community, our school and our families. But mostly, we represent ourselves."

The Bulldogs lost that day, 64-12. Egan said they still came out winners.

The decision was final: Either Coach Egan fielded at least eight football players by Labor Day or his season was over. "We have other teams relying on us," principal Leslie Molina said. "We can't just cancel game after game. It's not right."

The previous spring, Egan had considered quitting—after too many seasons waiting for enough players to show up to even hold a practice. Then three cousins promised to play in the fall. That August, a few boys appeared but not enough to field a squad. One kid, a 320-pound player who would have finally given the Bulldogs' anemic front line a solid anchor, quit after just a few practices.

Two weeks before the deadline, the Bulldogs canceled a scrimmage against a nearby team because they didn't have enough players. "Both Richard and I sat here grinding our teeth," assistant football coach Jack Smith said. "We both had great high school careers. We're competitive people. But it's tough to be competitive when you can't even field a team."

So Egan went to work, just as he's done in the past. One year, he and his son raffled off a 42-inch TV on the reservation to raise money to help fund the basketball team.

The coach called players at home, stopped them in the hallways. Many said they didn't have the energy to play football. "I did approach kids a few times, maybe too many times," he said. "Some gave me the cold shoulder. So I left them alone. I knew that if they wanted to play, they'd come."

Transportation has always been a big problem. Some students live hours from the school, and their parents lack both the time and money to pick them up after practice. So coaches have volunteered to drive them home.

Finally, Egan got some good news: Several players from the distant Kings River Valley finished their seasonal after-school farm chores and were ready to join the team. A few other walk-ons brought his team up to nine players.

The 2018 football season was on.

The dramatic efforts resonate with Humboldt County School Superintendent Dave Jensen. "Even if these kids aren't winning games, they experience a camaraderie that transcends ethnic backgrounds," he said. "They're relying on each other." None of it would happen without Egan. "The only reason we still have a football team is because of Richard," said Tildon Smart, the Paiute Shoshone tribal chairman. "It's tough to coach with just eight kids, but he has the passion to hold everything and everyone together."

Three plays into the Bulldog's second game, running back Ben Draunidalo, one of the team's best players, badly sprained an ankle and hobbled back to the huddle. Egan called over his freshmen and said it was time they started playing like seniors. Draunidalo stayed in the game. "It wouldn't have been fair for me to get hurt and not be able to help these guys," he said.

Win or lose—and mostly lose—the Bulldogs stick together, despite the odds.

On a recent afternoon, they practiced on their home field, performing drills on a donated, taped-up tackling sled. It's just another way Egan and his team work with what they have. Without a junior varsity program, the kids never learn the basics until they're on the varsity team. Without enough players to scrimmage among themselves, their tackling skills need work.

Quarterback Jagger Hinkey, a 16-year-old who weighs 205 pounds, gets frustrated in many games. "We're too small," he said of a line with a 225-pound top weight. "As soon as the ball is snapped, the opposing linemen are on top of me."

Last year, even after suffering an anterior cruciate ligament (ACL) tear, Hinkey showed up at games and stood on the field to convince the referees the team had enough players to compete. And he protects his smaller guys, especially Daniel Gomez, a 15-year-old freshman who stands 5-foot-3 and weighs 93 pounds. Gomez wouldn't make most teams, but he remains an integral part of the Bulldogs. In one game this year, a 280-pound lineman from an opposing team lifted the tiny Gomez in the air and slammed him to the ground. The freshman popped back up and went on to score two touchdowns in the loss. After the play, Hinkey was in the big man's face, defending his little scoring threat.

At practice, Egan patted Gomez on the top of his helmet. "He's got a really big heart for such a little kid," he said.

Still, Egan has to teach them everything. Leave that sweaty uniform in your locker on a Saturday afternoon, he preaches, and it'll smell ripe by Monday morning. And there's no such thing as any three-strikes disciplinary rule. If a player pulls a "no-call, no-show" for practice, he's allowed back, because the team needs him.

Following the 78-0 loss, Egan gathered his team at midfield and spoke solemnly, like he always does, reminding them to keep their heads up, their pride intact.

Sometimes, though, the Bulldogs surprise even themselves. In their opening game against Pyramid Lake, they led 38-20 at halftime. Egan warned them about getting cocky; there was still another half to be played. They eventually lost 58-38.

Even if they go winless, these kids will never forget playing with the Bulldogs, just like their coach never has. "Thirty years from now, they'll tell their grandkids what they did," Egan said. "They're making memories they'll keep the rest of their lives."

On a recent day, the coach walked across the school's dusty, weed-strewn former playing field, the place where he spent his glory days, when the fans lined up to watch their Bulldogs win a state championship. Even if his young Bulldogs can never follow in his footsteps, Egan dreams of seeing them savor what he considers the very pinnacle of high school football. Playing at home on a frenetic Friday night. Under the lights. "Just to see the looks on their faces," he said. "Imagine that."

Cowboy Ministers

■ **Winnemucca, October 2021.** The minister has cowboy hands, palms rubbed raw by the lasso, knuckles bruised from horse kicks and angry bulls. They're the hands of a man who in 68 years has known solitude, hard work and his share of heartbreak.

At first glance, Bo Lowe seems more Black Bart than solemn Man of the Bible. He wears a buckeroo hat with its wide flattened brim, Western boots, black shirt and suspenders, a maroon wild rag around his neck. His face is ruddy and whiskered, his white mustache waxed on the ends like some barroom dandy.

All in all, he doesn't say much, this sermon-giving man of the cloth whose words usually come painfully slow, if at all. He arrives early at the indoor rodeo arena here, his pickup truck pulling a trailer loaded with all the accoutrements necessary to perform his Sunday morning cowboy service before a rural flock—the wire-thin ranch hands, horse riders and young women wearing cowboy hats and embroidered Levi jeans. He produces his brown-leather bound book of scriptures and faith brochures, which are laid out on colorful Western blankets. He unpacks the speakers he sets up in one corner of the viewing stands. There are wires to run, sound checks to perform with his supporting cast and their acoustic guitars.

The men, Smokey and Blaine, show him deference, checking with the boss before performing any chore. They know time is tight: They must perform their service and break down their equipment before the first rodeo event starts at 9 a.m. sharp.

But there's a problem. As the first of three-dozen service-goers fill the stands, the electrical system fails. The guitars cut in and out, the acoustics sputter. Even though the temperature outdoors is in the mid-30s, Lowe begins to sweat as the men fiddle with wires and knobs. "Testing, testing," he says, as his voice finally projects into the stands. "Yep, she's a workin' now. We got her goin' on."

Then, finally, all is set. Lowe faces his audience and pauses. Then, with perfect comedic timing, he draws a laugh when he says, "That's just way too much electronics for an old cowboy."

For Lowe, the hours before each service are painfully the same.

Even when the equipment works, there's still a sense of stage fright punctuated by a nervousness and self-doubt that has in the past physically sickened him.

You see, it's just not in Lowe's nature to do this kind of thing—facing the prolonged gaze of curious crowds who look to him for guidance and polish and wit, like some Nashville performer carrying a Bible instead of a bass guitar. All across Nevada and the American West, cowboy ministers bring the word to rural folks on far-off ranches who might not otherwise get to church, outreaches with such names as "Church in the Dirt," "Steelin' for Jesus" and "Clint Country Gospel."

But none have made a more pronounced transition than Lowe to come to their religious calling. Growing up in rural Idaho, unable to read or write, Lowe never made it past the 10th grade, a moody and mischievous youth who as a teenager set out for the rough-and lonely life of a ranch hand buckeroo.

In those early days, he never said much around fellow cowboys, who joked that riding with Bo was like riding alone. When he finally did talk, he drank and raised hell, womanized and danced on tables, living an unleashed life that today, frankly, causes the grandfather-of-sixteen's face to redden a bit. "Bo is about as real as they get," said friend and fellow preacher Blaine Lilly. "When he got saved, no one could believe it. He was rough, and he was quiet. He could talk to a cow or a dog, but not a person. Bo rode alone, and that's how he preferred it."

But that's all changed. For almost three decades, Lowe and his wife, Cathy, have preached the faith—"Outfitting People for Jesus"—through their Morning Star Outfitters ministry (morningstaroutfitters.org), operated from a small ranch just outside the town of Jackpot on the Nevada-Idaho border. They've conducted services in corrals, tents, school classrooms, campgrounds, meeting halls, bars, libraries and ranch living rooms. They visit out-of-the-way places such as the Starr Valley or the Duckwater Native American reservation near Owyhee.

The couple reaches out to a chore-laden breed of Western men and women who might not otherwise have time for church, or who wouldn't feel comfortable in a town chapel with everyone wearing their Sunday best. Those who have heard Lowe preach know this: There are no $20 words spoken here, just a frank politically conservative view of a life steeped in cowboy culture. "Bo presents the word in a way that ranch people understand," said Teola Blossom, a regular service goer who raises bucking horses with her husband, Wally. "His sermons relate to our animals and our lives. He taps into a reality that, unless you're in this rural Western lifestyle, you're not going to get."

■ ■ ■

He was raised by his grandparents on a farm outside tiny Kuna, Idaho, a kid who rode horses and milked cows and acted up in school. It was easier to cause trouble than let his classmates find out he suffered from dyslexia and struggled to read and write.

At 16, he left home to join a passing cattle drive and never went back. That impulse started his life on the road, working as a buckaroo at ranches across the West, years punctuated by a brief stint in the Army. He was married by age 17 and, after having five kids, endured a painful divorce. Always independent, he went back on the road, on the lookout for the latest job notice, his next cattle drive.

All that changed in 1985 when Lowe, then in his early 30s, took a job on a ranch in rural Oregon. That's where he met Cathy, the woman he would later marry, who was then in charge of the horse program. An artistic woman who writes and does photography, Cathy needed help tending to a colt with an eye problem. Rather than a veterinarian, the cow boss sent her Lowe. She immediately took to this quiet man with a feel for animals. A year later, the couple married but Lowe soon left Cathy behind in Idaho for more adventure as a buckaroo. Later, working as a bouncer in a Jackpot casino, Lowe felt his life had hit bottom. "I was in self-destruct mode, and I remember saying, 'Lord, if you're real, I'll serve ya. If not, let me go about my way.'"

Lowe recalled that he soon got his answer: On a trip home to Idaho, he ran into Cathy after a three-year separation and they got back together. The couple moved to Jackpot and soon began hosting a Bible study group at their house. But there was something about religion Lowe couldn't figure out. "I noticed the way other Christians talked to God. You know, 'God said this, and God said that,'" he said. "As a new believer, I didn't understand. I took things so literally. When I opened the Bible, God didn't talk to me."

One day, he sat in a recliner in his house and vowed not to move until God spoke to him. "I was so wanting answers, I wanted him to speak to me," Lowe said. "Of course, he didn't. And it broke my heart."

Then in the summer of 1992, Lowe was driving on a backwater dirt road, delivering salt blocks for livestock when tears welled. "I was bawling my eyes out," he said. "I had to pull over." He resolved to take his Bible from the dashboard and read the first words he saw, which happened to be Psalms 32. He read aloud from the right-hand page: "I will lead you and guide you. I'll watch over you. Do not be like the horse or the mule that have no understanding."

That's when Lowe figured things out. "Sometimes, you just know that you know something, and you learn that's from God," he said. "You read the Bible, and the words lift off the page and you know he's speaking to you."

That started it. He soon enrolled in Rhema Bible Training College, just outside Tulsa, Oklahoma. But Lowe misinterpreted the brochure that described the 80-acre campus grounds near a town called Broken Arrow. He and Cathy arrived with a wall tent at a suburban campus teeming with white-collar intellectuals. Lowe even brought his horse to ride to class. "That Bible school didn't know what hit 'em," Lilly said. "Here was a real buckeroo who'd come to the Lord."

The couple eventually moved into a fifth wheel trailer and their evening campfires became popular among fellow Bible students. Cathy obliged, of course, thinking all the time, "Why don't you invite us to your house? For dinner?"

Lowe was making progress with his studies. But he was still dealing with his fear of public speaking. Soon after graduation, Lowe was participating in a buckeroo cow camp when the lead pastor had a surprise: He'd scheduled Lowe to give the sermon that day before hundreds of people. "It panicked me something horrible," he said. He picked up a few notes and went to the chapel. Removing his hat as he walked in, Cathy's 14-year-daughter, Shawna, whispered, "Dad, your hair!" Lowe walked to the pulpit and used his rough appearance to win the crowd. "If I'd have known so many people were coming," he said, "I woulda combed my hair!" Folks laughed, but that same stage fright would stay with Lowe for decades. "I learned early on that I'd be scared spitless when I had to minister," he said. "I'd get a bellyache and start to sweat, and I'd have to go to the bathroom. But once I'm at the pulpit, God takes over. I just have to get there."

Even with a degree in Bible studies, Lowe wondered about the future. He resisted going back to Nevada, "where people knew me." He also didn't know if he could actually preach, preferring to just go back to being a cowboy, answering questions from other ranch hands about the word of God. Oklahoma pastor Ken Stewart convinced Lowe to incorporate a new church and go back to where he came from. "The cowboy community is quite unique in the way they dress and think, who they respect, and that respect is very limited," he said. "They won't listen to just anybody, but I knew they'd listen to Bo."

For 27 years, the Lowes have taken the word across rural Nevada and the West. As cowboys looked on, they administered to cows in difficult labor and once to a blind sheep named Pricilla. They learned to start their services later in the morning so ranch hands had time to feed the animals and finish their chores.

Lowe made changes in his life and he made them stick. "People see the dramatic changes Bo has made, from the man he used to be," Stewart said. "Some people correct their lives, and it doesn't last. But after all these years, Bo's faith just gets stronger and stronger, and people see that."

Still, Lowe knows his limitations. He doesn't feel qualified to play the role of priest or pastor, relying on psychological training to counsel people through their problems. He sees himself as a simple minister, bringing the good word to those who want to listen. "I always tell people, 'I'm not a pastor. I'm all you have till one gets here,'" he said. "But it doesn't look like anybody is coming."

■ ■ ■

In the Winnemucca rodeo arena, Lowe is wrapping up his sermon as the first cowboys ride their horses around the dirt circle behind him. Mares whinny. Livestock bellow, but the minister ignores it all.

He didn't sleep much the night before, fretting about his sermon and his fears. He rarely smiles because he's missing a few front teeth and dental work is just too expensive on a ranch budget. But once he begins, the small congregation is rapt.

"He's as good as any TV preacher I've seen," said local Missy Luellen. "He's been a ranch buckaroo his whole life, and he brings things down to a cowboy level."

Lowe and his backup band play several Waylon Jennings songs, with the lyrics slightly adjusted to fit their needs, including one that goes, "There's no end to what he'd do, just because you ask him to."

In a rambling sermon, Lowe tells a tale of a cowboy reluctant to risk ruining his expensive boots in order to jump into a muddy tank and bring water to thirsty livestock. He advises his listeners to "cull the sacred cows" in their lives. "We don't need to wallow in the mud where we're at."

He pauses. "Can I get an amen?"

"I know," Lowe says, "because God is pointing out things I need to turn loose of."

He's referring to troubles that have convinced him to change his life. This year, Cathy was diagnosed with lymphoma. Then Lowe lost his son, Chip, to brain cancer. He knows time is fleeting and is considering doing less ranching on his spread near the Idaho border so the couple can take their ministry on the road full time. "Right now, I'm tied down to the ranch and the cows," he said. "I need to lighten my load." But for now, the cowboy minister administers to his flock whenever he can.

At 9 a.m. in the arena, Lowe tries to bring his cowboy service to an end. "Well," he says, "we're running out of time." But the congregation isn't ready. They want more. More Lowe. More of the word. A man calls out from the bleachers: "No, let's keep going till they kick us out."

And with that, the minister smiles.

Coach 17: Preserving Nevada's Railroad History

■ **Carson City, July 2018.** Wendell Huffman recalls the first time he saw the old passenger car he considers one of the most significant artifacts in American railroad history.

Known as Coach 17, it was sitting in a storage shed at the Nevada State Railroad Museum, collecting dust as it had once picked up passengers. It was a cruel twist of fate for this venerable vehicle, once the very symbol of streamlined movement, to become so stationary and so forgotten.

Huffman, then a museum volunteer, had read about the train car and knew of its freighted history. In its infancy, the private coach had ferried officials from the Central Pacific Railroad to Promontory, Utah, where they met their business brethren from the Union Pacific on May 10, 1869. A pair of locomotive iron horses from the two great lines, with their characteristic smokestacks, brass fittings and distinctive paint jobs, came face to face to complete the nation's first transcontinental railroad.

Railroad tycoon Leland Stanford was among the luminaries aboard the coach that day. Coach 17 also carried the golden spikes that were driven into a laurel tie in the ceremonial completion of a herculean project that had overcome political turmoil, American Indian raids and financial problems to revolutionize coast-to-coast travel.

The car had come a long way since then—pinballing from private rail coach for financial barons to standard passenger coach to historic prop for a host of Westerns and finally to neglected hunk of junk left to rot in the woods off the Malibu, California, coast, its once-elegant redwood frame feasted upon by hungry woodpeckers.

Now here it was. As a historian, Huffman couldn't believe his eyes. "It was so cool to finally see something you'd read so much about," he recalled. "Just to be able to touch that car was pretty special."

Yet something wasn't right. "The coach was there in a storage shed collecting dust. Nothing was being done with it," he said. "At least it had a roof over its head."

■ ■ ■

That was 1991. Seventeen years later, Huffman, now the railroad muse-um's curator of history, is overseeing the last bit of logistics that will move the car onto the facility's main display floor to mark the 150th anniversary of the event that helped usher America into the modern age.

This latest chapter in Coach 17's story is being spearheaded by a dedicated conservator who convinced museum officials they had a piece of history worth saving and promoting. The 70-year-old Huff-man has made critical restoration decisions that will preserve the old rail coach just as it is—warts, woodpecker holes and all.

He's also writing a book to chronicle Coach 17's place in American history. Soon after the completion of the transcontinental railroad, he said, the Cincinnati Red Stockings traveled by train to California for a series of exhibition games, the results relayed nationwide by telegraph in real time, to help solidify baseball's standing as America's national sport. And the fact that trains ran on schedules, Huffman said, also led Americans to heed the hands of the clock—a cultural develop-ment that stands alongside the introduction of the smartphone. And Coach 17 was right there in the middle of it all. One of the book's chapter titles pretty well captures its tale of the rails: "A History Lost and Found." "The amazing thing to me is that it's still here," Huffman said. "This car is really something else. It's a survivor."

In efforts to preserve Coach 17, Huffman ventured into Ameri-ca's past. Built in Sacramento, California, in 1868, the car belonged to Central Pacific Railroad executive Charles Crocker, who saw it as a showpiece of California workmanship. Able to accommodate a dozen people, it featured a dining room, a kitchen, bedroom, parlor and indoor plumbing. Its plush interior was constructed in California laurel with oak trim. "Crocker had an ego," Huffman said. "He knew the coach would be used by Leland Stanford and other railroad exec-utives, but once the project was complete, this was going to be his car."

The coach brought four special spikes to the ceremony: two gold spikes, one silver and the last made from iron, silver and gold—all of the ore coming from Nevada's Comstock Lode. When the gold spikes were finally driven home, a telegraph operator typed the word "done," and a war-weary nation still reeling from the assassination of Presi-dent Abraham Lincoln simultaneously reveled in its signature accom-plishment. "They'd just fought the Civil War," Huffman said. "So this was a very symbolic thing to tie the country together."

After that one shining moment, Coach 17 went back to work. In its lifetime, the car traveled back and forth to New York City four times. In 1876, as a private car, it was on hand at the nation's centennial celebration in Philadelphia. The Virginia & Truckee Railroad bought the coach in 1878, when it was reconfigured into a general passenger car, its plush interior lost forever. Then Coach 17 tumbled off the historical map. By 1938, the railroad was in bankruptcy and disposing its assets at a time when the nation's so-called rolling stock—passenger cars and steam engines—was being relegated to junkyards.

Eventually, Twentieth Century Fox Film Corporation stepped forward with an offer to buy the coach. The railroad instead agreed to lease the vehicle, and off it went, said Huffman, "to Hollywood to become a movie star." The coach snagged cameo roles in such movies as 1939's *Jesse James* and can be seen in Elvis Presley's first film, *Love Me Tender (1956)*. Kenny Rogers used it in his *The Gambler* movies. "But most of the time, it just sat there on the studio lot in downtown Los Angeles," Huffman said. In the 1960s, the car was stored in Malibu Canyon, near the set where the TV show *M*A*S*H* was filmed. "In the show's opening credits, you can see the woods where the train car was stored." The car made its last appearance in Clint Eastwood's *Pale Rider* in 1985, when "Denver-California Western" was lettered across its side. Finally, Hollywood had enough. When the Nevada Railroad Museum acquired the car in 1988, it was reduced to a humble state. "Several times, we tried to trade it away," Huffman said. "It was like 'Does anybody want this thing?'"

■ ■ ■

Wendell Huffman's life is defined by the railroad. When he was an infant in Carpinteria, California, his parents lived by some tracks. As the curator tells it, after passing trains blew their whistles at a nearby grade crossing, his mother had to nurse him to get him back to sleep. "Well, Pavlov did the rest," he joked. "Whenever I hear a train whistle, I salivate."

For Huffman, old trains were like dinosaurs with their huffing-and-puffing steam engines—creatures that would soon be extinct. He had to save Coach 17. But the answer was not to return the car to its 1869 splendor. In Huffman's eyes, there would be no Botox for this old railroad dame. She would stay as she was. After any restoration, he reasoned, the museum would have a mere replica, not the real thing.

"We all want to see historic things restored. But while this one may be ugly, it still tells a very important story."

Not everyone agreed. Some officials didn't want such unvarnished artifacts taking up coveted display space on the museum floor. "Past directors didn't think it looked as elegant as the restored items," said Dan Thielen, the current museum director. "People scratched their heads and asked, 'Why would you want to bring that thing up and show it off?' People still tell me the decision not to restore this car is the dumbest thing we've ever done." There was pushback, Huffman recalled. So he pushed back himself. "I told whomever would listen, 'This car has a national story that will bring in a bigger audience,'" he said. "We're not promoting it, and we need to be doing that."

Three years ago, Huffman got lucky. California Railroad Museum officials visited Carson City to make their own claim to history. They argued Coach 17 was really more of a Golden State icon and should be on display there. "We had the funds to restore it and suggested a loan situation where both museums could enjoy it," said Cheryl Marcell, president of the California State Railroad Museum Foundation. "At the time, they had no interest. Our offer fell on deaf ears. But we understood. After all, they owned it."

Huffman used the incident to step up his campaign. "I said we really have to get that car on the museum floor to show them that we're doing something with it." That apparently did the trick. The coach will be moved to the museum before the big 150th anniversary next May. After that, officials plan to let history speak for itself. Along with vintage pictures, the display will include a stuffed woodpecker to explain all the holes in the car's body.

Huffman is looking forward to retirement, but not before the old train coach gets the attention and respect it deserves. Looking back, he's just glad he was in a position to preserve and promote a small but valuable piece of railroad Americana.

So when Coach 17 finally basks under the limelight before curious museum crowds, will Huffman take any special satisfaction? The curator shrugs his shoulders. "Like that railroad car has always done," he said, "I'm just doing my job."

Frank Van Zant's Feverish Rural Dream

Imlay, July 2018. Fred Lewis is a spiritual guardian of sorts, the caretaker of a spread of man-made ruins that rest along a windswept expanse of Nevada between Lovelock and Winnemucca.

The hiss of traffic along Interstate 80 punctuates Lewis' story of a place that seems both an inspired altar to an ancient people and a backyard fort—a Burning Man-like artist's revelation envisioned long before that festival ever came to be.

The structures and surrounding fence are made of bottles, dented refrigerators, rusted engine parts, bedsprings, entire cars, scrap iron, dolls' heads, televisions, truck windshields, animal bones, helmets and old typewriters. All of it has been stubbornly scavenged from the surrounding desert and bound together with chicken wire, concrete and patient determination.

It's a rough-hewn temple overseen by 200 cement sculptures, faces and figurines depicting Native Americans of various nations and status—including Paiute peacemaker Sarah Winnemucca, Aztec god Quetzalcoatl and Ponca tribal chief Standing Bear, who was once imprisoned for leaving Indian country without permission. Surrounded by concrete totem poles are other ornate figures, some raising their arms in both joy and revolt; others dejected, peering out into the desert's nothingness. The site, known as Thunder Mountain, is the creation of the late Frank Van Zant, who underwent a spiritual epiphany when his pickup truck broke down near here one May morning exactly 50 years ago.

Van Zant was equal parts outcast, revolutionary and truth-seeker, a self-identified Creek Indian who soon changed his name to Chief Rolling Thunder Mountain. He spent nearly a decade constructing his testimony to the suffering and plight of the American Indian, often assisted by passing free spirits who shared the vision of the man they called Thunder. "I'm a castaway," he once said, "and I've sculpted a castaway thing."

■ ■ ■

Some call Van Zant a visionary, others an eccentric misanthrope, but most agree he had considerable talent; he was recognized with a Governor's Arts Award, and the monument was later listed as a state historic site. The last was a gesture Van Zant would never live to see. Three years earlier, in 1989, he took his own life by shooting himself in the head.

Today, the shrine located about 130 miles northeast of Reno sits in disrepair, targeted by vandals. Locks have been broken, the stoic faces of Indian chiefs chiseled away. The elements wreak their own damage—the main building was closed after an earthquake raised fears the roof might collapse.

As Lewis talks, a passing trucker sounds his cavernous horn, and the caretaker waves instinctively. "That happens all day—he's just wishing us luck," Lewis said. "Maybe they've been here and know about us, about what we're trying to do."

Lewis watches over the property as a favor to childhood friend Dan Van Zant, the artist's eldest son, who has tried to preserve his father's legacy—with mixed results. The Redding, California, resident travels frequently to the site to make repairs, providing upkeep through private gifts and visitor donations that average hundreds of dollars a month. He has offered to give the monument to the state but was turned down, he said, because officials lacked funds to preserve and maintain the five-acre site. "Ever since my dad passed away, I've done what I can to maintain the place and keep it open to the public so people can see his soul and learn about Native American culture and their mistreatment," Dan Van Zant said. "It was my dad's dream, and I don't want to see it disappear from existence."

Nevada, with its rich mining and pioneer history, is full of forgotten places like Frank Van Zant's monument, whether they're ghost towns that once housed thousands or private creations built for religious or political causes. The questions remain: Who should preserve them? And at what cost do we let them deteriorate into the desert dust?

"Frank Van Zant had something very important to say and, intrinsically, Thunder Mountain has a great deal of value," said Dennis McBride, director of the Nevada State Museum in Las Vegas. "These sorts of private monuments do have a place in our culture and somehow should be taken care of. But by whom I can't say."

Nevada officials draw a line between public and privates edifices. "Resources on private property really are a labor or love for the individual," said state historic preservation officer Rebecca Palmer. "We're here to assist with technical information, but it's within the property owner's right not to preserve what's there."

■ ■ ■

The monument can leave a lasting impression. Beneath one statue, visitors have left business cards, coins and trinkets such as a child's pink toothbrush, like the precious mementos left at The Doors' Jim Morrison's tomb in Paris. "Places like this are my favorite thing about traveling this beautiful land we call home," a Michigan resident wrote in the guest book, which rests on a covered wooden picnic table, secured by a rock so it won't blow away. "Let this place serve as a reminder of mistakes never to be made again."

Pierce Jensen and his grown daughter Ashley stopped after a brief discussion they'd had traveling east on I-80: She'd passed by Thunder Mountain countless times and decided it was time to stop; he'd never noticed the place. So they pulled over, checked out the site on the internet and later marveled at what they found. "It's living folk art, that's what I'd call it, a living museum," said Jensen, 61, an antiques collector. "The beauty is in the details."

No one knows for sure why Frank Van Zant loaded up his 20-year-old Chevy half-ton truck and headed east from California in the spring of 1968. Some believe he was embittered by a failed election run for sheriff; others say he'd received a diagnosis of inoperable cancer.

Whatever the reason, he had already been around in life, collecting some emotional scars along the way. The Oklahoma native came home from serving in the Army during World War II with posttraumatic stress disorder, then called battle fatigue, his son said. Frank Van Zant eventually married four times and had 16 children. Believing he was one-quarter Creek Indian, he'd take his family out looking for Native American artifacts and kept a home museum of what they found. He had worked as an assistant Methodist minister, forest ranger and private investigator before going into law enforcement. Years later, he declared that he'd had enough of the white-collar grind and hit the road with $36 in his wallet.

The truck's breakdown changed everything. After squatting with his wife on land in a remote canyon, he struck a deal with a local prospector to buy the land where he eventually built his monument—as the story goes, for $25 down and $25 a month.

In a documentary *Visions of Paradise*, filmed in the early 1980s, the white-bearded, chain-smoking artist, several of his eight children running around him, explains that his shrine is constructed of things he'd found within 50 miles. "I'm a builder, a creator of nothing from nothing," he said. "I'm just a guy who can take what everybody says is useless and make something out of it."

The main museum and living quarters were fashioned around the travel trailer Frank Van Zant pulled when he arrived at the site. And then whimsy took hold, an attempt by a man who had never before made any kind of art to explain the visions he saw in his head. He built a three-story hostel, roundhouse and other structures and sculptures. The site is full of faces, images that he called children watchers. Sometimes, he'd finish a piece, sleep on it, and then tear it all down the next morning.

The monument eventually became a commune for followers who would stay for days, weeks and in some cases years, living and working on the site as long as they followed Van Zant's ban on drugs and alcohol. Artist Lisa Gavon lived at the monument with her boyfriend for a year in the late 1970s. She has written a book about her experiences, dedicating the proceeds to the monument's preservation and the memory of its creator. "Perhaps Rolling Mountain Thunder's life did not turn out exactly as he had planned," she writes. "But Thunder remained himself. There was no one else like him."

Many see no small irony in the fact that the annual Burning Man festival is celebrated each year less than three hours away. "It's emotional for me. It's very hard to see something this significant kind of put by the wayside," Gavon said. "People go to Burning Man to cross the divide into the sacred for two weeks a year.

"Thunder did it for decades. He lived it every moment of his life."

Frank Van Zant always called working on his precious monument a happy time, one full of song and the impulse of the moment, always surrounded by the children he gave names such as True, Obsidian and Star. But the day came when his wife finally took the last three and left him alone. That's when he went to the roundhouse, wrote son Frank a note that willed him the monument, saying goodbye but never giving any reasons for what he was about to do.

Then he picked up his gun.

"As he described it, he swam in a wild and sacred river," Gavon writes. "At the end of his time here, he was caught in the swiftly moving current."

Nevada vintner Colby Frey stands before one of his casks of wine. Photo by Randi Lynn Beach.

A New Vintage for Nevada Farming

■ **Fallon, January 2016.** Even as a boy, Colby Frey knew there was something special about his house, the grand old home that anchors the family ranch in northern Nevada's expansive Lahontan Valley. Perched out in the growing fields, amid the crops and livestock, the multistory structure with ornate wooden floors and crown window moldings maintained its own stately style, the urban sensibility of some visiting city dignitary. But what the young Frey liked most were all those hiding spots. "I knew it was old and had a lot of history," he said. "And when I visited my friends, nobody else had all those secret hiding places under the stairs."

But there was more to the place, much more. The ranch is one of the state's oldest, operated continuously since the Civil War, back when Nevada was a Western territory. One of its earlier owners, Robert L. Douglass was an entrepreneur and politician who owned the first automobile in Churchill County, before Frey's grandfather bought the land in 1944. But it's the house that stands apart. Built between 1918 and 1920, designed by famed Nevada architect Frederick J. DeLongchamps, the centerpiece structure is rare in Nevada for it is designed in the Midwest Prairie-style architecture popularized by Frank Lloyd Wright in the early 1900s.

Now the so-called Douglass-Frey ranch has been singled out for preservation. In November, its core structures became Nevada's latest addition to the National Register of Historic Places compiled by the National Park Service. Said Jim Bertolini, National Register coordinator for Nevada: "The main house is one of the few examples of Prairie architecture in the state, designed by one of its premier architects."

Frey's mother, Debra Frey, said the house exudes personal charm. She recalls driving down Dodge Lane, under towering elms, to reach the soul of the ranch. "I'd get out of my car and say to myself, 'I'm just the luckiest person in the world to be able to live in this house,'" she said. "It's the best-built house you ever saw, a jewel out there in the middle of a farm."

The ranch's history is a story of surviving hard times with the pluck and rugged individualism for which Western settlers are famous. William Bailey, one of the earliest settlers in the Lahontan Valley, first settled the land in the 1860s. Following several harsh winters, Bailey sold much of his land in 1891 to Joseph Douglass, whose nephew Robert later took over operations, developing the ranch headquarters in 1917.

Frey's grandfather Charles P. Frey Sr. bought the ranch in 1944. Now 31, Frey is a fifth-generation Nevada rancher—his family owned Carson City property as early as the 1840s—and is the third Frey generation to make a living on the Fallon-area land. "You have to adapt to stay relevant," he said, dressed in blue jeans and an old Carhartt vest, his slate-blue eyes scanning the snowcapped Stillwater Range. "A lot of other ranch families are gone; the ones who didn't adapt."

Each generation of Frey had its own strategy for survival, he said. His grandfather, following a few hard years in the 1950s, bought some cows and built a dairy to supplement his income.

Decades later, Charles Frey Jr. faced his own reckoning with the land. In 2001, after several years of drought, he planted more water-efficient grapes for the newly formed Churchill Vineyards. "I remember my dad saying, 'This is not going to be the last drought here. We have to make a change,'" Colby Frey said. When his brother and two sisters decided to pursue other professions, Colby took the reins of the ranch with his wife, Ashley, growing alfalfa, wheat and corn.

One harvest season, he saw a program on the History Channel that changed their lives. The couple started a distillery, making alcohol with grains grown on the ranch land. He traveled to Kentucky to buy a specially made still, learning the conditions that made the state perfect for producing spirits. "You need four seasons, cold winters and hot summers, and we have all of that here," he said. Now, the family each year sells 10,000 cases of vodka, gin and brandy—growing the base grains all summer and turning into distillers during the winter months after the harvest is done. They also sell 1,000 cases of wine a year.

These Freys have put a stamp on the land the original owners never imagined. They turned some old horse stables into a state-of-the-art distillery and tasting room. Ashley Frey runs things from her Apple computer in the windowed office Douglass once used as his study. She's probably the first ranch wife here with braces.

In a December chill, Frey walked past a barking beagle named Jack to his boyhood house. Outside was the mammoth cast-iron bell the cook rang to summon the ranch hands to their meals. He worked the bell, its clang still heard for miles around, and then made his way to an old red barn straight out of Hollywood central casting, one popular with locals as a backdrop for family portraits. He looked out across his 1,400-acre operation. "We're farmers first," he said. "Everything else comes afterwards."

Now retired, Charles Frey Jr. still helps with the chores, unable to abandon the land, whose value soared. Purchased for $60,000, the place is valued at $8 million today. But it's not for sale. The young couple has a daughter named Alice and a son on the way. They dream of one day turning over the ranch to a new generation, with perhaps their son running the distillery and Alice operating the winery.

In 2017, the old ranch house will near its 100th anniversary. The milestone is significant, but so too is a bit of knowledge Frey holds close.

"I know my gramps would be proud of what we've done here."

The Denim Hunters

■ **Sulfur, January 2019.** The two amateur prospectors moved along a rocky hillside in the wooded wilds of the Humboldt-Toiyabe National Forest, picking their way across an unyielding landscape studded with juniper trees and pinion pines.

They were looking for holes in the ground.

Finally, they spied what they'd come for—an abandoned mine shaft whose tiny, jagged mouth was gouged into the side of a rock wall that flashed a signature of iron and copper. The men flushed with the excitement of archaeologists encountering a pharaoh's tomb, anticipating the riches that might be found inside. But it wasn't gold or silver they sought. It was blue jeans, the remnants of old denim work clothes—shirts, trousers, jackets and coveralls—worn by the countless grizzled veterans of the Comstock Lode, men who plied this same ground with picks, axes and caches of dynamite some 150 years ago.

Caden Gould, 41, a handyman and adventurer dressed in an old pair of Wranglers, flannel shirt and scuffed boots, set down his can of Coke and considered the task before him. He knows the most dangerous part of any mine excursion comes in the first 15 or 20 feet, where the exposed rocks and crushing boulders looming overhead are most likely to break free and come tumbling down on top of him. Ron Bommarito is Gould's sidekick and neighbor from the nearby town of Genoa, an antique dealer who at age 70 is old enough to be the younger man's father.

He sensed his hesitation. "OK, so get in there," he deadpanned.

Turning on his headband flashlight, Gould slid onto his belly and wiggled into the tight chasm. Soon, only the soles of Gould's boots were showing. Then he disappeared entirely. "This is where you get killed," he muttered.

■ ■ ■

The unlikely duo has formed a rustic brotherhood of historic pants, joining a handful of vintage-denim hunters who probe abandoned mines across the West looking for the mother lode of denim. They've searched the back rooms of old hardware stores, delved into retired outhouses, scoured the crevices in aged barns and once found a pair of old denim lying right there on the desert ground near the town of Mina, dyed white by the sun and alkaline crystals growing out of its seams. But most blue-jean booty lies underground, in often-forgotten mines spread across the Silver State, with names like Ben Hur, Silver Pick, Marble Monster and Sage Hen. Most wooden-ribbed shafts and crawl spaces they enter have no names at all, or if they did, they've been lost to the mounting dust of time. The pair pursue the holy grail of vintage denim—the line of apparel patented by entrepreneur Levi Strauss and Reno tailor Jacob Davis in 1873. The corners, rivets and pockets made the dungarees the sturdy favorites of not only miners, but also loggers, farmers and cowboys across the American West.

For the lucky finder of a vintage pair of Levi's, the payoff can be princely. Vintage denim is big, according to Daniel Buck Soules, president of Lisbon Falls, Maine-based Daniel Buck Auctions and a regular on PBS's *Antiques Roadshow*. He should know. Earlier this year, a pair of Levi's denim jeans originally purchased in 1893 by a dry goods store owner in Arizona Territory sold for almost $100,000, through Soules' auction house. The cotton jeans with a 44-inch waist and a button fly had no belt loops because most men wore suspenders back then. "People all over the country are coming to me with pairs of Levi's to sell. We have 15 to 20 pair coming up in our spring auction," Soules said. Among the items at that auction will be a rare pair of child's overalls from the early 20th century, he said.

Why are people so willing to shell out six figures for a pair of blue jeans? "In two words—iconic Americana," Soules said. "It really comes down to the fact that nothing says 'America,' especially to people in Asia, like a pair of Levi's." The brand—and some of the jeans—have stood the test of time. "There is a huge history to this apparel, from mining to its role in pre-earthquake and pre-fire San Francisco at the dawn of the 20th century," Soules said. "When you say the word 'Levi's' anywhere in the world, people know exactly what you're talking about."

Soules has been involved in the sale of more than a dozen pair of vintage Levi's but has never bought apparel from mine searchers such as Bommarito and Gould. Buyers of old jeans, many from Europe and Asia, include curators from Levi's own company museum in San Francisco as well as high-end clothing designers such as Ralph Lauren, who repurpose the material into modern apparel. Twenty years ago, Levi's even launched a vintage clothing line that featured replicas of

recovered pieces—including those with holes in the legs and without pockets. For many, the vintage jeans scream out with the colorful history of the Old West. Many hunters who come across vintage
jeans call the Levi Strauss company in San Francisco for assistance in
obtaining their value. Demand became so high that Levi's historian
Tracey Panek's telephone voicemail greeting points denim finders to
websites such as Denim Hunters and Denimology.

Gould and Bommarito haven't yet found their pot of gold in any
tunnel. Bommarito found his first pair of vintage denim in the 1970s
and has since sold numerous pairs for a few thousand dollars or more.
A veteran antiques picker with a major collection of Nevada artifacts,
he has the low-key humor of an aging Bill Murray. He's intellectual, a
storyteller, who plumbs not just for denim but any artifacts from the
state's territorial days, including a rumored lost box of gold plundered
from an early stagecoach robbery.

"There's all kinds of neat stuff out there," he said. "Nevada's funny
that way."

■ ■ ■

Gould, whose ancestors ran the Gould and Curry Mining Company in 1860s-era Virginia City, grew up on his grandfather's ranch
before becoming Bommarito's protégé five years ago. Quiet, muscled,
determined, he wields the energy of a settler who lived on the land
150 years ago, or a miner who went below it. He likes to repel deep
into the shafts, going far lower than the amateur spelunker, where
many of the denim finds lie, while Bommarito stands on the surface
to offer sage advice via walkie-talkie. Gould had traditionally looked
for minerals, not clothing. "Now I've created a monster," Bommarito
said of his partner.

Gould said he once drank to excess, but denim has helped him
overcome that crutch. "It's the thrill of the chase," he said. "It's like
the alcoholic chasing the drink. Now I'm chasing something else. I'm
addicted to the denim."

On a cool day in early autumn, the pair left Genoa just after day-
break in Gould's 2002 Ford diesel truck with 600,000 miles on the
odometer, two cracks that meander across the windshield, an ashtray
overflowing with cigarette butts and a pair of binoculars stashed on
the driver's side floor. In the back was a case of dog food and, under

the seat, a roll of toilet paper, which Gould calls "mountain money" because "it's more valuable than any currency once you get up there." Before they left, he had completed hours of computer research, scouring various internet sites for tips on the mines they intended to explore— information that included the years of operation, total depth, pro- duction numbers and types of yields. And, perhaps just as important, whether they're already claimed.

■ ■ ■

The excavations are not for the faint of heart. More than 50,000 of Nevada's mines pose public safety hazards, according to the state's Division of Minerals. Risks include "falls down inclined or vertical openings; rotted, decaying timbers; cave-ins; bad air; old, left behind explosives; poisonous snakes and spiders; disease-carrying rodents; and bats that can occasionally carry rabies," according to the agency.

Since 1971, when the state began recording mine injuries, more than one dozen people have been killed and many more injured exploring underground shafts. Gould and Bommarito have heard the ominous cracking of a mine's wooden supports, climbed on rickety 150-year- old ladders, dislodged rocks that have fallen atop their heads, denting skulls. But what the denim prospectors fear most is poisonous gas. Bommarito said the two follow a trusted rule of thumb: "If anything smells funny, you get the hell out of there."

On the most recent hunt, Gould walked upon the mouth of a mine shaft that had been fenced off with a sign that warned to stay out, adding, "Thank you for being on my trail cam! Evidence is going to BLM [Bureau of Land Management] at this time. Have a nice day!" Gould knows that mine owners can be a prickly crowd. The internet is filled with videos taken by amateurs who go poking into already- claimed mines looking to pillage gold and silver.

Gould claimed his first pair of vintage denim after watching an online video he recognized was filmed in a Tonopah mine. He saw the relic hunter step over a pile of clothing he figured contained some denim, and later went back to claim his prize. Now he and Bommarito know not to give too many details about where they hunt. Otherwise, the pair admit to be being amateurs in their quest. They know fall- ing rocks could kill them but rarely wear helmets and don't want to spend the $4,000 for an air-quality meter.

At mine sites, tempers can flare. Bommarito once had a fistfight with another denim hunter right at the open mouth of a vertical mine shaft. "We could have tumbled into that hole like in some cheap movie," he said. "If it's not that, God only knows what real stupid is."

Outside one mine shaft, Gould stooped low to throw in some rocks. "Snakes," he said.

Added Bommarito: "Caden has become a snake connoisseur."

A few years back, Gould was searching out a mine in central Nevada with Colorado-based denim hunter Brit Eaton. On a steep hillside, he felt an old wooden retaining wall give way beneath him and out rolled a ball of rattlesnakes that hit him in the leg before the creatures slithered into the sagebrush. He'd left his shotgun back in the truck a half-mile away, so he called out for his partner to start throwing rocks. But Eaton thought he was kidding and stood on the crest of the hill laughing. "Every bush was vibrating with rattlesnakes," Gould recalled. "There was so much sagebrush I couldn't see them, but I heard those rattles." He finally scampered up the hill untouched but will never forget the encounter. Sometimes, though, the danger gives way to jaw-dropping up-close views of history.

The pair have encountered underground scenes of half-filled ore carts still on their tracks, dynamite-packed walls with blasting caps at the ready, long-dead candles burned down to their wicks, the dirt floor littered with Wells Fargo receipts—as though those miners of another era had just walked way momentarily for a coffee break. "Those old miners worked hard," Gould said. "I wouldn't do it. It's scary down there, even with all the modern conveniences."

In the end, the day failed to yield any denim finds. The pair's best hope was a mine they believe was staked just after the end of the Civil War, pointing out the date "67" burned into a plank of wood with an acetylene gas lamp. Often, when a mine's era is in doubt, they scout for discarded bottles—canaries that suggest a mine's age. Finally, Gould called it quits on the search, saying he planned to return and rappel down into the mine system from another vantage point.

Earlier, the two wandered around the remnants of a century-old mill, inspecting cracks the walls for any secret spaces that miners could have stuffed with denim to stop the incessant wind. "Here's some old fabric," Gould said, turning the dirt with the toe of his boot.

That's when Bommarito surveyed the ceiling and uttered a truism about the vintage denim hunt: Rabies carriers and old blue jeans can inhabit the same space.

"There might be some stuff up there next to that nest," he said. "But I'm not gonna fight the rats for it."

The South

The Priest Who Conducts
Mass in a Casino

■ **Laughlin, December 2019.** Charlie Urnick stands in a backstage hallway at Don's Celebrity Theatre, tucked in the thrumming Riverside Resort Hotel and Casino. Smiling, shaking hands with well-wishers, he awaits the evening's events with the knowing calm of a veteran headliner. But in this brightly lit corridor, where musicians and magicians have signed autographs and greeted fans, Urnick offers something truly remarkable. He hears confessions. He's the administrator at St. John the Baptist Catholic Church, which sits atop a treeless hill some five miles away. But the 71-year-old Urnick is better known to parishioners and just about everyone else around this casino river town simply as Father Charlie.

After a deacon helps him slip into his flowing satin vestments, he quietly listens to the ways his fellow Catholics have gone astray. One by one, the believers wait outside for their turn. There's no confessional booth, and priest and penitent face each other on folding chairs. They are eye to eye, but Father Charlie puts them at ease. "Painless," said one confessor, crossing herself as she leaves the hallway. On this late-autumn Saturday afternoon, Father Charlie is continuing a 27-year tradition that's aptly suited to Laughlin. He celebrates Mass in a casino.

Yes, you read that right. Forget bingo. We're in the realm of hard-line games of chance. After hearing confessions, Father Charlie leads a small procession into the 700-seat theater with its bordello-red wallpaper, not far from the cartoonish squawks of slot machines. For the next hour, he preaches in a place where, for some, the real God is the almighty dollar. He faces his congregation from a floor-level pulpit, in front of a stage and its drum set looming in the darkness. Hours later, a Karen Carpenter impersonator will take this same stage. For now, behind Father Charlie stands a slender pole with a crucifix mounted on top.

Still, distractions abound in a place more associated with the seven deadly sins than 14 Stations of the Cross. Sharing the venue with acts that appear during the rest of the week, Father Charlie has given

Holy Communion before a huge backdrop of a Skyy vodka bottle and images of sultry Budweiser girls and Elvis, prompting him to jokingly remind the faithful they're praying to God the King, and not the King. Father Charlie has no problem with any of it. In fact, he insists that this implausible place is precisely where he should be. "The pope says priests should be where the people are," he said. "There are 11 casinos in Laughlin, so this is where we have taken our services. And to those who might say that God could not possibly be here, I say he is."

The theater's first dozen rows feature long tables where parishioners, some dressed in shorts and flip-flops, consult hymnals and church bulletins. One ponytailed man shoves a *Daily Racing Form* into his pocket just as services begin. As the collection basket passes, some toss in casino chips and slot machine receipts, which Father Charlie gladly accepts. He's even designed his own souvenir chip the parish sells for fundraising. Some refer to him as the "chip monk." "Pray with us," the chip reads, bearing a picture of the Riverside casino and Mass hours. "It's a sure bet." The chips—along with candles, medals and other items you'd find in religious bookstores, are arranged for sale at a long table-bar where workers sell alcoholic drinks at other events.

As the service ends, Father Charlie adds an encouragement not heard at other churches. "Don't forget to visit the bar on the way out," he urges. A retiree then slides into his electric wheelchair and heads for the door. "It's off to the casino," he said. "Let's hope I don't lose the farm."

■ ■ ■

In his sermons, Father Charlie forgoes fire and brimstone in favor of Andy Rooney-like humor. His talks also tend to mention such appetizing dishes as noodles with sauerkraut, ice cream pie, mushroom ravioli and other meals he's consumed that week—including pastries baked by doting parishioners for a roundish priest who admits he's never cooked a meal in his life and has rarely set foot in a gym. "God created angel food cake," he says in one sermon. "And it is good." Such is the power of Father Charlie's pulpit that whenever he offhandedly mentions a fondness for pineapple pound cake, bacon or cheese curds, the packages pour in from around the country.

Since 2008, when he arrived in Laughlin from his home state of New Jersey, where he served as an Air Force chaplain, schoolteacher and parish priest, Father Charlie has begun each sermon by referring to this city 100 miles south of Las Vegas as paradise on Earth. He loves the sunshine and mix of colorful snowbirds and locals, a place where he can play the penny slots to relax after a long day of being a priest. While he one day wants to go to heaven, he says, Laughlin will do just fine for now, thank you. He's a huge fan of magic and drives regularly to Las Vegas, where he's seen more than 350 magicians perform, some of whom refer to him as "Charlie the Chaplain." He insists his introduction to David Copperfield was "better than meeting the pope."

He's a priest without pretense, who has worn green florescent sneakers during Mass and greets people with his favorite phrases, "See you in church!" and "Pray for me, what harm could it do?" All with a boyish laugh and a propensity for the words "golly" and "gosh." He began one homily insisting the only tools anyone needed in life were WD-40 and a roll of duct tape. Many pulpit anecdotes involve his weekly parish adventures and his boyhood pet alligator and taxidermied penguin. Or how his mother, Mary, disciplined him by brandishing the family's parrot with its outstretched claws. When he refused to get out of bed, she'd threaten, "Don't make me get the parrot!"

He's come a long way from his first sermon decades ago, about which one priest said: "It was read, it was read poorly and it wasn't worth reading!" His sermons—compiled into three self-published books with such titles as *Live! Love! Laugh! Laughlin!*— are also spiced with jokes he gleans from the internet. On Father's Day, for example, Father Charlie said: "My father only hit me once—but it was with a Volvo." It got the laugh but then evolved into a meditation on the role of God as a loving father. Some anecdotes even target his flock. Father Charlie once told of a visiting priest who was shocked by all the sin he'd witnessed in Laughlin, commenting on "all those pathetic old people putting money into machines and they don't know God!" Father Charlie replied: "Those pathetic old people are my parishioners!"

The casino Masses were started in 1992 by Father John McShane, who sometimes encountered bits of skimpy showgirl costumes on the carpet. Even after the parish church was built in 2003, the Riverside services continued. Each weekend now features two church Masses and three in the casino—one on Saturday and two on Sunday. "We'll never leave here," Father Charlie said, adding that some parishioners attend the casino Masses only. "Once we close those doors, you're in a church."

For years, before he was assigned here, Father Charlie made annual pilgrimages from New Jersey, his mother in tow, as a guest pastor in Laughlin. Mary would attend a service and then spend the rest of the time working the slot machines. Once, both he and his mother won $5,000 on the same quarter-slot one day apart. Mary died in 2006, two years before Father Charlie moved here full time, and he received hundreds of sympathy cards. His sermons have related how Mary came to terms with him entering the priesthood after a friend consoled her, "Well, this way you won't ever lose him to another woman."

He also regales listeners with stories of two longtime actor friends he calls "the boys." Eddie Gelhaus is the priest's "illegitimate son," and Michael Serrano is his "brother from another mother." Some listeners don't always get the joke. John and Kathy Reed were visiting from Wisconsin a few years ago when they first met Father Charlie, and Kathy was shocked by talk of a priest having a son.

"I didn't know you were married," she said.

"I'm not," Father Charlie replied.

Reed still laughs at the exchange. "Well, my wife's jaw just dropped, until she got to know him," he said. The Reeds asked around town about this peculiar priest. "Everybody knew him," said Reed, a retired longshoreman. "He was a legend."

So, the couple moved to Laughlin to hear Father Charlie's sermons all the time and are now active church members. Reed notes that the priest keeps in his church office two slot machines, one called the "God Game," and has a stage-prop collection that includes a 14-inch dagger and a bed of nails. "He's so down to earth," Reed said. "We like that."

■ ■ ■

A few months ago, Father Charlie was visiting Ely in northern Nevada on church business. He stayed at a casino hotel and played penny slots. During the night, he suffered a stroke, which severely affected his eyesight. Then, around Halloween, Father Charlie tripped over a bag of books at his home and dislocated his right shoulder, damaging a nerve that caused him to lose all feeling in his arm and hand. He wears a sling and does not know if any sensation will return.

Friends and parishioners have rallied around their priest. With Father Charlie unable to drive, they now ferry him around town, including visits to dozens of sick residents each Monday. The boys bought him a watch with enlarged numerals for his damaged eyes. Another feature automatically alerts them if he takes another fall.

Gelhaus and Serrano cemented their friendship with Father Charlie years ago when they took rooms at his house in Las Vegas, turning what the priest had considered a personal refuge into a bachelor crash pad. Still, the older man was always full of good cheer and fatherly advice, they said, and none of it "preachy." In return, they helped a wide-eyed and yet somewhat sheltered priest experience life outside his religious flock. They insisted on calling him by his first name, saying he was Charlie long before he was Father Charlie. With the boys, Father Charlie also drank his first beer and kamikaze shot, rode his first roller coaster at Disneyland and bought his first cellphone. In turn, he has counseled them on girlfriends, and once sent a text to Gelhaus that urged, "Kick the girl next to you out of bed and give me a call." At one point, after a series of mishaps in which Gelhaus broke the TV remote, lost an expensive GPS device and then bumbled over filing his tax returns, a frustrated Father Charlie blurted out, "You're the son I never wanted!" The phrase stuck. Gelhaus now calls the priest "Pa."

Serrano always teased the priest for his "God complex" and, in one sermon, Father Charlie said he hoped he'd never lose his eyesight because he wanted to see the sarcastic look on Serrano's face whenever he talked about the Lord. But now it has happened. And the flock frets.

For years, church volunteer Bernadette Thompson has plied Father Charlie with homemade cookies, Rice Krispies bars and pineapple upside-down cake. Now she doesn't know what to do. "We worry about him," she said. Father Charlie is more worried about others. When a food bank needed winter coats for the homeless, he put out the call. Within hours, 220 coats poured in. "We couldn't survive without him," said Sandy West, the group's volunteer coordinator.

For now, the priest perseveres over his health setbacks. After a recent Mass, he stood in the casino lobby, using his good left hand to greet congregants. Some women moved in for hugs. The men joked. "Father Charlie, you gotta find some other place for that sling," one said, pointing to the lump in the vestments. "You look pregnant!" That got a laugh, too.

The casino Masses now have a new feature, something that's not his doing or his request. Along with a call to remember the sick and shut-in, the lay reader asks parishioners to pray for Father Charlie's eyesight and injured arm. That's when a murmur of concern rolls through this casino church crowd.

The Cowboy Commissioner

■ **Clark County, March 2015.** The cowboy commissioner arrives late, barging into the night meeting like one of his prized rodeo bulls broken loose from its pen. His Clark County Commission staff has collected residents of this ranching community to hash out a disputed federal land-use plan. Yet Tom Collins doesn't join officials up front in the meeting hall. Clad in worn Wrangler jeans and a plaid Western shirt, his black Stetson tilted back on his head, he eases his lumbering 6-foot-3, 250-pound frame onto a creaking folding chair in the back row. He takes his hat off his gray, balding head and sets it on the floor, and he leans back like a wisecracking high school senior. He digs into a Big Mac and fries amid the smell of grease and burger. "I haven't eaten since breakfast," he explains in a rough rural twang, wiping his fingers on his jeans.

The performance is vintage Collins. At age 64, the lifelong rodeo man continued to ride bulls until a few years ago and remains popular among voters who have religiously returned him to office—including five terms in the Nevada Legislature—despite personal peccadilloes that might have dynamited other political careers. For one, Collins likes to drink whiskey; his poison-of-choice is Pendleton, a Canadian blend. The one-time Mormon convert who later left the church has unapologetically professed to keep a bottle on his office desk, by his bed and by the TV. There have been alcohol-fueled mishaps, like being cited for excessive noise for shooting up a tree at his North Las Vegas home during a drunken 2012 holiday celebration. (Collins, who paid a fine, said he was mad at the tree. Voters reelected him four months later.) Tom Collins, some scoff: Even his name is a drink.

To grasp Collins' unflagging popularity is to understand politics in a state that has featured cocktail-swilling Las Vegas mayor and mob lawyer Oscar Goodman—a place where personal foibles and cheesy flamboyance are tolerated and even embraced, as long as a candidate delivers. Collins knows that all too well. At the night meeting, he playfully pokes a Boy Scout in the row ahead, giving a thumbs-up to the youth's uniform. Like President Lyndon Johnson, he leans imposingly into a group of men, invading their space, telling a private joke that makes everyone laugh.

He presses a wad of Copenhagen chewing tobacco into his mouth and fiddles with a smartphone video of his bellowing cattle. A staffer shoots him the slashed-throat sign to take it outside. He picks at his nails, sighing audibly at comments that displease him. A local activist and Collins critic asks if he can have the crowd's attention. "No," the commissioner says to himself. "Shut up. Sit down."

Then Collins limps to the microphone; his body battered by countless falls from angry bulls. He thanks people for their views and pledges to continue as their bridge with federal officials: "Happy New Year. I love you all." He knows such feelings aren't always mutual. "People out here either love me or hate me," he said later. "I can handle both."

■ ■ ■

Collins comes from country roots. Raised in Las Vegas, he rode a horse named Dogger Red to school as a boy. Decades later, the gruff political maverick insists he's not a politician, but an elected official who gets the job done: After flash floods, Collins distributed hay from his pickup to feed stray cattle and used his tractor to clear debris.

As a legislator, he intervened when officials refused to let residents use a county fair agricultural arena during off months. Collins snipped the lock with bolt cutters. Taxpayers had financed the building, he said; it was theirs to use. "Tom steps on toes," said Glen Hardy, an 83-year-old rancher. "If you're not a Democrat, you're not worth a crap—he'll tell you right to your face."

His public emails frequently launch the F-bomb; he leans over a trash-can-turned-spittoon at commission meetings, where he often addresses public speakers as "Bubba" and "darling." Commissioners once sought to ban him from the seven-member board over his public behavior. (They can't; only voters can.) Last year, the board chastised Collins after offensive remarks in which he called Utah residents "a bunch of inbred bastards." Collins admitted to battling some "personal demons," including a divorce from his longtime wife, Kathy. But he did not apologize. "He has such thick skin, he doesn't realize his words can be hurtful," said Clark County Commission Chairman Steve Sisolak. "This is a government body. We're not out on the range."

Collins says he's accountable only to his constituents: "I have won elections by a landslide because I'm honest and I'll tell you what I think. And if I tell you I'm going to do something, you can take that to the bank."

At home, he often watches the Westerns Channel, shows like *Bat Masterson* and *Maverick*. He espouses "cowboy logic" and his cell-phone message tells callers to "cowboy up." He tweets under the handle @CowboyCommish. And his diesel pickup—its vanity plate carrying his cattle brand, "T Bar K"—is such a behemoth he struggles to fit it into his county parking space. He says his guiding ethos comes from John Wayne in the 1976 movie *The Shootist*: "I won't be wronged; I won't be insulted; I won't be laid a hand on."

He briefly attended Midwestern University in Texas on a rodeo scholarship and is an inductee in the National Senior Pro Rodeo Association Hall of Fame. He rode bulls until a bad fall five years ago and says he may yet ride them again. He has a house in North Las Vegas and a 40-acre spread farther north with 30 rodeo-stock cattle.

Collins did construction and worked for a power company until he first ran for public office in the early 1990s, concerned over "do nothing" government. Campaigning as a "union Democrat" conservative on social issues, he was elected to the North Las Vegas City Council and then the Nevada Legislature, often capturing 60 percent of the vote. In 2005, he began his first term as a county commissioner.

The cowboy commissioner has also used social media to blast fellow officials. Last year, Darin Bushman, an official in Piute County, Utah, called Collins about a ranch issue. That's when Collins made the "inbred bastards" remark. The comment floored Bushman: "I'm like, 'Really dude? You're a public official?'" Collins says his sarcasm is misunderstood. When reminded of the Bushman fray, he smiles. "That inbred bastard? He's related to half the people in Piute County."

But Collins can be contrite. At a meeting after his insults to Bushman, he dropped his bravado. "I've been in a downward spiral for a couple of years, I admit it. I've done some rude things and some not pleasant things, and real friends come and talk to me," he said. "A lot of it is when there's sarcasm or trying to turn pain to humor."

■ ■ ■

Through it all, Collins remains a drinker; no excuses. He often boozes out of anger over politics and his personal life, including personal debt and estrangement from his two children and his eight grandkids.

Recently, at a North Las Vegas watering hole, a staffer plays designated driver. Collins orders a bottle of Coors Light—his first of four—saying he's loyal to Coors and Pendleton for sponsoring rodeo shows. He spits tobacco juice into a Styrofoam cup, addressing his critics with the F-bomb, a salvo he fires often.

He calls himself "a binge drinker" rather than alcoholic, saying he doesn't booze as often as people think. He admits he's come to public meetings with a buzz. But again, no apologies: "Even drunk, I can do more by accident than many people can do on purpose." When his commission term ends, he may run for city council. Or governor.

Close friends have forgiven his reckless behavior. Decades ago, Collins was out drinking when his truck struck a parked tractor-trailer. He was injured, but his passenger, local pig farmer Bob Combs, suffered serious head injuries that still slur his speech. "I held Bob's head to keep him from bleeding," Collins recalls. "That accident taught us something: that we're both mortal."

As Collins battles his demons, Combs still calls him a brother. So does Combs' wife, Janet. "I love Tom; he stands his ground," she said. "All in all, he's a pretty darned good man. A man's man."

Queens of the Mexican Rodeo

■ **Sandy Valley, June 2020.** Viri Colon was just 19 when she first saw the women riders parading on horseback, perched sidesaddle, dressed in ornately embroidered sombreros and colorful dresses, boots with pointy rodeo spurs, their long black hair tied into neat braids.

In an arena called a *lienzo charro,* the women moved to the beat of traditional Mexican mariachi music, eight riders guiding their horses in a synchronized routine that was equal parts rhythmic ballet, historical fashion show and demanding equestrian gymnastics, where female rider and horse moved as one in an elaborate athletic dance. The presentation, a feature at Mexican rodeos, is called *escaramuza.* Colon fell in love with what she saw. It looked so regal, so romantic. She and her two sisters were raised by a father who trained horses for a living and competed in the local rodeos, known as *charreria.*

But those horse-riding contests oozed machismo, with the men always at center stage. Attending rodeos with her family, Colon could only watch, along with the mothers, sisters and daughters, but never participate. Now, she saw her chance to perform, to become part of a historic tradition prized by her culture. She wanted to try these exotic *escaramuza* routines herself. "I remember telling my sisters, 'That looks so pretty; let's do it. We all have horses. How hard could it be?' Well, little did we know."

The year was 2013 and Colon, now 26, joined one of the Las Vegas Valley's few *escaramuza* teams. Seven years later, she leads a competitive drill squad that puts in long hours of practice, the women gently encouraging their horses, repeating their self-designed routines—all with an eye toward earning the right to compete at the national *escaramuza* contests in Mexico.

And they're cheered on toward success by an unlikely sponsor. At 75, Marilyn Gubler spent a career empowering women. In the early '80s, she chaired Nevada's Republican Party, then became a political consultant, a role model for ambitious women of both parties. Several years ago, Gubler bought a 160-acre spread in the Sandy Valley, 45 minutes south of Las Vegas, where she created a working dude ranch and corporate retreat. Along the way, the woman known as "Boss Lady" discovered the subculture of Mexican rodeo, which is considered Mexico's national sport. She and her husband, Tommy DiGiacomo, built a traditional *lienzo charro* for local riders to practice and compete. Shaped like an exclamation point, with a rectangular area that connects to a circular arena, the space hosts rodeo events year-round.

Gubler first heard about *escaramuza* when the daughter of one of her ranch hands approached her about starting a team. Her research revealed the history behind the riding drills, whose name translates to "skirmish." During the Mexican revolution, *adelitas* or women soldiers, often fought alongside the men against the Spanish, riding into battle dressed in flowing gowns, their galloping horses creating clouds of dust designed to confuse the enemy.

Gubler quickly fell in love with these young queens of the Mexican rodeo. She marveled at the gorgeous costumes, pageantry and dedication. She loved how the family events helped preserve a rural Latino culture often lost in today's urban life. "When I saw the women perform, tears came to my eyes," she said. "I do not want this sport to die. It's too important to local Mexican culture."

Gubler built a separate practice arena for the *escaramuza* riders, but that's not all. She bought the team its first performance dresses and sombreros and has covered expenses for out-of-town competitions, mostly in California, home to 50 teams.

Each year, statewide contests are held across the U.S. to decide which teams will qualify to compete in the Mexican national events each November, where the top team is awarded a trophy and $15,000. Nevada's five teams, based in Clark and Nye Counties, were set to square off in Pahrump in early April, but the event was rescheduled for September because of the coronavirus pandemic.

Colon's *escaramuza* team, named Altaira, an Arabic word for a high-flying bird, has enjoyed success both in the U.S. and Mexico. They've won every state competition since 2013, and in 2017, placed 67th out of 200 teams that competed in Mexico. For Colon's riders, the season starts in January, when the women begin practicing in earnest, hosting fundraisers and raffling bottles of tequila to collect money to pay for their coach, gowns and equipment.

Recruiting members remains a challenge. Riders, who range in ages from 14 to 26, must commit to a year with the group, own their own horse and be available to practice at least once a week. Often it means juggling jobs and schoolwork. Colon works in the corporate office of a dental firm. Others are casino workers and students studying accounting and nursing.

■ ■ ■

Each rider has reasons for devoting so much time to the sport. Vanessa Jauregui, 24, revels in competing in a sport denied to her mother, Isela. Her grandfather, Jesus, was too conservative to allow his daughters to compete in a rodeo arena he defined as a man's realm. "In his eyes, only men rode horses," she said, "not women." In the years before his death, Jauregui's grandfather eventually relented, allowing her aunt— her mother's younger sister—to ride. Now, each time she enters the rodeo arena atop her horse, Jauregui thinks of Jesus. "He's there riding next to me," she said. "He helped instill in me this passion for horses." Her parents also have rallied around her. Her mother is there at competitions along with her father, who suffers from a physical disability. "If there's a wheelchair available, he's there, along with my mom, rooting me on," Jauregui said.

The practices require discipline. Each season means a new routine to choreograph. The women meet when they can. On weekends, they might practice for three hours in the morning before taking a lunch break to enjoy a light barbecue prepared by their parents and let the horses rest. Then it's back to practice for another few hours.

Often the girls carp at one other when someone stumbles out of line, but they make it work. "They're feisty," Gubler said. In the first years, she said, she battled an attitude problem among some younger members, who became jealous of opposing riders and each other. "They were falling into a trap, torpedoing and bad-mouthing each other," she said. At one point, Gubler suggested that she would withdraw her support if the situation didn't improve. Nowadays, the women are more relaxed and even socialize with opponents, who ride on teams with names such as Amazonas, Prestigio and Colibris.

On a recent Sunday, the *escaramuza* women prepared to perform in an afternoon rodeo event. They were nervous, knowing they would be practicing new sequences while the men watched, for a moment giving up their coveted rodeo stage, resting their boots on the wooden corral fences. That morning, in a ranch dining hall, the women donned their red and white dresses, brushing one another's hair, laughing the way teenage girls do. "Is this mine?" one girl asked, rifling through a handbag for a red hair bow. "No," another said. "But you can use it."

The women know their gowns are nearly as important to their success as riding skills. In competitions, the team's uniforms must match perfectly and judges deduct points and teams can even be disqualified for the slightest variance or imperfection. The dresses worn by Altaira are made by a Tijuana seamstress, who is revered for making gowns with form-fitting flair—mixing function, historical accuracy and femininity. To mimic those worn by the original *aldelita*, the gowns for Colon's team feature designs on the torso that resemble the ammunition belts worn by the women soldiers of old. Considering the expensive lace and the various layers of fabric required by judges, each garment can cost up to $500.

Most riders buy two new dresses a season. With accessories such as sombreros, boots, horse care and coaching fees, expenses run into the thousands of dollars a year. New dresses are coveted over the old. "You know women don't like hand-me-downs," Colon said. "Your dress is your showcase. You're representing the female soldier ready to go to war. Your gown has to fit you perfectly. It must be flattering. You must wear it well."

At age 16, rider Linsy Enriquez's gown bestows an aura of glamour. "I feel like I'm wearing tradition, representing something that comes from my cultural roots," she said. "I feel beautiful." In many ways, each performance is like going to the prom. "There's competition among girls to see who shines most in their dress," she said. "You can put on a dress and call it a day, but if you know the right way, you stand out from those who don't."

As the *escaramuza* riders readied themselves, younger girls, too young to compete, hovered at the edges. They watched intently, knowing in future years their turn will come. One performer stepped into a *crinolina*. The fabric piece is boiled in cornstarch to give it the consistency of papier-mâché, providing a bouncy lift beneath the flowing skirts. One girl joked the garment looks like a corn tortilla fresh off the grill. The wide-brimmed sombreros are more helmet than hat, often made of rabbit but adorned with art designs. In Mexican ranch culture, the wide sombreros protect cowboys from the harsh sun. The last bit of apparel were the riding boots. Most of these women far prefer wearing spurs to high heels. Finally, the team walked outside to ready their horses. "Let's rock and roll," Colon said.

■ ■ ■

That's when her father, Osbaldo Colon, rode up, looking majestic on horseback, like a figure from a romance novel. A lifelong horse lover, he provides horse-shodding services at the ranch. But on this day, he's just a proud parent.

He helped both of his daughters, Viri and 23-year-old Alondra, brush down and saddle up their rides. He has become a surrogate father to the entire team, watching after both the women and the horses. In seven years, he has yet to miss an event, or even a practice.

In the background were the sounds of a working ranch. Horses whinnied amid the thundering gallop of hooves. Rodeo fans have backed up their pickups to the arena, sitting on chairs arranged on their truck beds like tailgaters at a football game. A woman peddled Mexican wheat flour *duritos* smothered in hot sauce. The *escaramuza* riders also sold corn on the cob to help raise money. Children hung on the stable fences, pointing to baby goats, pigs, colts and ranch dogs.

Osbaldo stood between his two daughters, both mounted on their horses. Viri rode a red roan named Canelo, or cinnamon. Alondra rode a quarter horse named Bandolero. "I have always had a passion for horses," he said in Spanish. "And now my daughters do, too. That makes me proud."

Moments later, the eight Altaira team members led a procession of rodeo riders into the arena. They formed a vertical line, the horses moving in slow, perfect step. A cowboy took a picture, a bottle of Modelo in his hand. The rodeo performers, both men and women, paused and dipped their heads as the announcer recited a cowboy prayer. Then the rodeo was on. As the men performed, the *escaramuza* awaited their turn.

To calm their nerves, they described the goal of the day. "We must embody beauty, grace and strength," Viri said. "You have to ride with elegance. It's a challenge to ride side-saddle, but you must do everything with grace." Added Alondra: "People see our routines and say 'Oh, it's beautiful!' But it takes so much work to achieve that beauty."

Alondra has two small sons and her husband babysits when she practices and performs, playing a support role while his wife follows her passion. "It's addicting," she said. "To be able to handle a horse that strong. The animal can think for itself, and yet he follows your commands." She paused. "It's amazing."

Enriquez said the women are sometimes as hard to choreograph as the horses. "You have eight girls with different attitudes piecing together a seamless routine," she said. "To make it flow is just so difficult, but we make it happen."

■ ■ ■

An hour later, the women reentered the circular arena, their right hands held aloft, hoping that the many hours of practice have paid off. Even though this display is not an official competition, the women are perfectionists. They pretended the judges were there. They had eight minutes, timed to the second, to enter and leave the area. That left five minutes for a routine that consists of 12 movements. This brief time on the rodeo's center stage left little room for error.

Before each competitive performance, teams submit to the judges a detailed sketch of their planned routine, which is then videotaped in progress. In state competitions, there are two judges, but in Mexico, there are five. That means many sets of eyes looking for the slightest defect, Viri said. The rules allow for teams to challenge judges' calls. Once, in Mexico, Viri questioned a verdict that two of the team's horses had collided during the routine. Colon consulted the tape and won her argument, saving Altaira 42 points. She felt like a lawyer who had prevailed before some high court. "I thought to myself, 'Oh my gosh, the process works! I used the rulebook to my advantage.'"

On this Sunday, the routine involved riders and horses moving around a large square marked in the dirt. The team kept moving, working through choreographed maneuvers. They veered off in groups of two and three, circling the edges of the arena and moving back to the center, crossing one another precariously close, the horses sometimes pausing to perform small pirouettes. "*Va!*" Viri Colon commanded, "Go!" urging the riders on. The program resembled a balletic rendition of soldiers in battle, horses of different sizes and gaits all moving as one, the women straight-backed, determined, elegant.

When it was done, the *escaramuza* riders were pleased with their new routine. As they left the arena, Gubler was waiting. So was Osbaldo Colon. "My dad never says a bad thing," Alondra said. "He's biased. He always says, 'You guys did really good.'" He knows that for those shining moments, this team, these women, his daughters, have commanded the rapt attention of a male-dominated world.

With grace, beauty and power.

Melissa Mevis, known as "Sarge," helps guide recovering addicts in Nye County. Photo by David Becker.

Former Addict Helps Keep Rural Addicts Clean

Pahrump, June 2016. The drug crowd shows up outside the Nye County Courthouse with the morning sun still an upstart; many, it seems, dressed in the same clothes they had worn the night before. Some peer ahead in a trance, not yet awake. Others stand at the door, cigarettes hanging from their lips, arms crossed defensively, squinting into the hard-slanting light. Mothers pull children. One 3-year-old girl guides a stroller bearing a Cabbage Patch doll, unaware a judge has termed Mommy a habitual offender who must appear here at random times each week to urinate into a bottle and prove she's not using. "I gotta get to work," one woman complains. "I ain't got time for this BS today."

The regimen is called The Drop, and nobody wants to be here. When the doors open at 7 a.m., men with pants dangling on their hips and women without makeup congregate dourly in a waiting room where "One Day at a Time" is scrawled across a mirror. They make cynical cracks, rolling their eyes, waiting for their names to be called.

On this morning, like most others, "Sarge" is there to meet them. She's a boss lady, a petite drill instructor and, sometimes, a knowing confidante. Just don't cross her; that's the street-corner wisdom here. Because Melissa Mevis once walked in these same drug-doing shoes. Twelve years ago, she made these same post-dawn courthouse appearances, dragging her two young daughters, trying to show a judge and anybody else who cared that she was clean, ready to start a new life. But that was long ago, when Mevis had a taste for meth and pot and bad choices. Now, at 34, she helps coordinate the county's drug program; she's a graduate-made-good who analyzes urine samples rather than gives them. With a practiced eye, she sizes up these street players to gauge whether, on this morning or any other, they're telling the truth. These drug users know they lie to Sarge at their own peril.

The day before, participants in Nye County's drug court—a get-help program that is an alternative to prison—called in to hear a recording in which Mevis reads off the colors being summoned for the next

57

day's drug test: Red. Purple. Pearl. Lime. The voice is no-nonsense, a bit weary, coming from a woman who has attended that party, taken that drug. Mevis assists 5th Judicial District Court Judge Kim Wanker, who oversees the drug court program.

Mevis takes the urine samples, stands by in court and keeps an eye on those now-familiar frowning faces as Wanker hears their cases. The judge gave Mevis that nickname. "Melissa is no-nonsense; she knows crap when she hears it," Wanker said. "She'll barge right into my office to get her answers. She wants stuff done, and she wants it done now." Mevis says the Sarge name fits. "Maybe it's because I'm bossy, impatient," she said. "I need things done now."

That morning at The Drop, Mevis rolls open the window to the crowded waiting room and calls a woman's name. A thirtysomething blonde jumps up and walks down the narrow hallway, her spiked hair rising like weeds. Her arms bear purple tattoos; she wears a black shirt with the word "Blessed." Her 5-year-old daughter trails behind her.

The testing takes place in a jury deliberation room, where participants leave their valuables on a table and step into either a men's or women's bathroom. Mevis follows the blonde into the restroom, little girl in tow, and closes the door behind them. The chatter is bright, considering the circumstances.

"How you doing today?"

"I'm great! Yourself?"

"It's too early to tell."

Mevis is all ears. Tell her you lost your job, and she'll make calls to help you find another one. She's got a soft spot for mothers struggling to feed and clothe their kids. But do her wrong, give her an attitude, and she will be there like a drill sergeant dropping you for 50 push-ups. Walk in a minute late, and Mevis will turn you away cold. Dress down, wear pajamas to her drug test sessions, and you're a goner.

"Melissa's always right there to call you out if you get out of line," said Alana Murphy, 22, a brothel worker who wears a T-shirt bearing the phrase "Bunny Ranch. Eat Fresh." "She's smart, and she's been there. I can lie to my friends, but not to her."

Nearby, 18-year-old Blake Drouillard, whose heroin habit landed him in drug court, shook his head in a sort of dark admiration. "Yeah," he said. "It's like, before you even do it, she's right there, knowing you're gonna do it."

Sherie Winn, 54, a blonde whose looks have hardened from her heroin habit, has seen Mevis go from light to dark when she suspects she's being played. "She'll seem real nice, and then, if something happens she doesn't like, her whole attitude changes, and you're like, 'Oh no, I'm busted,'" she said. "But if you're behaving, she can be your best friend. I think Melissa gives us all hope: Because if she can do it, if she can beat these drugs, then so can we."

■ ■ ■

Mevis grew up in Pahrump, the daughter of a butcher. She wasn't a bad kid, but she hung out with troublemakers. She first did meth at age 16. She liked the rush but hated the next day, when she felt depressed coming down. She did a stint in juvenile hall and later, after high school graduation, started waitressing. But she couldn't give up her drug crowd. She lost her job, and crashed. "I wasn't used to doing meth and then not having any more," she said. She lived in a succession of trailers and cheap motels. For a while, authorities took custody of her first daughter. Then she got arrested for receiving stolen property.

In 2004, she ended up in drug court, bitter and angry. "I didn't like it at first," she said. "I thought my counselor was against me." Turns out, drug court didn't much like her either. "She was just hard, abrasive," 5th Judicial District Court Judge Robert W. Lane said. "She annoyed the heck out of me."

But Mevis got the hang of the system, which she says gave her life structure: regular drug tests, counseling sessions and group events such as potlucks where she brought her daughters. She rarely, if ever, missed The Drop.

Along the way, she knew when fellow drug court goers were high; she read through their lies, how they said they weren't still using, when she could tell they were. And that, Lane says, is a talent few judges possess. "It's the beauty of her role in the program," he said. "I'm a Mormon; I've never had a drink. So I can't relate these people's lives. But there's a saying that in drug court, that when their lips are moving, they're lying to you. Melissa sees through the lies."

And she brooks no excuses. When newcomers learn the rules of making a $30 contribution to the program, they complain that they don't even have a job; how are they supposed to pay? "Do it the same way you got your drugs without a job," Mevis tells them. "If you could get the money then, you can get it now."

Mevis finally finished her drug court stint in 2006. Then she did something no graduate had ever done: She came back, looking to volunteer. Then-program coordinator Tammi Odegard saw how Mevis wanted to put her drug past behind her and gave her a chance. She soon saw Mevis grow as a woman and as a mother; in 2009, Mevis took a paying job with the program.

As she got on her feet financially, Mevis did something else Odegard had never seen before: She took herself off government aid programs. "She did her research and then got on the phone with Section 8 housing and other programs," Odegard said. "People said they'd never had anyone call and take themselves off the program. Seeing that, it was just my proudest day for Melissa."

■ ■ ■

It's just after 8 a.m., and results from The Drop are in: Out of 37 clients, two failed their tests. Mevis could smell booze on one man's breath. There were six no-shows. Gritty work lies ahead: Mevis empties the urine vials and mops the bathrooms. She doesn't mind because she is seeing success in many people here.

Her own life continues to progress. She's now a mother of four, with twin 5-year-olds. Her two eldest, now teenage girls, are good students. Their mother sees to that.

Sometimes, Mevis will a see a face from the old days, somebody she met during her drug court stint who is back again, on drugs and in trouble. "It's sad to see," she said. "Because you know how hard they worked to get clean the first time."

In a few days, she planned to accompany Wanker on a trip to Tonopah to celebrate one man's graduation from drug court there. Those are the stories Mevis likes to see: people who beat the drug life. "I don't think I could ever live like that again," she said. "I have four kids; that's chaotic enough."

The Beard of Knowledge

■ **Clark County, March 2021.** Mark Hall-Patton faces the camera, ready to reveal nuggets of wisdom about the colorful events that once took place in Las Vegas and Clark County. In this era of COVID-19, he wears a red kerchief over his mouth, looking a bit like an aging Billy the Kid—that is, if the Wild West outlaw had also worn a wide-brimmed Amish hat and long, white beard. On this day, the longtime administrator of the Clark County Museum, hosts his weekly live Facebook Q&A for those history buffs trapped at home during the pandemic.

A woman wants to know if Las Vegas casinos had Cold War-era bomb shelters. Hall-Patton patiently explains how most casinos had basement rooms reserved for that purpose and that authorities even identified abandoned mines in the area to house people in case of a nuclear attack.

Then a man asks: Why is Nevada known as the Silver State? "Nevada at once became known for its silver as a result of the famed Comstock Lode," Hall-Patton says cheerily. "And, well, the name just stuck."

Rather than a stuffy academic exchange, the event feels more like a virtual autograph session for a humble administrator turned international celebrity. For countless fans, Hall-Patton has become the much-revered "Beard of Knowledge," the most-recognized public museum spokesman on earth. "People see me as accessible and excited about history, which I am," he said. "That's just me. I've been a geek all my life."

Since 2009, Hall-Patton has played a cameo role in 200 episodes of *Pawn Stars*, the History Channel's Las Vegas-based reality show whose quirky, off-the-cuff bargaining scenes between opportunistic sellers and jaded buyers quickly turned it into one of cable television's most popular programs, now dubbed into 32 languages. Hall-Patton has become the show's most-consulted expert, bringing him such acclaim that fan letters and emails daily pour into his Henderson museum office. He's recognized at gas stations, hounded in restaurants, called out on the street. On a visit to Ireland and Luxembourg some years back, he couldn't buy his own beer in any Irish pub. The lads just wouldn't let him.

Now 66, Hall-Patton is about to do something many find unfathomable. In the spring, he plans to retire from his museum post. While he still will make *Pawn Stars* appearances, the move will make him decidedly less accessible to followers who flock to meet him in the facility's hallways.

A few years ago, colleagues posted a life-size cardboard cutout of Hall-Patton as a consolation to fans who came to the museum in search of the friendly figure they normally encounter in the comfort of their own living rooms.

During the recent half-hour Q&A, queries turn decidedly personal. Questioners want a piece of the man himself: How many cats does he have? (one) Where does he buy his Amish hats? (mostly online) When did he start growing his beard? (1976) Do strangers mistake him for a rabbi? (yes)

Most grasp the fact that he is not a normal museum administrator. The Santa Ana, California, native is a lifelong collector of stuff, a history hoarder with highly specialized pursuits—odd items that over the years have included old beer cans and vintage postcards, museum guard badges and decorative fraternal swords, not to mention a personal library of more than 20,000 historical volumes and counting. Hall-Patton lives within the realm of books, in the course of his research of all things past and their vivid retelling. For more than 40 years, he has traveled the nation to carve out his own place in the rarefied realm of running history museums.

Hall-Patton's story is one of stubborn persistence, about settling upon a professional path and sticking to it, even during painful periods of unemployment. It's also about learning how to live in the public eye and sacrificing your privacy for the good of the museum, that hallowed realm, which has become his raison d'être. Thanks to Hall-Patton's celebrity, the Clark County Museum—which has no advertising budget—saw its pre-pandemic attendance soar more than 50 percent.

So, how on earth is the county going to replace him? "His are big shoes to fill," said Jeanne Brady, a former museum guild president. "He knows so much about the area's history."

County officials do have their work cut out for them, agreed Michael Green, a UNLV associate professor of history. "People see Mark on TV and forget that he had a day job," he said. "My hope is that the county can bring in someone who shares his commitment to the community, luring museum patrons into that little jewel in the desert."

Like any seasoned performer, Hall-Patton knows when it's time to make his exit. After 28 years in Las Vegas, he says, he's accomplished what he set out to do at the museum. Still, some people can't quite accept that he's leaving—like the host of a recent retirement seminar he attended.

"I know who you are," the man said. "You can't retire!"

"Oh, yes, I can," Hall-Patton replied. "I've been doing this job for forty years." Frankly, he deserves a bit of privacy, he says, time for his own pursuits. "I'm not dying," he told the instructor. "I'm just retiring."

■ ■ ■

Hall-Patton was one of three children born to Navy veteran Arthur "Pat" Patton and his wife, Mary Jane, who worked as a nurse. He was an instant collector. When he was 5, his father told him to empty the contents of his pockets into a grocery bag. The result: five pounds of everyday stuff, including an old lock the kid had found interesting. By 13, he already was playing the role of amateur museum curator. He'd force his younger siblings—sister Catherine and brother Michael— on tours of odd home displays he'd arranged, including a .50-caliber machine gun round turned lighter. Both brothers developed their own passions: Michael later played bass for nationally known punk band the Middle Class.

While he studied for his history degree at the University of California, Irvine, Hall-Patton held the first of the unconnected jobs that would later give him an understanding of the backgrounds of people who would patronize his museums. He sold patio furniture and worked the graveyard shift at a mortuary. He did a year of postgraduate work in American history and museum studies at the University of Delaware. Finally finished with school, he landed a position at the Bowers Museum in 1977, in his hometown, where he worked as a part-time security guard and later as a grants developer. He also married the girl he'd met in high school, a fated union that has lent the museologist his last name. Fiancée Colleen Hall, a budding academic as well, didn't want to surrender her last name, so the couple decided to call themselves Hall-Patton. Reversing the order to Patton-Hall, he says, would have made it "sound like a residence dorm."

After his grant-funded position ended at the Bowers, Hall-Patton worked for three years at the Siouxland Heritage Museums in Sioux Falls, South Dakota. But he lost his grant funding there and once again became jobless, this time with a mortgage to pay. For months, he worked on the assembly line at a microwave factory, reading 16th-century satire on breaks and learning something about himself. "I was a horrendous assembly line worker," he recalls. Looking around at men who did their job well, he sighed, "I saw how incompetent I really was." The couple returned to California in 1983, where Hall-Patton counted election ballots and was a manager trainee at an automotive parts store. Friends began asking tough questions. His father urged him to take a training course to become a bus driver.

"Maybe you need to get into something else, because it doesn't look like a career in museums is going to work out," people said.

"No," Hall-Patton responded. "That's not who I am. What I am is a museologist. And that's what I am going to continue to be."

Finally, in 1984, he landed a position as director of the new Anaheim Museum and never looked back, later moving on to a job at the San Luis Obispo County Museum, a post he held for eight years. But Las Vegas eventually beckoned. In 1993, Hall-Patton was named the administrator of the Howard W. Cannon Aviation Museum in McCarran International Airport. He moved to Henderson with his wife and two children—5-year-old Joseph and 2-year-old Ellen—and bought a house in a residential community where he and his wife live to this day.

By then, Hall-Patton was a man surrounded by collectibles such as first-edition books, chunks of the Great Wall and Golden Gate Bridge made into paperweights, a candleholder fashioned out of a piece of the London Bridge. "I don't collect easy things," he said. "They have to be unusual—objects I can use to tell a story." He has, for example, hundreds of enforcement badges—not the police type, but those worn by guards and ticket-takers at zoos, museums and libraries. And by church ushers. "Think about it," he said. "How tough does a church have to be for ushers to wear a metal badge like a cop?"

Hall-Patton's son, Joseph, recalls that the family home could be a dangerous place. "One of our constant annoyances was the book-o-launch, when towering stacks of books would just topple over," he said. Especially when the family cat, who negotiated by sense of touch since it was blind in one eye, slunk past a wobbly stack.

Joseph and his friends suspected that behind his father's easy chair sat some mysterious black hole to an alternate universe of stuff. "I once read about this piece of gear the Army called a Jeep cap," he said. "I asked my dad where I could find one, and he literally reached behind his chair and produced one. He did that all the time."

And through the annoying history lessons that took the place of bedtime tales, the father taught the son a valuable lesson. "History is a story," said Joseph, now a PhD candidate in history at the University of New Mexico. "My father made that clear." The younger Hall-Patton has followed that lead. His YouTube channel, "The Cynical Historian," where he tells his own tales, has more than 150,000 subscribers.

In 2009, three years after he was promoted to administrator of the Clark County Museum, Hall-Patton struck publicity gold: He began appearing as an authenticator on *Pawn Stars,* which tracked the daily sales and acquisitions of the Gold & Silver Pawn Shop in downtown Las Vegas. "They sought me out," he said. "The show needed experts, and somebody said, 'Call the guy at the museum.' So they did, and it turned out I had no shame on camera."

Hall-Patton was an instant hit for just being himself—a chatty, avuncular man with a booming baritone and the same grandfatherly beard he'd begun growing at age 22. He also wore a series of distinctive Amish hats—a look he'd fallen in love with in college while attending farm auctions in the Pennsylvania hill country. On TV, he was anything but pedantic, but he drew the line on commercialism—relating only the fascinating backstory of an object while never offering a monetary value, because that's just not what a museologist does. *Pawn Stars* host Rick Harrison said, "On camera, I only know so much, and so we have Mark, who knows everything. The guy is just brilliant. He's the only rock star museum curator I know."

The crew reveled in Hall-Patton's everyman zaniness. One director even talked of producing a short horror film in which Hall-Patton invites unsuspecting visitors to his museum—victims who later turn up as statues in his growing House of Wax. "The joke," Hall-Patton explains, "is that I'm such a good-natured collector that I had to have this creepy alternative ego."

One day, Hall-Patton's bearded visage inspired a long chain of postings on Reddit, with one writer saying that the museologist wasn't really that smart, that he was just the current owner of the mystical "Beard of Knowledge" handed down by such visionaries as Leonardo Da Vinci and Michelangelo. When Harrison used the phrase on the show, it stuck.

There was another Hall-Patton touch that viewers noticed—the red shirts he wore as a salute to his membership as a "Clamper," part of the eccentric E. Clampus Vitus fraternity dedicated to the preservation of the heritage of the American West, a group whose motto is "Credo Quia Absurdum," or "I believe because it's absurd." Hall-Patton is a former Clamper Noble Grand Humbug now recognized as a Dead Salmon because "after a few years as an ex-Humbug your advice begins to stink." Members have handles such as "Chainsaw" or "The Butcher." Hall-Patton's nickname, of course, is "the Beard of Knowledge."

"Mark finds everything fascinating," said fellow Clamper Dennis Robinson, who is also Hall-Patton's accountant. "One day, he said, 'So, tell me something about the history of accounting.' And I said, 'Are you serious?'" He was. He loved that modern-day auditing standards evolved out of scandals, and later gave Robinson accounting manuals from the 1800s and an original *Forbes* magazine from the 1920s on the history of the Big Eight accounting firms. "He is the Beard of Knowledge," Robinson laughs.

Still, Hall-Patton has paid a price for his fame: lack of privacy. Colleen Hall-Patton, a UNLV sociologist specializing in women's studies, years ago wrote an academic paper on her husband's celebrity status— how fans stopped him in the grocery store and waved from passing cars, how women wanted to touch his beard and children tugged at his coat. "Unfortunately, Mark has gotten the worst of both worlds," she said. "He got the fame, but without any of the fortune."

■ ■ ■

Hall-Patton is walking on the Clark County Museum's 30-acre property on Boulder Highway in Henderson, along a shaded lane named Heritage Street, filled with acquired local buildings that look like they could be found in any American small town. There are original structures from the area's mining days, construction of Hoover Dam, and the 1931 Boulder City train depot, all expertly restored.

A man and a woman pass by on the sidewalk. The man turns.

"Hey," he says, "you look very familiar."

"There's a reason," Hall-Patton says with a smile.

The visitors are on their way to the Candlelight Wedding Chapel, a onetime Strip institution, which now perches in a grove of trees here since it was acquired in 2004 and restored under Hall-Patton's watch. The woman says she was married in the chapel many moons ago, and she is among thousands who visit the little structure every year. Hall-Patton encourages her to send a wedding photograph and a copy of her license to become part of an exhibit the museum is building. "Wow," she says. "I'm going to do that."

Time is running out on such chance encounters. Hall-Patton will soon retire from the beloved job he's held for almost three decades. For Hall-Patton, the move is bittersweet, but he's ready. "I have done what I intended to do here," he said. "Finished all the major restoration projects."

He's proud of the public record of Clark County history the museum has amassed, including one of his favorite artifacts—a Southern Paiute bow and arrow collected in the Las Vegas Valley circa 1900, a piece of sinew-backed wood that shows the sophistication of early Native Americans here. That sums up Hall-Patton's creed for residents: Know your own local history because "if we don't understand why something is the way it is and we change it, we may make old mistakes all over again."

Oddly, his own favorite museum addition is a new storage facility complete with rolling shelves and fire protection. Because Hall-Patton believes his task is not just to display the county's historic artifacts, but to protect them as well. "As a museologist, you are responsible for the physical memories of your community," he said. "And while not very sexy, a new storage facility is critical to that mission, a way to preserve the community's memories for the next hundred years."

Even in retirement, some things with Hall-Patton will stay the same. He'll still be a talker, busier than two men his age. He'll work on completing four books that include an autobiography, a humorous look at museum work, a second edition of *Asphalt Memories*, his 2009 book exploring the origins of area street names, and a book tentatively titled "This Day in Local History," with an important event for each day. There may even be a new television show in the works.

The Beard of Knowledge still will be recognized most everywhere he goes. If you see him, say hello. And don't be surprised when you're told some character-filled backstory about the place where you live.

That'll just be Mark Hall-Patton, lifelong geek who is obsessed with the past, stepping onto what he calls his newest "bully pulpit, to describe just how cool history really is."

Miss Kathy's Way or the Highway

■ **Crystal, June 2018.** Hey, partner, listen up. If you're gonna drink at the Short Branch Saloon in the high desert outpost of Crystal, home to hookers, high hair and hootenannies, you best be forewarned—you gotta play by the rules. Miss Kathy's rules.

Yep, she's the owner of the joint, as sharp and lethal as a rusted nail. What she says goes. Don't be fooled by this grandmother in blue jeans and strawberry-blond hair whose signature meat loaf once brought them in for miles around. Or that every Christmas she sponsors a cookie bakeoff, the results distributed among the road and utility workers who help keep life nice in the little settlement of 100 residents, not counting the working girls. She runs a respectable place out here next to a shuttered brothel and a cluster of trailers, a community where the mostly unpaved roads bear such cowboy-themed names as "Pinto," Corral" and "Bridle."

Miss Kathy, her regulars know, will as soon throw you out as look at you, as a few now-pitiable former patrons can tell you. She slaps possible troublemakers with one-or-two beer limits, and after that they're done, no arguments, she says, because they've shown in the past that that they can't be respectful.

The drinker folks here call "Loosey" learned his lesson. He'd run his mouth, used a few too many cuss words. But he is a big man, over 6-foot-4, and he climbs high-voltage electric poles for a living, so Miss Kathy waited until he walked out and then locked the front door behind him. He had car trouble and was back a few moments later, pounding on the door, demanding to be let back in. Not on your life. "Don't mess with me," Miss Kathy said. "That's pretty much fact."

After two decades of serving drinks and not taking any lip, she owns the bar and motel outright, which gives her a bit of leverage in laying down the law. She opens her doors Tuesday thorough Saturday, from noon until 7 p.m., or whenever she damn feels like closing. Complaining that you drove all this way to find the place closed? "Well then, come when I'm here!" Miss Kathy said.

Her full name is Kathy Bragg, and she bought the Short Branch in 1999 while working for Sears down in Las Vegas.

Don't even ask her age: "You don't need to know."

Husbands? "No need to talk about them," she said. "I just don't know how to pick men. I can't even count the total, but they had this in common: They were bad."

Miss Kathy's outspoken ways harken to Nevada's pioneer era, when single women had to look out for themselves or be taken advantage of by all those men. This bar owner is no damsel in distress. A poster hanging near the bar could very well define Miss Kathy's self-image, right there for all male drinkers to see: There's an image of a witch, along with the phrase, "Broom rides 25 cents." Other placards show, quite plainly, what Miss Kathy thinks of men. "Men are like parking spaces," one reads. "The good ones are taken; the rest are handicapped." Or try this one on for size: "Men are like coolers. Load them with beer and you can take them anywhere."

On another wall hang memorials to departed regulars now drinking at that big bar in the sky. Country music plays, a sickly Christmas tree leans year-round into a corner.

Miss Kathy is a staunch Trump supporter. Just sit down, shut your trap, and she'll tell you all about the horrors of being a small business owner under that other party. "Only those people who don't look around and read get in trouble in here," she said, pointing to a sticker under that TV that read "#Trump Train" and another disparaging House Speaker Nancy Pelosi.

She also doesn't cater to those sophisticated city types who walk in ordering drinks with fancy names. You want a vodka and orange juice? Then say so. She doesn't want to hear the words "screw" or "driver."

Over the years, Miss Kathy has devised ways to pack the place. She sponsors the annual bordello run for charity and brings in thousands of bikers. But her movie day came to a screeching halt when the TV broke down.

On a Saturday, the regulars roll in like tumbleweeds. There's Charlotte LeVar, who once worked as prison warden's secretary, and her husband, Dan, dressed in bib overalls. He says a visitor can use his name, "as long as you're not from MSNBC or CNN, or else I'll get in my truck and leave right now."

Then Gordon and Jackie Steffek arrive with their dog Sadie. "Hi, sweetie," Miss Kathy coos at the animal. "Hi, baby girl." Jackie walks behind the bar to peruse some women's lingerie, then sighs. "My husband won't let me buy one more stick of clothing, shoes or even a purse." Gordon Steffek says proudly he's been coming to the Short Branch for 19 years "and I haven't been thrown out yet." Yes, he adds, he and Jackie are married. "Well, we were when we walked in here."

They all rave about Crystal's quiet life, seeing the occasional badger or long-necked crane on a winter morning, not to mention those gorgeous summer sunsets.

Miss Kathy also likes it here, despite its lousy phone service and lack of good help. Mostly because she stays busy. "There's always towels to wash, floors to mop and nine toilets to clean."

Wiping down the bar, Miss Kathy laments that she might have wasted 32 years working at Sears; if she'd only known how much darned fun she'd have running the Short Branch out in Crystal. Because this is no department store. Out here, it's Miss Kathy's way or the highway.

The Coffee Cup: Tending to Hearts and Stomachs

■ **Boulder City, February 2018.** The customer at the Coffee Cup Cafe has had a bad night. Sandy Nelson's left hip hurts, putting him back in his wheelchair. That's after a stroke left the 1960s rock drummer with a bit less command of his sticks. "Hey, Terry," he calls out from his counter stool. "You were a paramedic. Can I ask you a question?" Just as Terry Stevens, co-owner of the venerable downtown breakfast fixture, leans in for another customer consultation, a group shows up to solicit a donation for a local baseball team. Of course, Stevens handles it all—along with a quick refill of their coffee.

For nearly a quarter century, the Coffee Cup has been synonymous with good eating and a sense of community. California transplants Al and Carri Stevens first fired up the grill in 1994, and decades later, in a new location five storefronts down, they're still at it—now with the help of their grown children, son, Terry, and daughter, Lindsay.

More than a restaurant, the Coffee Cup, open from 6 a.m. to 2 p.m. seven days a week, offers a culinary slice of the American West. Al's pork chili verde omelet, which celebrity chef Guy Fieri featured on his Food Network series, *Diners, Drive-ins and Dives*, and the tall-glass Bloody Marys served with a thick wedge of bacon as a stir-stick, have earned the Coffee Cup a national reputation as a stopover for RVs and SUVs en route to nearby Hoover Dam.

The family is recognized almost everyplace they go—from the DMV office to the bike paths of Southern California—where people stop them and say, "Wait, aren't you the owner of the Coffee Cup? Great Bloody Marys!"

Al's occasional grouchiness and Carri's motherly demeanor are part of the diner's draw, and the couple works hard to preserve the Coffee Cup's local touch. Customers and waitresses know one another by their first name. Conservative politicians stump for votes come election season, especially among the morning coffee klatch of old geezers who call themselves the Circle of Knowledge.

The eatery is so popular the family doesn't need to advertise, so they earmark that money for community donations—sponsoring youth events or purchasing uniforms for kids who couldn't otherwise afford them.

When Nelson lost his keys, Coffee Cup waitresses tore the place apart on a fruitless hunt to return them. Now the drummer's gold record hangs over the counter. Carri keeps a chalkboard list of cherished daily regulars near the kitchen—if they don't show up by noon, she calls them at home to make sure they're OK.

At the Coffee Cup, customers are considered family. The restaurant and its familial bond have wielded its own gravitational pull on Terry and Lindsay—who in their youth wandered from the fold. But it was Al's two dramatic bouts with throat and blood cancer that have most helped the Stevens children and the entire Boulder City community to better appreciate the little diner gem at 512 Nevada Highway as a precious, irreplaceable thing. "This restaurant means so much to Boulder City—the whole family does," said longtime regular Bill Burke, a retired National Park Service ranger. "When Al got sick, it was hard on everyone. We pulled for him. And we all pulled for Carri to stay strong."

The concern over her husband's health has made Carri emotional. Even crusty old Al is impressed. "I'm not the world's friendliest person—I haven't always played well with others," the 67-year-old said. "But this restaurant allowed me to meet some special people. They're here because they want to be, not because they have to."

Nelson can't stay away from the place. "The food is damned good, but I really come to flirt with the waitresses," said Nelson, a well-known session drummer in the 1960s, who scored such solo hits as "Teenage House Party" and "Cool Operator." "It's not fair; they're all in their 20s, and I'm almost 80. Good thing I have a sense of humor."

Al Stevens came to the desert as a way to get away from the politics of the ocean; he got into a fistfight over a surfing run off Huntington Beach, California, and retired his longboard—which now hangs on the wall of his signature diner. He landed in Boulder City in 1977 and later met Carri Ham, a native of Norwalk, California, who bagged groceries at the supermarket where he worked as a meat cutter. They dated six months and got married.

After the couple took out a home loan to open the first Coffee Cup in 1994, Al, the cook, sometimes wandered around the tables in his white chef's cap and apron to inquire about the food. Delighted customers wanted to know more about this sphinx from the kitchen. But Carri shooed him back to his post for insubordination. She fired him, he quipped. Once Al told a customer to shut up so he could hear the TV. "Oh, my God, Al," Carri remembers telling him. "You just cannot do that!" If a group wanted their bill split, Al suggested they pay the check and then go outside and figure it out for themselves. He'd never heard of Fieri when the chef called about visiting the restaurant for his show. "I don't want any," Al said and almost hung up.

The couple put their teenage kids to work. Lindsay was hostess, and when the place needed waitresses, she'd bring friends from the high school, starting a Coffee Cup tradition. Terry, too shy to greet the public, stayed in the kitchen. He soon tired of the all-consuming restaurant life—how even at home his parents would rehash the day's events, the thing the customers at Table Two had said, and how they had to bail a dishwasher out of jail.

In 2004, the owners moved the restaurant down the block to its present location. The local newspaper featured a front-page photograph of the family rolling refrigerators down the sidewalk. Al and Carri relived that day over dinner, for sure.

Four years later, the Stevens kids had left the Coffee Cup. Lindsay attended college in San Diego, and Terry was racing boats and studying to get his EMT license as a firefighter. Then disaster struck: Al was diagnosed with throat cancer. Terry went to visit his father, who couldn't speak. He asked how he could help, and Al wrote down some chores that needed doing: cleaning the bathrooms, repairing the roof, making stock runs in the family Suburban.

Meanwhile, word got out about Al's cancer. Customers offered to drive him to his daily radiation treatment. Carri couldn't go to the post office without people inquiring about her husband. She was crushed, worrying about losing her lifetime partner in crime, and quietly put the restaurant up for sale.

In San Diego, Lindsay told friend and Navy SEAL Shane Patton about plans to sell the restaurant. "Wait, what?" she remembers him telling her. "You can't do that! That's your family business!" The exchange brought Lindsay to a decision: She had to go home to do what she could to help save the Coffee Cup. Patton was later killed in Afghanistan. His picture now hangs on the restaurant wall.

In Boulder City, Carri had a buyer. But on her way to the real estate agent's office to sign the papers, she had a change of heart. She arrived with a bouquet of flowers and told the agent the news. "I can't sell the Coffee Cup. If I ever lost Al, what would I do?"

Al eventually beat his death sentence, returning to the restaurant six months later and counseling customers as a cancer survivor. But in 2014, Al was diagnosed with a new, more aggressive form of cancer. After a year of blood transfusions, he checked into City of Hope Hospital in Duarte, California, and Carri rented an apartment nearby while the grown kids ran the Coffee Cup. "We'd dreamed of turning over the restaurant to them," Carri said. "But not like this." Al remained in a hospital isolation unit for 172 days. Once, wearing a respirator, he pointed heavenward, making a circle gesture for his family to surround him. He wanted to die. Lindsay slapped his hand. Her father was going to fight, she insisted.

At the Coffee Cup, customers bought votive candles for Al and bused their own tables to help out. Terry emerged from his shell. After once guarding his privacy, he engaged with customers, showing pictures of his wife, Kristin, and young son, Cruz. He also bonded with Lindsay, who has her own daughter, Kyra. Al survived, but the cancer convinced him to let his kids start pouring the coffee. He rolls in now and then, cleans the bathroom and riffs with customers.

The family has a newfound ethic of balancing work with their personal lives. Al and Carri run the packed restaurant on Saturdays—when an hourlong wait for a table isn't uncommon—so their grandchildren get some needed bonding time with their parents. Still, they love seeing Kyra, now 7, help her mother swipe customer credit cards at the register or 9-year-old Cruz walk behind the counter to make his own milkshake.

Just ask Al and Carri, and they'll tell you: Cancer has taught them a valuable lesson. "Money doesn't rule everything," Carri said. "Family counts." Customers, too.

Death Squad: Sorting out the Remains of the Rural Dead

■ **Pahrump, May 2018.** Some death scenes stay with Ginger Stumne, disturbing her sleep. Like the man found a year after his suicide, a troubled soul reduced to bones hanging from a rope. Some of the dead she knew in life, like the close family friend she found in bed, his once-vital body withered, already gone for weeks in the middle of summer. She only recognized him from the photo on his driver's license. "That one gave me nightmares," she said.

Stumne isn't a homicide detective or medical examiner; they collect government checks for their labors. But not Stumne. She's Nye County's public administrator, filling an elected position for which there is no budget—a baffling fact considering her macabre duties. Because the county has no coroner, Stumne must appear at the scene of each unattended death (one where no family member is present) across this vast but underpopulated county—the nation's third-largest at 18,000 square miles, home to just 43,000 residents. While she's not there to collect evidence or discern cause of death, her role still looms large. Because when people die without wills, they leave behind a financial and emotional quagmire for their grieving families.

That's where Stumne excels. The 45-year-old grandmother protects all assets until family members arrive to claim them. At death houses, she and her volunteers pull the blinds, unplug the toaster and electrical appliances, secure the car keys and resolve the fates of pet dogs, cats, birds, a squirrel and, once, even a snake. She's a fixer, social worker, consigliere, financial adviser and family hand-holder. And a custodian. Her staff is also responsible for cleaning up the death scene, even after suicides. They walk into homes wearing gloves, booties and masks, and sometimes hazmat suits because of the blood and risk of infection.

She pays for everything out of her own pocket, shelling out for death certificates, cremation and burial fees, electric and water bills for the estate, even gas for her truck. Because she draws no salary from Nye County, Stumne must rely on money she makes from a small percentage she earns from the estates she handles. And those can be few and far between and not be worth much, so her salary each year varies wildly. Once an estate is settled, Stumne receives a percentage, after scrutiny by a county judge. But many cases drag on for years, and there is no guarantee that she will ever collect a dime. In 2016, for example, she made $8,000, but last year she made a more respectable $52,000.

Nye County Sheriff Sharon Wehrly said she is amazed at the quality of work Stumne performs and thinks she should be paid by the government. "I've been around a very long time, and I've seen a lot of people do this job; some did it well and others took advantage of the position," she said. "Ginger has taken this job and turned the office around. She's done an admirable job, and I'd really like to see her continue." Wehrly said she thinks Stumne should be paid through the district attorney's office but that despite recent conversations about the issue, that has yet to happen. "It really needs to be a paid job," she said.

In Stumne's makeshift trailer-turned-office, grease boards detail the 40-odd ongoing cases and $4,000 in fees and expenses that remain uncompensated. In a storage closet, she keeps the cremated remains of those deceased and still unclaimed. Inside a safe kept closed with duct tape—there's no money to fix it—she keeps weapons used in suicides. On one wall, Stumne keeps a placard from a family that reads, "Be Fearless." "Because you're dealing with death and an often-angry public," she said.

Stumne responds around the clock to deaths that occur hundreds of miles away. She conducts nationwide—and even international— searches to locate the family members of those who die on her watch. "I know if my mother died, I wouldn't want (anyone) to learn about it on Facebook or TV," she said. "I want to let them know the deceased's home and estate are secure until they get here, and not be bombarded with what-ifs."

The job can age you. Stumne has encountered family who want nothing to do with the deceased. Like the man who said of a brother who took his own life, "Good, I'm glad he's dead. But if I have any money coming, you better get it to me fast."

In training seminars, would-be volunteers walk out after seeing photos of death scenes, saying, "Whoa! I'm not up for this!" before even encountering their first body. Many nights, after tending to the indelicate details of death, she removes her clothes in the garage, deciding whether to toss them in the washer or throw them away. Sometimes, her boyfriend does a sniff test before he even opens the door.

But Stumne carries on. A compact woman with dirty-blond hair, she dresses in blue jeans and wears an oversize smartphone on her belt like a gun in a holster. As for guns, she has one of those, too. She recently bought a 9 mm handgun as protection against a public that both misunderstands and threatens her work.

Over the years, the Nye County public administrator's office has been rife with bad luck and bad press. Twenty years ago, Public Administrator Robert "Red" Dyer and his wife, Jennette, were charged with siphoning money and goods from county residents whose estates they were responsible for administering. In 2010, Robert Jones resigned from his public administrator's position after he was tied up and robbed at gunpoint by assailants who targeted him because they knew he handled valuables as part of his job. When Robin Dorand-Rudolf suddenly resigned in 2016, Stumne—then a public administrator's volunteer assistant—took over to complete her four-year term. The move has put her in the public's crosshairs. Not long ago, after she bought her dream vehicle—a "white Ford diesel jacked-up pickup truck"— Stumne was confronted by a man in a newer-model Mustang. "You stole that truck," he shouted at Stumne. "You can't afford that truck."

Neighbors call the police when she arrives to remove items from a house. Then there are friends and roommates who don't like the fact that without a will, the estate of any deceased legally goes to family— even if the person had little contact with relatives or had talked about doing something else with his or her money. Two roommates with criminal records have left Stumne threatening voicemails. "I can't believe you can sleep at night," one began. "We're coming after you." Her response was pure Stumne: She told them to have their attorney call her. Her job was to follow the law. Still, the threats give her pause. "I'm the bad guy," she said. "They know what I drive."

Such chutzpah represents a remarkable turnaround for a mother of three who was once physically abused by two former husbands, who at age 40 found herself unemployed, undereducated and struggling to provide for three teenage children. Raised in Pahrump, Stumne began running her family's gym at the end of her first abusive marriage. When her parents sold the business, Stumne was out of a job. Back then, she didn't even know how to apply for unemployment insurance. But she learned.

She harnessed a compassion to help others and threw herself into a life of public service. While working marketing jobs for a law office and senior center, she volunteered as a sheriff's dispatcher, and opened a licensed day care center and later a nonprofit that advocated for senior citizens, U.S. veterans and the disabled. She volunteered at a hospice center and became a court-appointed advocate for children. She also became a legal guardian to a physically and mentally disabled couple brought to Pahrump after being abused in a California mental hospital. All the while, she received her paralegal certificate via an online course and continues to take prelaw classes with the goal of becoming a probate lawyer. This semester, she once again made the dean's list. All this from a mother who once had to tell her children she was too busy to stop at a McDonald's when in reality she was too poor to afford a burger and fries. "I want to show my kids that as long as you want to improve yourself, age does not matter," she said. "You can do it. There are more than just eight hours in a day."

In 2016, when Stumne stepped up to lead the troubled public administrator's office after her boss resigned, her family worried she was going to ruin their good name. Stumne disagreed. "I told them I wasn't going to ruin it, but I was going to take our good family name and clean up this office."

One California woman witnessed Stumne's style firsthand when she handled the death of an older brother and thanked her in a card that hangs on the wall. It cites Stumne for "taking the pressure off us and I was able to focus on grieving the loss of such a fine man that was my brother."

With her own children now grown, Stumne is helping raise her boyfriend's two teenage boys. He's helped her redefine her self-image and reclaim the self-worth taken from her from two abusive marriages. His message: It's OK to have your own life and not work around the clock.

But for Stumne, slowing down takes work. While she pursues her legal degree, she plans to run for re-election next year. "I have to keep busy," she said. "That's who I am."

The Center

Longtime friends Lina Sharp and Minnie Perchetti visit in Perchetti's living room in Tonopah. Photo by Randi Lynn Beach.

Outback Nevada's
Women Pioneer Pals

▪ **Tonopah, May 2016.** Lina Sharp arrives, like she always does, with a polite knock, waiting under the stately front-yard elm tree for the familiar face of a cherished old friend. For decades, she has come calling on Minnie Perchetti, who lives in a tiny one-story house just off the main drag of this high-desert eye-blink without a stoplight. On this day, as always, Lina is here to catch up on goings-on around town and in the surrounding back country: who has landed in jail or in the hospital, who has made that last sad procession to the graveyard.

"How are you doing?" Lina says as the door opens.

"Pretty good," Minnie answers softly. "My eyes aren't so good."

Lina's response is unhesitating: "But you are."

They're two pioneer women who have witnessed both boom and bust in Nevada's mostly unpeopled outback, a pair of stubborn frontier characters who, having long outlived their husbands, were left to navigate a tough-as-leather landscape not always kindly to widowed women. Theirs is a friendship that has endured both time and distance, a bond between great-great-grandmothers of Croatian lineage that got its start during the last gasp of the Great Depression, when Franklin D. Roosevelt was president and the nation was soon to enter World War II, a time when the roads out here were still dirt tracks.

Lina is 96. Minnie is right behind at 95.

▪ ▪ ▪

In many ways, their lives are mirrors, but there are differences. Lina is unsentimental, a college graduate who loves to read and whose wanderlust took her across the globe after her husband died. Minnie is a homebody who married young and dropped out of high school, a person who can count on one hand the times she has left Tonopah. She's also a romantic, like when she describes meeting her husband the day he delivered milk to her home decades ago: "I came to the door and fell in love." Lina is more practical. "He was earnest," she said of her mate. "The pickings out there were pretty slim."

In 1940, Lina Pinjuv (pronounced pin-you've) arrived here from Las Vegas to take a job as a country teacher on a ranch in Railroad Valley, 100 miles east of Tonopah. She married a young cowboy named Jim, who liked to memorize poems as he drove cattle on horseback. Years later, after Jim died of a heart attack, Lina stayed on at the ranch, raising five daughters who were homeschooled, taught to tend to the chores without a man around to supervise.

But she always made time to visit Minnie, the girl she'd met on trips through Tonopah en route to her classes at the University of Nevada, Reno. She recalled once taking a photograph of Minnie dressed in a fuzzy turquoise sweater popular in the day. On the long bumpy ride north to Reno, Lina thought of how she wanted that sweater. The two women still laugh about that.

If Lina was worldly, Minnie was a townie from the start, a woman who still lives next door to the house where she was born. While still in high school, she eloped with Tony, a mine worker; the two stealing off to Hawthorne for a fly-by-night wedding. Nobody knew about the marriage until Minnie's mom suggested the two shop for a new dress for Minnie's senior year in high school. "I'm not going to school," Minnie announced. "Tony and I got married. I'm going to move in with him and keep house." Later, Minnie climbed ladders to help her husband in his roofing business. They eventually raised four children. And now, nearly a half century after Tony died, the four grown kids still stop by to visit their mother each morning.

Lina comes, too. For years, she has left her sprawling Blue Eagle Ranch, situated 12 miles from the nearest paved road, for the long drive along U.S. Highway 6, past signs for places such as Silver Bow, Golden Arrow and Stone Cabin. She drove Jeeps, trading them in every few years to avoid the dreaded middle-of-nowhere breakdowns. As years passed, and she drove less, Lina hitched rides to town with the mail delivery woman, riding home the following day with some kindly neighbor. She's always stayed overnight; the spare bedroom off of Minnie's kitchen was reserved just for her.

On a recent morning, the two confidantes sit on the couch in Minnie's parlor, talking about the days when people sat on their front porch and watched the world go by; before TV, smartphones and social media. Minnie laughs self-consciously about a set of Western figurines she keeps on a long shelf, wondering aloud if people like them. Lina jumps to her best friend's defense. "That's you," she says. "If people don't like them, they don't have to come."

As World War II raged, Lina began her life as a country teacher at a ranch named after the figure of a blue eagle early settlers said they could spy on a nearby mountaintop, if the season and sunlight were just right. She wasn't exactly a city girl, but she was far from country. Back then, she didn't know how to build a fire, cook on a wood stove, feed the cows, chickens and sheep—skills she would later teach her children. She blanched at mannerless ranch hands who ate beans, potatoes and canned prunes out of quart jars. Her pay was $64 a month, plus room and board, to teach eight children. The job included sweeping the floor and starting a daily fire. At night, she slept in a nearby cabin. She missed her access to books but soon fell for the mountain vistas and iron-red sunsets at the ranch that had been homesteaded in 1868 and bought by the Sharp family in 1895.

Jim Sharp was a young family wrangler whose poems included one about a cowboy who prized an old hat. He soon fell for the young schoolteacher, and they were married a year after Lina's arrival. Those first years were the hardest, without phone service or electricity. Well water was pumped by hand. Winters were so cold clothes froze on the line and snowdrifts blocked the sun. "Mom was definitely out of her element," daughter Jeanne Sharp Howerton said. "But she persevered." In 1961, when Lina was just 45, Jim suffered a heart attack after scaling the crest of an isolated mountain peak. During a long painful night waiting for help, his daughter Jeanne by his side, he weakened and died in the rescue helicopter. If people expected Lina to flee the ranch, they were wrong. Someone suggested she could take her daughters to San Francisco. Lina thought that was nonsense "It's just part of me," she said. "I am part of the picture. I've spent most of my life out here."

Things eventually got easier. Phone service came to Railroad Valley in the 1970s, and electricity followed a few years later. Lina hung a map of the world on the wall so her girls would know there was a big universe outside the ranch. After she retired from teaching, Lina took flight. Often traveling alone, she visited the places she'd read about in her books. Soon, she'd set foot on all seven continents. But she always came back to the ranch, where the old one-room schoolhouse still sits, its desks and instruction books intact. Lina likes her rustic life; she still doesn't "know the language of computers."

Several years ago, Lina was just one of four people who lived in the entire valley, which is 100 miles long and 13 miles wide. Whenever she got the urge, she'd jump into her Jeep "and just go," the vehicle kicking up a cloud of dust on its way to the paved road. She'd be off to visit Minnie, eager to tell stories of Antarctica and South Africa, just as anxious to hear about the people whose simple lives and common sense had helped shape her into the woman she had become.

■ ■ ■

Minnie Boscovich grew up as a tomboy; her three older brothers often pointed out the girls—and boys—in the schoolyard they wanted Minnie to go and beat up.

Later, her marriage to Tony was a shock to the family. Minnie worried her brothers might take revenge on her new husband; ending her dream of domestic bliss before it even got started. The family was poor and lived without indoor plumbing. Minnie and the kids would help Tony on his roofing jobs and on weekends go hunting and fishing in the surrounding countryside they came to know so well it appeared in their dreams. "I've lived here all my life; I loved Tonopah," Minnie said. "I knew everybody. I didn't need a car. It was a nice place to live."

After Tony died in 1973, Minnie lost her interest in men and romance. "I never looked at another guy," she said. "I never wanted to get married again." Not that her kids didn't try to play matchmaker. "Mom was just 53 when dad died," said son Bob, who runs a motel in town. "She was still attractive, but she was a one-man woman. She loved my dad and that was it. Once we got her to go on a date with a geologist. He took her to dinner and helped her hang clothes on the line. He never got inside the house, though."

Minnie always looked forward to Lina's visits, when they'd go gambling at the casino in town. Minnie teased her friend for being a cheapskate, slipping a single nickel into the slot machines instead of five. Recalled Lina: "I'd buy a book and pay a horrendous price, but to put money into a machine and pull the handle. . . "

As the years want by, Minnie's friends passed away, but not Lina. She kept up her visits, just like always. They'd talk until 8 p.m., when Minnie got tired and went to bed. She'd leave Lina in the living room with her book and drop off to sleep knowing her best friend was there nearby.

In the parlor, Minnie tells about her trip to the eye doctor up in the Smoky Valley. "We had a nice trip," she says, "but my eyes aren't in the best of shape." "Can you read?" Lina inquires. "Do you need glasses?"

As time passes, the two settle into their personalities like comfortable chairs. Minnie laughs about killing chickens as a girl, putting their heads between two nails and giving their bodies a tug, watching the headless animals run across the yard.

Lina says she wants to visit the bookstore before she goes home. She kicks herself for not bringing a few fresh eggs from the ranch. Soon, the two old friends go their separate ways, always happy with each other's company, no matter how long it lasts.

Because Lina knows you can take nothing for granted out on the frontier. "Your life was handed down to you, and you lived it," she said. "That's just the way it went."

Where the Drinkers—and the Chickens—Come Home to Roost

■ **Manhattan, July 2016.** The bar regular known around these parts as Chicken Dave Sweetwood is telling a tale about his largesse of freshly laid eggs. A few years back, the white-bearded desert roustabout found himself out of a job at one of the Big Smoky Valley's mines. With time on his hands, he bought a couple of chickens and, with his roost soon boasting 30 hens and counting, he did something that embodies the generosity and community spirit of the place called the Manhattan Bar:

He gave his eggs away. Each morning, he would walk the town's single main street in the western foothills of the Toquima Range, leaving cardboard boxes full of eggs for friends and neighbors. Often, he'd bring them into the bar and people would buy him drinks. "I didn't make any money," said Chicken Dave, now 60. "But a lot of those same people often lent me a hand, bought me food, offered loans, when I was unemployed."

Now, on a late spring afternoon, standing in the historic old bar, Chicken Dave talks about how he eventually got his mining job back and sold off his poultry brood. That's when Sam Lauver, a big strapping miner and volunteer firefighter in a white T-shirt and red ball cap, swivels around on his bar stool, loaded with a one-liner. "Well," the 24-year-old says, "now you're Chickenless Dave, aren't you?" The drinkers all laugh—it's more of a cackle, really, that once might have been heard in Chicken Dave's henhouse. Backs are slapped, and this tight-knit assemblage of boozers out in the middle of Nevada's nowhere turns back to their beers.

All across the Silver State, old-time saloons such as the Manhattan Bar are stubborn holdouts from another era; many established a century or more ago in the region's gold-and-silver boom days. Then, these tiny towns teemed with hundreds of hardy residents, each looking to strike a vein and get rich quick.

Nowadays, these places have regressed into near-ghost towns, the often-lonely domain of the independent few who prefer a rural life, living comparatively unfettered under big Western skies. For them, places like the Manhattan Bar provide a sense of community, like a town hall or an urban barber shop, where blue-collar men and women can get a drink, revel in some gossip, buy a round, laugh, get drunk, maybe dance on the bar, sometimes fight, and realize that they're not alone out here after all. Some regulars slouch at the bar nursing sodas, drawn not by the alcohol, but by the camaraderie.

On moonless nights, the neon beer ad in the bar's window might be the only welcoming light for 50 miles. And the regulars, drawn like moths to a singular florescent bulb, return to this century-old wooden shack with its clapboard frontage reading, "Emporium: Wet Goods for Dry People." They arrive in dirty pickup trucks, four-wheel drives, motorcycles, all-terrain vehicles, on foot and even on horseback. They're miners, ranchers, retirees and those not inclined toward work. They're a life-hardened crew, with many faces furrowed with age lines; the men sporting cowcatcher beards and ponytails, wearing NAPA Auto Parts caps, cigarettes and toothpicks dangling from their lips; the women often adorned in handmade jewelry, or none at all. Many patrons have taken turns as hired bartenders because out here, where jobs are scarce, you do what you can just to survive another year. Dogs are also welcome, because almost everybody has one. If not exactly barflies, these regulars are all bar birds-of-a-feather. "This is it; this is what we do in Manhattan," Lauver said. "If you live out here and don't stop in to the Manhattan Bar, you're either a hermit or you don't like people."

There are actually two bars in Manhattan, about 50 miles north of Tonopah (year-round population is 45). The other is the Miners Saloon, where owner Sharon Pauley—who has run the place for 26 years and is also the town's postmistress—runs a tight ship. She quickly shushes anyone who cusses as she perches watchfully behind the bar, near the window, keeping an eye on her unattended post office across the street. Many frequent both establishments but some prefer the Manhattan Bar, where beers are supposedly served colder and where the management once staged a weekly Dirty Song Night, when patrons took turns playing jukebox ditties with naughty lyrics.

The Manhattan Bar is also the spot where they hooted over the Chicken Hit game. Regulars bought numbered squares in a tiny coop, rooting for the bird to poop on their spot so they could take home the cash. It's a bar where a former owner known as One-Eyed Fern would pocket your cash when you slunk away to the restroom. Even though the chicken game is retired and Fern is long gone, the regulars still flock here to watch *Jeopardy!* on TV and practice their horseshoe tosses out back for the regular tournaments that take place in Manhattan and nearby Belmont.

At the Manhattan Bar, the humor is often as rough-edged as the decor. Along with mementos and photographs of the town's mining heyday, and the stuffed mountain lion that peers down at the pool table, the place bristles with a man-cave sensibility. In the men's room hangs a sign: "Please do not throw cigarette butts in the urinal: It makes them soggy and hard to light." On the front door, two signs beckon: "Please unload guns and remove ski mask before entering" and "Save a Flag: Burn a Protester."

A visitor at the bar asks a regular, "What do you do?"

The local lights a cigarette and responds: "I don't."

■ ■ ■

Ever since they discovered gold 110 years ago, Manhattan has remained a rough town, a realm of rowdy miners and drunken gamblers.

In 1906, Tom Logan, then the popular Nye County sheriff, came to a bad end in Manhattan. Logan, a silent partner in a local brothel, was asleep there one night when he was roused by the madam about a recalcitrant patron. Dressed in a nightshirt, Logan challenged the man and was shot five times. He died after bleeding out from a leg wound when a doctor failed to use a tourniquet. Nightlife, it seemed, often came at a steep price.

In the early 1930s, settlers hauled in several pre-built buildings from surrounding towns, including those that house the Miners Saloon and Manhattan Bar, ensconcing them in view of an area so contested by mining companies and their lawyers that it earned the name Litigation Hill.

Over the decades, wild times ensued. If the mines were booming, the men had money. And when the men made more money, they drank and played that much harder.

Bobby Bottom is a Manhattan mainstay, unofficial mayor and official volunteer fire chief. He likes to tell colorful tales of when One-Eyed Fern, whose full name was Fern Vetsera, ran and lived in the Manhattan Bar until her death in 1978. One day, a customer spotted Fern washing her undies in the same bar sink in which she swabbed her highball glasses. "Nobody drank highballs after that," Bottom said. "They all bought bottled beer."

At 74, Bottom is himself a character who spent decades mining a claim outside town. Sitting in the Miners Saloon with a can of Diet Dr Pepper, he pulls out a "pocket piece" that he says every bona fide miner carries. In Bottom's case, it's a 1¼ ounce gold nugget worth several thousand dollars. These days, Bottom doesn't frequent the Manhattan Bar. He'd had words with a bartender there. In small towns like this one, personal grudges can die hard.

But the place has gone on without him. In 2001, Las Vegas car dealer Jim Marsh—at age 82 a longtime rural Nevada regular—bought the bar, adding a half-dozen motel rooms next door so people had a place to bed down if they drank too much. A few years back, the town got a relay tower and Wi-Fi coverage, so drinkers no longer have to drive seven miles down the mountain to talk on their cellphones.

Most nights, hijinks still ensue. One old-timer tells of the night a man rolled in from Louisiana—his last name was allegedly Turdwater—danced on the bar and got whacked unconscious by a ceiling fan.

On slow nights, Chicken Dave says, the regulars take bets on whether one heavy drinker leaving the joint will fall down before he gets to his four-wheel drive. "One day, he came in and I told him, 'Hey man, your quad's running off.' It was rolling down the street. He had to take off after it."

These days, Tony Grimes works as an assistant at the town library, but in a previous incarnation he tended bar at the Manhattan. He recalled the night a regular nicknamed Bronco Billy rode into town and hitched his horse in front of the bar. Many drinks later, Billy mounted his horse and fell off the other side. Billy's gone now, and Grimes jokes that he's in the running to take his place. "I'd like to be the town drunk, but some people have more money than me," he said. "So I have to settle for being the assistant town drunk."

And he couldn't think of a better place to hone his craft than the Manhattan Bar. "We're like one big semi-dysfunctional family," he said. "People come in to cash their checks and get the scoop. It's a raucous mix of bank and social center." On Thanksgiving, locals throw a plywood board over the pool table and serve a turkey dinner for the town. When patrons pass away, the bar's regulars hold a ceremony with the drinker's ashes at Boot Hill, the town cemetery, then return to the bar to get drunk and celebrate the life of the deceased—the bar providing a rite of passage both in life and in death.

Bottom can't stay mad forever. But just in case, he's built his own cozy bar called Tommy Knockers on a hill overlooking his home. The boys have had some doozy nights drinking up there at 7,200 feet, where the view stretches for a hundred miles. "But most often, when I get mad at all the bartenders in town, I'll go up there and drink all by myself and give the middle finger to everyone down below," Bottom said.

It's early June, and the Manhattan Bar regulars are gearing up for the big horseshoe tournament in Belmont. There's always something going on up in the hills. The regulars travel a bar circuit of sorts, bouncing from bingo night at the Half Moon Saloon in Hadley, to Dirty Dick's in Belmont, or they might stop for a round at the bar in nearby Carvers, where fists are known to fly on Friday nights. There are favorite bars south in Tonopah or north in Austin, where they frequent Zack's Lucky Spur Saloon. All of them are beacons of light and sociability in the rural darkness. Sometimes, a cowboy band featuring the mayor of nearby Bishop, California, plays the circuit and people dance—both with partners and by themselves.

One afternoon, Manhattan bartender Sandy Crawford is serving drinks and stirring up nostalgia. At one point, she describes the famous flood that warped the bar so badly patrons had to watch that their drinks didn't slide away when they set them down. But she's not good with dates, so Crawford turns to the crowd. "What year did that flood come through and the bar sagged so bad before it got fixed?" Chicken Dave turns from his post at one of the three slot machines. "They fixed it?" he asked, sounding bewildered.

Now Chicken Dave is back working hard at the mine. He also sells art at his shop, the Manhattan Country Store.

One day, drinking a beer at 2 p.m., Dave admits he's not going anywhere. "I love it here," he said wistfully. "I'm gonna die here." And when he does, his fellow drinkers, horseshoe-throwers and gossip-swappers will throw him a life-celebration party down at the Manhattan Bar.

Jack Malotte: A Rural Native Artist Gets Political

■ **Duckwater, September 2021.** One night not long ago, Jack Malotte was awakened by the sound of a woman's laughter. At age 67, the Native American elder has for decades inhabited a remote reservation redoubt amid central Nevada's vast Great Basin.

Other than the wind or the howl of a coyote, rural nights are peaceful. Women don't laugh out here in a community of 192 people. Not at this hour. Not this close.

But Malotte wasn't dreaming; Chad, his Australian Shepherd, had heard the noise, too. Malotte got up, walked out the front door and fired off a few rounds from his .22-caliber rifle. Then he then did the same thing out back.

Who knows what he heard. Perhaps it was the shadowy figure Malotte calls "the spirit that follows me," one that appears in much of his work. His subject matter ranges from the spirituality of his Shoshone and Washoe ancestors to the injustices non-native culture has perpetrated upon these sacred lands—U.S. Army massacres, atomic testing, military bombing trials, open-pit mining and massive water diversion projects.

He takes the episode in stride, admitting that this place and its history are both violent and mysterious. "My motto is that Duckwater is where the pavement ends and the fun begins," he said. "The place where the real meets the surreal."

Born on northern Nevada's South Fork Reservation but raised in Reno, Malotte has spent his life and career not being boxed in. He's not content to be defined as a silk-screener, a painter or even an activist who expresses his political views through line drawings or sweeping Western landscapes.

Over the decades, he has done all of the above, capturing vital Native American causes in paint, pencil and ink. He's worked such diverse jobs as a newspaper graphic artist and U.S. Forest Service wild land firefighter, all while lending his artist's eye to Nevada's indigenous protest movement. He's worked beside Mary and Carrie Dann,

Artist Jack Malotte poses inside his studio on the Duckwater reservation.
Photo by Randi Lynn Beach.

the Western Shoshone sisters who in the 1970s challenged the federal government's use of their tribe's traditional lands, a case that went all the way to the U.S. Supreme Court.

Throughout Malotte's career, marijuana has been his muse; he's found that alcohol and other drugs just got in his way. Getting stoned helps connect him to an abstract world that combines the modern and the ancient, making the invisible turn visible. His paintings depict mythical renderings of ghostlike whirlwinds and geometric cones that hover over an electrical storm moving across the high desert at night. There are commentaries on such challenges as toxic dumping on Native American lands and alcoholism within indigenous communities, There's a scene of U.S. Air Force bomber jets strafing revered mountains colored yellow and purple. In Malotte's paintings, the mountain ranges and basin valleys come alive with color.

For much of the artist's life, he was on the move, each new place more isolated than the next. He married three times, had a daughter, but always felt the press of partners trying to make him something he wasn't. He lived on people's couches, becoming more solitary, the "spirit that follows me" always on his trail. As he dispensed with cellphones and official addresses, friends had to contact his mother to learn of his whereabouts. In 1999, he arrived in Duckwater to produce a mural for the high school gym, fell in love with his fourth wife, activist Virginia Sanchez, and never left. Duckwater now serves as his base, where he works in a trailer-turned studio, situated off a dust-swirled dirt track, the property line marked by a forlorn white truck. When he moved out here, he jokes, people thought he'd died.

But it is just such isolation that fuels Malotte's creativity, far from the distractions of the city, allowing him the space to create. It took him a full two years to get used to the quiet and endless space. But now when he hears the city's car horns and shouting, he longs for the tranquility of the reservation. He takes long wandering rides in his Toyota Tacoma pickup truck to find promising landscapes—such as nearby Diamond Peak, creating images of the mountain top reflecting ethereal light after a recent snowfall. His work has been shown worldwide, from European galleries to the Smithsonian.

Four years ago, Malotte converted the old trailer into his art studio. For the first time in his life, he had a place to store all his art. He recalls visiting folks across the West to collect pieces he'd left behind on loan.

He'd meet with old friends, spot a long-ago piece of his hanging on the wall and say, "Geez, where'd ya get that?"

In person, Malotte is quiet and quirky. He uses leftover paint to create unorthodox designs on his studio's inner doors. He's like a stoner who takes a hit and stares at the stars. Yet the body of work, while lush, is always pointed. For audiences, it speaks loudly, much more so than the man himself.

"Jack gives Nevada's issues a global relevance," said Ann Wolfe, curator at the Nevada Museum of Art, which in 2019 hosted an exhibit of Malotte's work. "He depicts events from open-pit mining to experiments at the Nevada Test Site, that have a huge influence worldwide. His work shows a world that's out of the way, in the margins, out of sight, out of mind, the places people don't get to see but are still so important."

■ ■ ■

Jack Malotte sits in his trailer studio and talks about the past. Soon to be a great-grandfather, he still exudes a youthful energy—his silver hair shaved close at the sides, the back shaped into a ponytail. He wears bib overalls and laughs a lot.

As a boy on the reservation, he fished and swam down at the river and did small crafts when the mood struck him. He encountered his first serious visual artist at his grandmother's kitchen table, as he sat across from his uncle Bobby, a draftsman for the power company who drew cartoon caricatures in pencil. The boy marveled at the flow of creativity and wanted that outlet for himself. He took drafting classes in high school. When he wasn't playing football, he was drawing— figures of animals and native American spirits.

He attended what is now called the California College of the Arts in Oakland, where trips to record stores influenced his growing style. Album covers were their own art forms and he would buy vinyl for the messages on the cover, most times never even having heard the music. While he never graduated, Malotte's college training made both his art and his worldview more disciplined. Even while his instructors discouraged him, Malotte incorporated Native American culture and commentary into his work, which included a portrait of the Lakota leader Sitting Bull, and another of U.S. Army officer George Custer, with blood drops sprayed across the paper.

After leaving the Bay Area, Malotte began a peripatetic life, never living in one place for long. He learned to dislike the assembly-line drudgery of what it took to sell his paintings in galleries, redoing the same images if they became popular, like a singer with one hit song. Malotte decided that his best audience was Jack Malotte. He experimented with silk-screening, drawing, drafting and painting. He became partial to T-shapes and triangles in his art, always trying to loosen up, stretch his artistic muscles, using a base in geometry to develop his own free-flowing style.

By 1978, Malotte was back in Reno, where he found his personal groove. "I was an easygoing pot smoker who used to party like hell," he said. "In the 1970s, you made a lot of friends when you walked around town with a garbage bag full of weed."

One day, while getting high, a friend said, "Jack, we gotta get you a job." He picked up the newspaper classified ads and pointed to one: "Artist Wanted." Malotte soon began working as a paste-up and editorial artist for what is now the *Reno Gazette-Journal*, illustrating news articles and advertisements. Since then, he's always been open to assigned work, but his heart had always been in his own art.

In the 1980s, Malotte began designing posters, pamphlets, murals and publicity materials for Native American activists and environmental groups, including the Western Shoshone Sacred Lands Association, which was pressuring the U.S. government to return traditional native lands. That's when he met the Dann sisters, two tribal leaders who were making headlines as native activists. He found out he was related to the pair, who told him about his ancestors. Malotte's father and mother are both descended from the Te-Moak Band of Western Shoshone.

While Mary Dann was reserved, Carrie stayed in your face. Malotte recalls the time the sisters were assisting a cow caught in a difficult birth. The mother was splayed on the ground, the calf halfway out, with the Danns arguing whether they should push it back or keep pulling. Finally, Carrie gave the newborn a yank and out it came. "I'd meet them for breakfast, and Carrie gave me advice," he said. "It was like she was yelling, bawling at me to come see them more often and to get more political."

But Malotte shied away from waving banners on the political front lines. "I knew I wasn't a speechmaker," he said. "I wasn't out there yelling and shaking my fist. As an artist, people came to me like a hired gun. That wasn't my thing." His wife agrees. "Jack got pulled into situations," she said. "He likes choices. As he gets older, he's just as political, but probably more wise."

Lately, Malotte's activism has mellowed, though the military jets still hawk the landscape in many pieces. He's also at work on a large painting about little-known U.S. Army massacres of tribes in central Nevada. The political edge remains; he just expresses what bothers him on any given day. He gives his silk-screened art such design names as Indian Uprising, Sagebrush Heathen, Pesky Redskins and Wretched Savages, playing off the derogatory phrases often applied to Native Americans. "They're little political jabs," he said.

In one recent work entitled *Shot in the Heart*, he depicted the controversy surrounding Cave Rock, a formation on the shore of Lake Tahoe that has long been sacred to the Washoe tribe. Now the cave had been taken over by rock climbers, the rock pierced by two tunnels used by gamblers and tourists. The Washoe see the move as cultural theft. Malotte's work shows blood seeping from the tunnels, as though they were wounded by bullets. Above, mysterious figures rise and flee from Lake Tahoe, representing the loss of its spiritual powers.

Such work satisfies him. Yet every time Malotte does art on commission, he ends up asking himself why. Like the woman who wanted her late husband's ashes mixed in with the paint. The artist politely declined; that would be messing with the spirits.

Or the time he painted a boardroom mural for some Reno executive. The customer was a pilot and wanted a scene of jets flying on the horizon, so like he always does Malotte painted his mountains in technicolor. The man wasn't pleased. He wanted his mountains to be a realistic drab brown. So the artist went back to work, mixing up a color he likened to baby poop. "OK!" the man said when the work was done. "That's what I want!" Malotte sighed. "I didn't like it," he recalled. "But he was the boss."

■ ■ ■

To find inspiration, the newest sweeping landscape to mark his art, Malotte still takes ponderous drives in his white pickup. After two decades, he has to scout hard for new images, absorbing all he can, joking that at least the trips have shown him where to find all the good firewood in the valley. "I look for drama, the changing colors, the light through the clouds," he said. "In Duckwater, all you have is a lot of horizon."

Much of Malotte's artistic vision comes via memories. Once, while climbing a cliff as a boy, he looked up to see an eagle soaring directly above him, hovering in the wind. The creature looked down at the boy and then flew off. "But the way he looked at me, I'll always remember those eyes," Malotte said. When he draws eagles, the eyes come first. It's the same thing with mountain lions or wolves. He's spotted both in the wild, their yellow orbs burned into his cortex.

His renderings of nighttime desert downpours come from moments as a child when he sat in an outhouse, keeping the door open, so he could watch the electrical storms move across the darkened landscape, lightning flashing on a far horizon.

And he will always remember the time when his young daughter, Cora, discovered a wild coyote resting beneath the family car. The father had never before seen a coyote that close up, but the girl wasn't afraid and neither was the coyote, and for the longest time, she squatted there, talking to it. "In Shoshone culture, the coyote is like our father, the person who brought us here," Malotte said. "People say the coyote must have been someone we know, whose spirit had come back to talk to us."

These days, Malotte still communes with wild animals. Not long ago, he and Virginia began feeding four feral cats who turned up on the property. Pretty soon, several skunks and ravens also found the food and began showing up at mealtime. "So, we feed them, too," Malotte said. "I say they're all part of my tribe now."

Meanwhile, Malotte continues to make new art. Surrounded by cherished works of the past, he might smoke a joint to get to that creative place in his mind. Then he sits down to produce. "I'm trying to do as much as I can before the end comes," he said. "Sooner than later, the 'spirit that follows me' is finally going to catch up."

The Circuit Judge Upholds
an Old-Time Tradition

■ **Goldfield, March 2016.** Kim Wanker has a serious case of lead foot. Trained as a professional race driver, she thrives on the exhilaration that comes with going fast, pedal to the metal, as the high desert hurtles past her car window. For Wanker, (pronounced wonker), speed takes her mind off stressful work—encountering accused wife beaters, molesters and drug abusers across central Nevada.

She's a traveling circuit judge, one of two 5th District judges in Nye County who dispense justice the way it was done when the Silver State was still a territory. The task requires a lot of driving, thousands of miles each year, sometimes at a pretty fair clip. The bespectacled black-robed judge doesn't wait for lawbreakers to come to her. She goes to them, gavel in hand, to administer a disappearing brand of road justice.

Wanker covers two vast counties, Nye and Esmeralda—a combined area about the size of West Virginia. Based in Pahrump, she also holds court in Goldfield and Tonopah, county seats whose meager populations don't merit a full-time judge.

The job is indeed a throwback: Both Wanker and her rotating counterpart, 5th District Judge Robert Lane, have received death threats from fathers who thought they deserved custody of their children and parents who didn't think their sons merited prison. Just for that reason, she packs a 9 mm handgun, drives an unmarked car and is often accompanied by a bailiff, just to be on the safe side. Still, she holds court in old buildings without metal detectors, her bailiff as her only backup.

But even he can't protect her from run-ins with Nevada Highway Patrol troopers who spot her Chrysler zipping through the desert like the roadrunner in those old cartoons. Some take Wanker's highway faux pas in stride, joking, "Late for court again today, are we?" Others demonstrate a stern fortitude. "Hey judge, you need to slow down," one officer said tersely, standing by her driver's window. "If I catch you again, I am going to write you a ticket."

Wanker slowed down. She never asks for leniency, knowing the officers have a job to do, just like she does when she takes the bench. In court, she's known for her fairness and work ethic, often staying up overnight to best prepare for the following day's cases. Her acquittal rate is near 50 percent in an era when many conservative justices convict at a 90 percent rate.

Yet prosecutors, defense attorneys and defendants alike know her as "The Hammer," a no-nonsense judge who doesn't suffer liars in her courtroom, who may well offer one chance at redemption but rarely a second. She's an adjudicator whose quiet smiling demeanor can change swiftly if she's pushed too far. "I'm speaking, so zip it," she tells a defendant during a proceeding in Goldfield. With another, she's more like a miffed parent.

"You're clean, really?" she asks a young drug offender.

"Yes."

"You know your drug test came up dirty, so cut the bullshit."

Wanker's job has deep roots in legal history. King Henry II, who ruled England from 1154 to 1189, instituted the custom of judges roaming the countryside "on circuit," rather than hauling defendants to London. Much later, a young Abraham Lincoln traveled on horseback alongside Illinois justices who often rode in more comfortable stagecoaches. Today, circuit judges are mostly found in the West. Most of mammoth Montana's 56 counties, for example, are served by circuit courts.

Wanker each month hits U.S. Highway 95, which cuts a swath through the wild heart of Nevada between Las Vegas and Reno. She dodges wandering burros and windblown tumbleweeds, rousting resentful crows from roadside kills. Her legal domain averages three people per square mile—population density that rivals Siberia. With just 600 registered voters in sprawling Esmeralda County, she struggles to seat juries in which the members aren't all related.

In Goldfield's vintage-1907 stone courthouse, the lawyers are set, audience in their seats, the accused already ushered into court. Just one thing is missing.

"Where's Judge Wanker?"

"Oh, she's probably stuck in traffic in that construction on 95," someone says.

Soon Wanker rushes into her chambers, looking hardly justice-like in slacks, a red University of Nebraska sweatshirt, a gavel-shaped pin on her lapel. Donning her black robe, she takes her place on the court's original steel judge's bench, sitting beneath faux Tiffany lamps, under a majestic mounted bighorn sheep head confiscated decades ago from some luckless poacher. She bangs her gavel in a courthouse steeped in history. Famed lawman Virgil Earp was once deputy sheriff here. Each seat in the courtroom still bears a holder for a Stetson.

Courthouse hallways offer up relics of another era: letters from lawyers written in 1911 and a sign warning that "Those who expect to rate as gentlemen will not expectorate on the floor." There are displays of long-ago cattle brands and a glass case displaying a blackjack and a handwritten card saying the "leather-covered bludgeon" was used to "subdue a person by giving them a good whack. Very effective."

A century ago, Goldfield was a thriving mining town of 20,000 wanderers and rapscallions. "Defendant ragged and filthy," a judge wrote of one accused. "Nothing but a cigar stump found on him." In a case involving another vagrant, the court ruled: "He is too lazy to work but is harmless. Given a warning not to come back this way."

On this day, Wanker heard a plea from an alleged Oregon drug runner who missed one court appearance because his private plane ran out of gas in Death Valley. Next came a man accused of numerous sex offenses that could bring a life sentence without parole. He insisted on representing himself at trial. Wanker didn't think that was such a good idea. "You seem to have all the answers," she tells him. "You might want to talk a little less and listen a little more. This isn't my first rodeo." And she warns a drug offender in court on a probation violation: "Do not lie to me. You mess up, you tell me the truth. One thing I cannot stand is lying."

Wanker hears almost 1,000 civil and criminal cases a year. Many involve sex crimes and drugs. Some feature speeders found with opiates in their cars during a traffic stop out on that long, lonely highway.

The morning breezes by. Finally, Wanker leaves the bench for the drive to Tonopah, where she will hear a docket of afternoon cases.

Wanker grew up in Nebraska and spent most of her career as an attorney working in employment law, with several major Las Vegas casinos as clients. Single, with no children, she's a tomboy who collects vintage cars and rides motorcycles, mountain bikes and jet skis. One draw of being a judge in Pahrump is the opportunity to light out each month for open territory, reveling in the freedom of the road. She admires the independent spirit of the rural West. Near the 10-acre spread in Pahrump she shares with her three Labradors, one of her neighbors keeps a pet lion.

In 2011, Governor Brian Sandoval appointed Wanker to fill a vacancy on the bench. She won the subsequent election after attending barbecues and town hall meetings to get to know the communities she represents. She handed out gavel-shaped pieces of chocolate at most stops. "Rural Nevada is a collection of small towns," she said. "You do what you can to fit in."

The judge's reputation has spread beyond the Nevada desert. An independent film crew is marketing a TV reality show called *Travelin' Justice*, based on the exploits of Wanker and Lane. Another outfit is working on a script, based on Wanker, about a rural Western judge with an all-female staff. "Just the amount of cases these two judges handle blew us away—from murder and rape to business squabbles and name changes," *Travelin' Justice* producer Ken Brisbois said. "I mean, there aren't metal detectors in these courtrooms. The bailiff has to be a better shot than the person coming through the door."

The trailer for the show shows a ground-view closeup of Lane and Wanker walking a lonely highway, their shoes crunching on the asphalt, until they turn and face the camera, arms crossed. Subtitle cards read, "Rural Nevada is the modern-day Wild West. In these parts, when they ride into town, everyone knows the law's a comin'."

And when Wanker is behind the wheel, justice arrives at a high rate of speed.

Political conservative and Trump supporter Victor Antic walks out of his International Cafe & Bar in rural Austin. Photo by David Becker.

At this Joint, You Swallow Your Politics with Your Food

■ **Austin, July 2016.** They're known as this town's campaign odd couple. Victor Antic and Gail Morehead get along fine, like two peas in a far-right political pod; it's other residents of this former mining boomtown—not to mention the tourists who ramble along meandering U.S. Highway 50—who find them rather peculiar.

Take the couple's no-holds-barred endorsement of Donald Trump. A few months after the outspoken billionaire declared his long-shot candidacy for the White House, the owners of the International Cafe & Bar began plastering Trump signs outside their historic 1860s-era building in the heart of town. Suddenly, as in literally overnight, the sleepy little establishment became an unofficial, unapologetic, in-your-face, join-us-or-be-gone Trump headquarters. A half-dozen Trump placards, including the ubiquitous "Make American Great Again," are posted near a vintage pioneer wagon wheel and a Miller High Life neon sign that blinks in the bar window.

Many in this unincorporated community of 175 residents have gasped, while their neighbors applauded. Others refuse to do business here. Weary road travelers have chosen to drive another 100 miles for food and rest—but not before stopping for a few selfies in front of the campaign spectacle.

Over the months, the couple's aggressive brand of politicking has been marked by pilfered campaign signs, heated political arguments and lots of shaking heads. Their reaction? Well, like their chosen candidate himself, they are outspoken and defiant. They just don't give a damn. "We don't care if they don't want to eat here. We'll tell them: Get out!" said Morehead, standing at the register, wearing a Trump cap she bought off the internet. "If you're not a Trump supporter, don't come in here. Otherwise, you might get eaten alive."

All across America, the political battle lines are drawn as the nation moves toward November's presidential election, but perhaps nowhere are they more indelible than in this little mountain burg in Nevada's central expanse.

Like much of the rural U.S., Austin is politically conservative territory—many here vote for a straight GOP ticket come Election Day. Some liked Senator Ted Cruz of Texas or Floridian Marco Rubio. At the International Cafe & Bar, they weren't having any of it. "They're just representing what they believe," said Julie O'Hara, who runs a motel directly across the street. Other than that, she wanted to stay clear of the couple's political steamroller.

In the café, Antic, who shuffled along with a slight limp he didn't want to talk about, is a refrigerator repairman with a shock of gray Albert Einstein-like hair who keeps the place running. He was born in a small Serbian town and traveled around Russia and Eastern Europe before landing in the U.S. He met Morehead one Thanksgiving at a karaoke bar in Reno. A decade ago, the pair relocated here to put what Antic calls an international brand on Austin.

He stood at the counter, in front of a picture of Depression-era comedian W. C. Fields, and talked about the political uproar of the last few months. Nearby was some reading material left out for customers, including a book titled *How to Cope When You Are Surrounded by Idiots or If You Are One.* Said Antic: "It hasn't hurt my business one bit." He admitted, though, that he senses hostility among some passersby. "I can feel their attitudes," he said. "I see them pull up in their cars and then drive off."

Some Trump signs have been stolen—replaced the very next day with spanking new ones. He said the young liberals cruising the venerable coast-to-coast highway are the most vocal, arguing their case for Democrat Hillary Clinton. Antic responds with his no-nonsense political beliefs—that both foundering political parties helped create Donald Trump, that police no longer work for the people, that Walmart is the future of socialism in America with so many of its employees on the dole and that Senator Bernie Sanders of Vermont should head on down to Venezuela to help out with that country's socialist revolution.

Just that morning had come a typical face-off when a motorist got into a tiff with Morehead. "He said Trump was a stupid SOB and that he didn't want someone so ignorant to have his finger on the nation's nuclear button," Antic said. "Some of these people get defensive. He just rattled on and then he left—wouldn't give Gail a chance to say her piece."

Many motorists don't even make it in the door to start an argument. "We hadn't even gotten to the door when we saw the prominent

Trump banner and realized that we wouldn't be welcome here," one wrote. "The food could have been wonderful. . .but nothing would have been worth eating in that poisonous atmosphere. No one complained as we left and drove another hour and a half to get lunch." Another Yelp reviewer added: "Try the food if you must, but the gas station down the road is a better decision if you have any type of moral compass."

The couple has their supporters. When two people sitting on a bench in front of a bar were asked for their take on Trump, one gave a thumbs-up sign; the other voted thumbs-down. "Women in town won't go in there," one said. "How could they?"

Gail Utter, who works at the county courthouse, said she stopped in the café and when she left, noted that someone had put a Trump bumper sticker on her car. She didn't take it off and wouldn't say which candidate would get her vote. "When you go into that little voting box, nobody knows your business," she said.

Back at the lunch counter, Antic speculated on what might happen if Trump loses: The U.S., of course, will descend into political chaos like the former Soviet Union. "Even if he loses, he's woken up a lot of people," he said

Still, Antic won't be able to help Trump come Election Day: He's not a U.S. citizen, so he can't vote. But rest assured, Morehead will be the first to put the stamp on her mail-in ballot. And that, Antic hopes, will make America great again.

The Coyote Hunters

■ **Austin, December 2018.** The two brothers shot pool on a cool October afternoon in the Silver State Saloon, along the main drag of this former mining town, just down the street from a sign that reads "Prayer Spoken Here." The eight-ball matches, waged over laughs and beers, weren't really about billiards; the men were working on their hand-to-eye coordination, honing their hunting skills. Jesse Anson and his younger brother, Worth, were preparing for the next day's contest against several dozen practiced marksmen in an animal-killing event.

Coyotes, to be exact. *Canis latrans*. Kill the most, win some money.

The brothers and their fellow sportsmen have practiced names for the animals: They call them "varmints," "pests," or "apex predators run amok." But when they make their kills and lift their prizes by the tails, they call them "dogs." Estimates of their population in Nevada run from about 50,000 to several times that.

Jesse, 35, and his brother are from Battle Mountain, 90 miles to the north, another struggling, blue-collar, central Nevada town. They're both miners—Worth, 22, does his job above ground, Jesse below. Their father taught them to hunt when they were kids. "We're Nevada boys," Jesse said, lining up a corner shot. "This is what we do."

Coyote hunts are a fixture among rural outdoorsmen nationwide, a response to the animals' perceived threat to livestock. In many states, coyotes are unprotected by wildlife laws, meaning they can be hunted without a license or bag limits. Some states, including Utah, Texas, Colorado and South Dakota, pay coyote bounties. As a result, a contest circuit has sprung up in 49 states. The events have names such as the Iowa Coyote Classic, Idaho Varmint Hunters Blast from the Past and the Park County (Wyoming) Predator Palooza. On a recent weekend in Austin, the much-anticipated Coyote Derby drew hunters from as far away as Utah and Las Vegas.

Environmentalists and animal-rights groups have petitioned to halt what some call "killing for kicks." In 2014, California became the first state to ban all wildlife-killing contests, and similar efforts are being waged in Vermont, New Mexico, New York and Oregon. In 2015, critics petitioned Nevada wildlife officials to prohibit the contests. Putting a tally on the number of animals taken in a day, they said, is the very definition of frivolous killing. The Nevada Wildlife Commission voted 7-1 to deny the petition.

Nevada has one of the nation's most pronounced urban/rural splits, according to the 2010 Census. So the brothers know many urban residents view their activities as a senseless extermination and were reluctant to give detailed answers to questions about their tactics—using calls that mimic injured animals to lure out their prey, again and again, as many times as the daylight will allow—and motivations. "You're calling out a wild animal, but you're also getting out into the country and having fun," Jesse said. "Out there, it's all about good times and great friends."

He was decked out in brown camouflage, while Worth wore a black Jack Daniel's T-shirt and blue jeans. At the registration table, a poster advertised an upcoming "Varmint Hunt" in nearby Carvers. Both said they could compete in a coyote-killing contest just about every weekend if they were willing to drive a few hours.

Each time he pulls the trigger in the contest, Jesse said, he's helping the Nevada economy. "Every coyote we kill saves 13 calves a year," he said. "This is ranching country. We're helping save people's livelihoods. All those people who criticize us, we call 'em Californians. Nobody should call this bad until they find out the true facts and go out and try it." He even offered some advice to get started: "Go get yourself a little .22 and start shooting ground squirrels. They're the biggest menace of all. After that, you'll pretty much be hooked."

■ ■ ■

Austin's Coyote Derby has been held annually for more than 15 years. With its promotional poster showing a howling coyote in the crosshairs of a gunsight, the one-day hunt promised more than $6,000 in prize money. There were "big-dog" and "small-dog" competitions, and a "Calcutta" bracket that allowed teams to bet on each other, adding a wagering incentive similar to playing for "skins" on the golf course.

The chief organizer is Phil Marshall, a 65-year-old California construction company owner and rancher who spent much of his childhood in Austin, helping out at a general store his late grandparents ran. "Many of my relatives are buried here," he said. Now Marshall and his family have purchased a half-dozen buildings along the main drag and staked a claim in the future of this community of about 200.

Marshall sees the hunts as a way to inject some energy into Austin's flagging economy. "The purpose of the hunt isn't just to kill a bunch of animals," he said. "The contest brings people and commerce into town. In the slow months here, you might as well lock the doors and wait the winter out." Coyote contestants need a place to eat, drink and regale one another before and after hunts, and Marshall's Silver State Saloon and restaurant are there to serve them. A bar sign reads: "Beer! Because No Great Story Ever Started with a Salad."

The rules of the hunt are straightforward. Participants must show up at the bar to register on the night before the hunt, and return by 6 p.m. the following day to have their animals assessed and weighed. Hunters can take their prey from any county in Nevada. They can use calls and dogs to flush out the animals. No night hunting, no helicopters, no snowmobiles. Hunters are advised to stay off public land, but that rule is rarely enforced. A few entrants go it alone, some using a shotgun so they're forced to get close to their prey. But most hunt in groups, and the really prolific killers use semiautomatic weapons, which Marshall's older brother Kenny called the "fun gun of the hunt."

Sitting at the bar, he described the various weapons used to take out coyotes. "Most guys use either an AR-15 with a scope or a .204 Ruger bolt-action rifle," he said. "The high-velocity rounds go in real small, tears 'em up on the inside and exit. They're sure-kill rounds. You don't want those coyotes walking away." But some hunters prefer to take home their pelts. "In that case, they use the .17 Remington Fireball," Marshall said. "The bullets travel at 4,000 feet per second, and they explode on the inside, but they won't go through."

All Friday afternoon and evening, the pickup trucks, many with jacked-up suspensions, arrived outside the bar, prompting stares from the RV drivers who rolled through on Highway 50. The weekend in Austin came with a dress code: camouflage. Men in green and brown earth-toned uniforms walked the streets, some chomping on cigars, eating in the restaurant and ordering rounds at the bar. "We tried conference-calling those coyotes, but they refused to leave the state and relocate to Florida," one hunter said. "So now they're fair game." Another said he was there to drink, not hunt: "I'll shoot any coyote that walks through that bar door."

As the game of pool wrapped up, Jesse talked about the cautious nature of the animal he hunts. "Coyotes are graceful," he said. "They're a dog." His brother hadn't said much, but finally stepped in. "They don't do any good," Worth said. "They eat all your useful food." Jesse nodded. The brothers planned to get started early the next morning. Jesse had a phrase for those minutes just after dawn and just before sunset. "That's shootin' time," he said.

■ ■ ■

Dawn arrived at 7,000 feet amid a steady rain and a 40-degree chill that hunters suspected would keep the coyotes in their dens. Marshall was up before the light; he wasn't killing coyotes, but he still had work to do. He perched at the end of the bar, drinking coffee, the stools still upside-down from the previous night's cleanup. He divided several piles of cash and put them in envelopes for the winners in each category, using a calculator to make sure he got his accounting right.

Asked about the motivation to join the coyote hunt, Marshall pointed to a pile of tens, twenties and fifties. "This is the thrill of the chase right here," he said. "You get to do what you love to do and compete for money. Get paid for doing your hobby."

Marshall had flown into Austin on his private plane and had invited some friends from the Bay Area. He allowed some novice hunters to take along guides. "Some of these old guys couldn't find the back door if they weren't shown it," he said. "If you don't know the area, you don't do very well."

The registration board showed 21 teams, the last entrants arriving after long drives from around the state. Marshall acknowledged that the hunt didn't do much to fill the town's motels, because most hunters sleep in their trucks to get an early start.

Down the street at the International Cafe & Bar, waitress Angel Walker said she wished the coyote hunts would help other businesses than Marshall's bar. "Hunters are like pack animals," said one customer, drinking coffee at the counter. "They all stick together." Walker scoffed. "Last year, I saw them all walking in the street with their bloody kills in their hands," she said. "Nobody came in here."

For Marshall, there wasn't much to do but wait. He and two brothers kept tabs on the contest from hunters who called in. By 9 a.m., one team had already dispatched five animals. The chase was on.

Last year, the hunt tallied 37 coyotes, but organizers expected more this time. In lean years, all the hunters combined might kill one coyote. The Austin event is small compared to some others. In 2013, for example, the World Coyote Calling championship in Elko claimed more than 300 killed.

The big events bring out many hunters' competitive nature—and for some that means cheating. A few years ago, Marshall disqualified a team from Fallon after he found that many of the group's coyotes had been killed earlier and stored on ice until hunting day. "If someone brings in a stinky dog, you know that animal is at least a week old," he said. "We told those guys to get out of town and not come back."

About 2 p.m., when news came in that the U.S. Senate had voted to confirm Brett Kavanaugh's nomination to the Supreme Court, hunters celebrated by firing their rifles into the air.

Later, Marshall received a report from the field. One of his Bay Area pals had shot a coyote out near the dump. Then he got the real story: The man had forgotten to load his gun, so the animal got away. Another caller said a group had killed four coyotes near town. The tally would have been five, but one was wounded and slipped away.

Marshall had one qualm about the hunt: The animals aren't good eating. As the rule goes, he said, you don't eat anything that eats meat. "One year, I was firing up the barbecue for a cookout next to a pile of coyote carcasses, and a guy walked out of the bar and said, 'You know, you can't eat those.' And I told him, 'I know, heck, I know.'"

Patrick Donnelly opposes coyote-killing contests for two main reasons. The hunts are based on bad science, he says. And they're unethical. Donnelly, state director for the Center for Biological Diversity, insists that predators such as coyotes, wolves and mountain lions are essential to healthy ecosystems.

Each kill saves 13 calves? Not true, he said. "The science very clearly shows that killing coyotes, rather than reducing livestock kills, probably increases them. Killing coyotes creates more coyotes; that's been documented scientifically. When too many animals are taken, females will have bigger litters of pups. The killing of coyotes also obstructs the hierarchy of groups so that the more aggressive coyotes are encouraged to fight over territory and potentially kill more livestock to assert their dominance."

Just as troubling, he says, is the arrogance of some hunters. "Many want to kill coyotes so there are more deer for them to hunt, which puts more venison in their freezers," he said. "This is a blood sport, the slaughtering of living animals for a game, and it's antithetical to the compassionate and empathetic society we want to be." Nevada's wildlife commission, he added, is dominated by hunters and ranchers who have "unlawfully reneged on their responsibilities to manage wildlife." He added: "They're giving in to guys who think it's their right to kill as many animals as they want because they have dominion over the earth."

Brad Johnston, chairman of the Nevada Board of Wildlife Commissioners, rejected that characterization. "None of the commissioners believes we have the right to kill what we want, any time we want," he said. "We pay close attention to hunting in this state." If you ban coyote-killing contests, he asked, where does it end? "Do we ban fishing derbies for kids?" he asked. "Why is one acceptable and not the other? Where does it stop?"

"Our wildlife belongs to everyone, not just ranchers and farmers," said Michael Sutton, who was president of the California Fish and Game Commission when it voted to outlaw all wild animal hunts. "Just because you have permission to use public land doesn't give you dominion over all the animals who live there." He called the coyote contests an anachronism. "They should be relegated to the history books. That cowboy mentality to shoot anything that moves, it's outdated. These days, we know a lot more about predator ecology than we did in the Old West. We can no longer keep killing these wild animals just to satisfy some farmer's or rancher's ego."

■ ■ ■

The rain had stopped, and the late-afternoon sun poked through the clouds as the coyote hunters began showing up at the Silver State Saloon. Their trucks were muddied, their kills tagged and piled into the beds of their pickups, coyote jaws cinched tight with plastic straps. Men hovered around the registration board, comparing shots.

John, a rancher who would only give his first name, said the competition wasn't among hunters but between man and animal. "The man who hunts a coyote loves the coyote," he said. "It's a standoff between you and him."

Donnelly balked at this. "The tradition of respect from hunting comes from peoples utilizing the prey for sustenance," he said. "I'm not saying that some hunters don't have a relationship with the animals they hunt, but there is nothing respectful about a coyote-killing contest." Nothing respectful or fair about mimicking prey to dupe the animals into shooting range. "These people slaughter large numbers of animals and then pile them up for a photo op before tossing the carcasses in a ditch. Where's the respect in that?"

For the weigh-in, the contestants moved outside into an empty parking lot next to a youth center. Some opened the beds of their trucks and showed off their kills. Others threw the bloody corpses onto the ground. Two officials assessed each animal, cutting through a hind leg to hang it from a line attached to a rudimentary scale. One sportsman lamented: "That dog would have weighed more, but we shot half his ass off!" As officials worked, more hunters arrived, providing a running commentary. "He was on his way to becoming one big bad coyote," one said, "until those guys with camouflage came in."

One contestant produced an animal that weighed in at more than 30 pounds. "That's a wolf right there," one man said. "That's not a coyote." John sized up the big carcass. "Fortunately," he told his friends, "we're above them on the food chain, or we'd be running from them." Still, he insisted it wasn't all about the kill. "I had a little blue-eyed guy come up in my scope," he said. "He was just a pup, so I didn't shoot. That little bastard has a little more time to live."

When the counting was done, the competition had netted 78 coyotes. A few hunters skinned their kills there in the parking lot. But most took a few photos and walked away. Marshall said that in past years, a man trucked the carcasses to Utah to collect the bounties. Other times, the bodies are dumped outside town. "That way," Marshall said, "the other animals can feed on 'em."

Just before sundown, an older hunter leaned against his pickup and talked about his success with a call that mimicked a wounded rabbit. But his best tactic, he said, was a call that imitated a wounded coyote: "The others come in to finish the job. "Well," the old man added, taking a draw off his beer, "that was a fun day. Profitable, too."

A California Family Breathes New Life into a Historic Nevada Town

■ **Tonopah, February 2016.** Each time she walks into the exquisitely preserved lobby of the Mizpah Hotel in this old mining town, Nancy Cline feels a tremendous sense of peace. Not to mention accomplishment, pride and even a sense of belonging. After all, she owns the place.

The successful California vintner, who founded the Sonoma-based Cline Cellars winery with her husband, Fred, runs a rich harvest of other business interests nationwide, but none is more special than the Mizpah, which opened in 1907. "This is the one we love the most," she said of the fabled five-story inn, which in its heyday was the state's tallest building. "Really, it's a respite from an incredibly brutal, technological, fast-paced world. I feel the escape every time I go there."

The Clines bought the hotel five years ago, when many of the community's 2,500 residents might have considered them newcomers, but Nancy Cline's family roots here date back more than a century, when the twin frontier towns of Goldfield and Tonopah were the bustling center of the state's epic gold and silver boom.

Cline's grandmother, Emma Ramsey, was once the postmaster of Goldfield. And her great uncle, Harry Ramsey, one of Tonopah's first settlers, owned the first saloon in town, a crude affair with a tarp roof not far from where the Mizpah now sits. He later earned his fortune ($26 million in today's dollars) after staking a claim in one of the area's most prosperous silver mines.

But for 58-year-old Cline, becoming absentee owner of the Mizpah isn't enough of a footprint in the central Nevada region her ancestors helped settle. So the family has embarked on a plan to breathe new civic and financial life into a town that many Las Vegans write off as a mere gas-and-bathroom stop on the daylong drive to Reno. With renovating the Mizpah, which had been shuttered for more than a decade, the Clines have built a new microbrewery in town and this summer plan to start converting the 19th-century Belvada building across the

An employee is silhouetted in front of a stained-glass window at the Mizpah Hotel in Tonopah. Photo by Randi Lynn Beach.

street into hotel, retail and apartment spaces. They also plan to open a small casino next to the Mizpah, to be called The Mizpah Club.

■ ■ ■

The goal is to create a bustling new community in the high desert that stays true to its historical roots—representing a new American West that is emerging from the old. Visitors can relive the luxury of boom days in a modern setting while exploring mines, museums and ghost towns, Cline said. "We want something that's authentic where people can experience something that's true," she said. "Not Disneyland, not Las Vegas, not an illusion."

The fates of Tonopah and Goldfield and other towns here, Cline said, helped build the West. Much of the profits that came from the ground went into building San Francisco, she said. "This place is such a significant part of Western history."

According to legend, Tonopah was founded almost by accident by silver prospector Jim Butler. About 1900, he went searching for a burro he had lost during the night and found the animal seeking shade under a rock outcropping. Butler picked up a rock to throw at the beast and noticed that it was unusually heavy: He had stumbled upon the second-richest silver strike in Nevada history. A few years later, a local writer penned a poem from the perspective of the mule titled, *Me and Jim Found Tonopah*, which was published in the newly minted Tonopah newspaper. The poem read in part: "So when you erect Jim's statue / don't omit your long eared friend / So gratefully I'll 'Haw! He! Haw! / Yes, ME and Jim found Tonopah."

Soon, dreamers, wanderers and East Coast malcontents flocked to the area, including Texas-born Harry Ramsey, who opened the then-dusty mining camp's first saloon. Wyatt Earp and wife Josie also briefly opened a bar here. Years later, as the sagebrush gave way to streets and buildings and the area swelled with money and investors, central Nevada's gold-and-silver towns became so popular they received more mail each year than even New York City, historians say.

The Mizpah was named for a Bible reference meaning bringing people together. The word was engraved on the wedding ring worn by Butler's bride. The town would keep its cachet: Jack Dempsey once fought at a local arena (a meeting room at the Mizpah bears his name), and in 1957, Howard Hughes married Jean Peters in town.

After making his turn-of-the-century fortune, Ramsey sent for

his sister Emma, who spent several years as one of Goldfield's leading ladies. Eventually, the wealthy brother and sister relocated to the
San Francisco Bay Area, where Cline's ancestors continued to thrive.

■ ■ ■

"Tonopah was generous to my family," said Cline, who grew up in
nearby Marin County. "I look at the place, and I am grateful. I feel
compelled to honor it."

On family excursions to Las Vegas as a child, Cline passed often
through Goldfield. Decades later, as a married mother of seven children, she and her growing family returned to the area and took a
shine to exploring Nevada's outback. "We'd lose ourselves in the history, appreciating the perseverance, ingenuity and strength of character it took to make a life in such tough, isolated places," she said.
"The desert is a very wild and brutal environment. The fact that people
could build communities there in the middle of nowhere fascinated
me." But when they decided to invest in the area, they instead chose
not Tonopah, but Goldfield.

For years, they tried unsuccessfully to buy the hotel there but could
never reach the right price. Then in 2011, a real estate agent informed
Cline that the owners of the Mizpah suddenly decided to sell the hotel,
which had been closed since 1999. "They paid $1.9 million," the agent
said. "But I think they'll take $250,000." "We'll offer them $200,000
and close in five days," Cline shot back. "Tell them we need to know
by Friday." She hung up and turned to her husband, "Dear, I think
we just bought a hotel in Tonopah." The price was the same as original owners spent to build the hotel in 1907.

Since then, the Clines have hired dozens of residents in a town that
has long relied on the mining industry, the nearby military test range
and commercial solar project for its main sources of employment.

Recently, hotel manager John McCormick sat in the Wyatt Earp
bar in an elongated Victorian lobby with gilded pillars, maiden statues, period furniture and a 19th-century bank vault that now serves
as a gift shop. A veteran in hotel management, he drove out from
Kansas to run the Clines' new venture. He had never even heard of
Tonopah and admits his reaction driving into town was not love at
first sight. "I thought, what am I getting myself into?" he recalled.
Then he saw the Mizpah, walked through its doors and was sold. "It
was the 'Wow!' factor."

In the months before the hotel's August 2011 premiere, Cline scrambled to make things ready, while she also completed plans to spend several months in Florence, Italy, with her two youngest children. Two days after the Mizpah opened, Cline left for Italy. "It was giving birth and letting someone else take care of your new baby for its first nine months," she said. "I'm probably the only person in the human race to have been in a beautiful apartment in Florence and wishing they were in Tonopah. I was just out of my mind over a special project that's dear to my heart."

Cline visits Tonopah whenever she can. She likes being known by her first name by people she meets on the street. She calls the town "the California of forty years ago." And Tonopah likes her, too. "She's so down to earth and easy to approach," said Bobby Jean Roberts, a former newspaper publisher whose family has lived in Tonopah for five generations. "What she's done is such a shot in the arm to our community. How can we not like her?"

Cline's experiences have been free of the hassles of any similar project attempted in Sonoma, California. "In Nevada, we were able to renovate a building in six months, something that would have taken five years in California."

Now a new generation will join in the celebration of the family's Nevada roots. Cline's son Ramsey, named after his great-great uncle, is leading the new casino project. His entrepreneurial mother knows that challenges lie ahead. "I tell him that real life starts when you try to run a business in Tonopah."

Dodging a Virus in Esmeralda County

■ **Esmeralda County, August 2020.** When news hit rural Esmeralda County that a lethal global virus was on the march, Linda Williams knew precisely what to do.

For 42 years her family had run the general store in tiny Dyer, an unincorporated assemblage of farmers and retirees four hours north of Las Vegas. She knew most residents because her store was a longtime central gathering spot, 75 miles from the nearest chain grocery store.

Every day, she monitored the governor's latest health mandates and helped organize an effort to knit homemade face masks she gave out for free in her market, where a sign at the door announced that customers were limited to enter no more than three at a time. She cleaned and disinfected the store, constantly, like a woman possessed. "I was on it like Donkey Kong," she said. "My message to customers was 'I will protect you. You are my responsibility.' We reminded them as soon as they walked through the door about wearing a mask and keeping their distance."

And, so far at least, it has worked. Esmeralda is the only Nevada county to report no COVID-19 cases, a rarity in a state that has seen some 58,800 cases and 1,030 deaths. There are reasons, of course. With a population of just 974, Esmeralda County is among the nation's least-populated counties. Social distancing is a way of life in a place with no incorporated communities, no high schools, no traffic signals and just a handful of stop signs.

The county features three population hubs: 350 inhabitants live in the county seat of Goldfield, 150 in Silver Peak and another 350 in the westernmost Fish Lake Valley, on the California line, home to Dyer and Williams' general store.

Residents are proud of avoiding the virus, pointing to a sense of community and collective common sense necessary to carve out a life far from the big city.

■ ■ ■

Health officials have yet another possible explanation: They've dodged a bullet. "They are really lucky to not have COVID introduced into their community yet," said Trudy Larson, dean of the school of community health sciences at the University of Nevada, Reno, and a member of the governor's medical advisory team.

While most of Esmeralda County's residents live away from main state highways, Goldfield sits along U.S. Highway 95, the main route between Reno and Las Vegas. "This virus travels with people, so it may just be a matter of time," Larson said. "Distance between people helps reduce transmission, but it takes just one person to introduce it into the community. Especially along a busy highway, where someone stopping for gas or getting something to eat could bring the virus."

In Esmeralda County, testing for the virus has also been low. Without a hospital or clinic nearby, Esmeralda County residents must travel to Tonopah in Nye County to be tested for the virus. Through early August, only 73 people had done so, about 7 percent of the population, which is about half the statewide rate of 15 percent, Larson said. More may have gone out of state to be tested in Bishop, California.

Ralph Keyes, a farmer and one of three county commissioners, said Esmeralda has formed a health board in response to COVID-19 that is investigating bringing a National Guard mobile testing unit that could visit even isolated locations. "I think our success is a combination of local vigilance and our lifestyle," Keyes said. "This is a rural community. Everybody is spread out."

In the mine town of Silver Peak, regulars at the Old School Bar toast one another on their success at staying one step ahead of the virus. Still, Goldfield resident Patty Huber-Bath keeps her fingers crossed. "I tell people that Esmeralda County still has zero cases that we know of," she said. "I always add that last part."

Esmeralda County Commissioner Timothy Hipp says he knows the virus will come one day. "I'm nervous even talking about it, that I'm going to jinx it," said Hipp, 47, a mineworker. "As soon as it comes out that we're acting proud of not having any cases, we (will) get one the very next day."

And when that day comes, he said, it could hit the county hard. "We have the state's highest proportion of elderly people, who would be susceptible to the virus. And we're so small that all of our services are located in one building. So if someone with the virus walks into the

Goldfield courthouse, they could infect the court people, jail inmates, district attorney, public defender. We could be in serious trouble."

■ ■ ■

For the most part, the virus has meant locals looking out for locals. Keyes said Fish Lake Valley residents donated gloves and masks. A woman's club there that got its start in 1929 making quilts began knitting masks that were handed out to classrooms and among senior citizens. Everybody did their part. "We normally get kind of huggy-huggy out here, but we started resorting to elbow bumps," Dyer resident Patty Hudson said.

Not only that, but the Saturday night cribbage game at the Fish Lake Valley Saloon was put on hold. The Fourth of July festival in Goldfield was reduced to a few fireworks, and the county seat also canceled its popular Goldfield Days in early August.

While judges in the Goldfield courthouse required workers and defendants to wear masks, they often had to ask them to pull them down to be understood during hearings. After each run to the nearest hospital in Bishop, EMTs scoured their ambulance with sanitizer and even changed their clothes.

Locals who left town on monthly shopping trips took orders from neighbors, especially the older ones, so they didn't have to leave home. State health officials did video inspections to ensure businesses were following the latest disinfecting protocols.

Rather than feel isolated, Esmeralda County residents revel in the cultural and geographical detachment. One of Nevada's original counties, it was established in 1861 and ghost towns now outnumber peopled communities. Writer Mark Twain spent time in the area as a miner while researching *Roughing It*, his 1873 book. Neither paved roads nor electricity arrived until the early 1960s. With no building codes, Esmeralda County attracts outsiders tired of big-city regulations. While serious crime is low, residents pack concealed weapons, and a sign posted in the Dyer general store bears two six-shooters and reads: "We Don't Dial 911." A T-shirt for sale there reads "Where the hell is Dyer?" while another shows a road mileage sign that says, "End of the World: 9 mi. Dyer, Nev: 12 mi."

The national shutdown has meant fewer outsiders. Goldfield has seen less U.S. 95 traffic and fewer tourists passing through Dyer en route between Yosemite and Death Valley national parks. "People think little communities like ours don't pay attention just because a lot of big cities don't," Williams said. "It's not as though we like having to take all these precautions, but we realize we're all in this together."

Following the shutdown, Gemfield Resources, which operates a local mine, donated $150,000 to the county for economic development, including $50,000 to create vouchers at local food outlets to help keep residents close to home. For seven straight weeks, until the money ran out, each Esmeralda County resident received a $20 voucher. The move not only provided food for the community, but kept employees in their jobs and the doors of businesses open.

Still, at 82, Fish Lake Valley resident Jeanie Amick took no chances. "I followed the rules," she said. "When I went to the Dyer store, I disinfected my hands before and after. When I left, I used my body to open and close the door." And if Amick and others spotted vehicles with out-of-state license plates outside the general store, which attracted outsiders looking to buy fireworks before the Fourth of July, well, they just drove on by.

There have been struggles to keep the peace. Since the conference room at the Goldfield courthouse is too small to maintain social distancing, somebody suggested that county commissioners move into the courtroom for their regular meetings. But the judges weren't having it. "We told them, 'We're willing to work with you, but this is a courtroom and we will be having court,'" said Court Judge Kimberly Wanker, who hears cases in Goldfield. Commissioners rescheduled their meetings for when court was not in session.

Williams has an extra reason to fear the virus. Now in her 70s, she is undergoing chemotherapy for an autoimmune disease. She knows she's vulnerable. When some store customers refused to wear masks, she took it personally. "We had some confrontations," she said. "Some locals pride themselves on their mountain ruggedness. They have this attitude that they're invincible. They live in God's country, they trust in God and they've got strong immune systems."

But for the most part, Esmeralda County residents are proud of the way they've handled the novel coronavirus, whether it finally reaches them or not.

Williams, who recently sold her business to concentrate on her health, told the story of a California Highway Patrol officer who walked into the market without a mask. "I told him, 'Hey, you're welcome here, but where's your mask?'" Williams said. The officer responded,

"Oh, yeah, you're right" and returned to his car to get one. The next thing you know, Williams said, he walked back in "wearing one of those big honking N95 masks, like he meant business."

Later, he saw the pile of free masks and donated $100 for a handful, which he planned to hand out to shut-ins. Williams used the money to buy food for four needy families. "We all came together," she said. "And all the little things, they add up."

Steel and Sweat:
Forging Yesterday's Tools

■ **Tonopah, December 2016.** John Campbell stands in his machine shop, a solitary figure flipping a switch into another time when the mines burst with gold, silver and opportunity. Suddenly, amid the dust and scattered parts, a 19th-century lineshaft groans to life overhead—a system of spinning wheels and pulleys that runs the grease-blackened contraptions that for decades have created and maintained mining's often-complex heavy machinery.

At 66, the towering 6-foot-4 Campbell feels at home here, the third generation of his family to stand at the controls of these same humming behemoths in this very building. Before him came his father and grandfather—two visionaries who built Campbell & Kelly Foundry and Machine Works, a company that helped pour the iron and steel that shaped the American West.

Although the gold runs have tapered, Campbell uses the same century-old lathes, drills and grinders his grandfather once sweated over to promote a 21st-century endeavor: preparing parts used to mine the lithium that fuels Tesla's new line of cars. The unlikely practice of using yesterday's tools to help build tomorrow's economy comes straight from the Campbell clan's personal playbook: "If it ain't broke, don't fix it."

And if these machines do fail, there are no fast-and-easy factory replacement parts; Campbell must often forge new ones to continue his work as a heavy-metal engineer. It's not as much out of any spirit of preservation as sheer necessity: These throwbacks are still hard at work. "You're just hoping to get the job done with these old machines before they quit," he said. "And the next one and the next one."

Many here say Campbell has become such an important cog in the workings of Tonopah, they'd be at a loss to carry on without him. For decades, as Bobby Jean Roberts and her late husband, Bill, ran the newspaper, they frequently called on Campbell to fix aging press machines that had long before gone out of production. "John kept the newspaper running for years," she said. "He can fix anything."

Old-school toolmaker John Campbell poses in his Tonopah machine shop.
Photo by David Becker.

■ ■ ■

With the Campbells, that's the way it's been for 110 years. The family's stubborn longevity mirrors the story of this historic outpost between Las Vegas and Reno on U.S. Highway 95, a former boomtown that refuses to crumble back into the high-desert dust.

Over the years, the Campbell business suffered two debilitating fires, the first burning the enterprise to the ground in 1915. In the second, in 2012, John Campbell put out the blaze mostly by himself, before volunteer firefighters could even get there.

John's grandfather, Horace P. Campbell, also died on these grounds. In 1944, he was nailing tin onto a shop roof during a windstorm when he was blown onto a live 480-volt wire. His son, Horace Joseph Campbell, took the reins from there, and continued building the business he eventually turned over to his own son.

When Campbell was a boy, he learned from his gentle father. "It's the love you develop between yourself and your parents—and the result is the work ethic they instill in you," he said. "With men like my father, you go through life watching over their shoulder over the years. I did that a lot."

Grandfather Campbell was a Scottish immigrant who in 1905 saw opportunity in the Nevada minefields: When machines broke down, a new part often had to be cast at far-off shops in Reno and even San Francisco. He soon went into business with partner Reuben "Rube" Kelly to fill the gap, moving on to fashion mine cars, pumps and well drillers.

Winters were hard in the shop. Before anti-freeze, machines were cooled with water that froze when the temperatures dipped into the 30s. But the men liked the challenge of taking a customer's unformed idea and shaping it into a working product.

■ ■ ■

A few years ago, Nye County honored John Campbell's life with a biography that consists of several interviews with the craftsman. The idea came from former County Commissioner Joni Eastley, who calls Campbell "a quiet unassuming man with a heart as big as any piece of machinery he's built."

Eastley said rural Nevada was built by craftsmen like the Campbells. "Many were self-taught engineers like John's grandfather," she said.

"Was he formally trained? No, he didn't go to school a day in his life. But that organic know-how was instilled in his son and his son's son."

Early on, Campbell decided to follow in his father's footsteps, which meant staying in Tonopah. "Back then, I thought the earth was flat," he said with a laugh. "Like I'd fall off if I wandered too far from home." Back then, he and his father were inseparable. Each morning, the kid would accompany the old man to the Tonopah Club, where the elder Campbell and Emerson Titlow would sit around over coffee, trading town gossip and complaining about things. In the afternoon, they'd come back and do it all over again.

One recent morning, dressed in jeans, a sky-blue shirt and dirty boots, Campbell wanders the 10-acre tract outside his machine shop; land littered with dozens of vintage Chevrolet wrecks from the 1950s and '60s. Nearby, the unofficial guard dog, Roy the Rooster, squawks from his pen.

If television junkman Fred Sanford moved to Tonopah, this is where he'd do business, in a field of rusting pickups, sedans left with their doors wide open, a lost tumbleweed trapped beneath one steering wheel. There are disembodied car doors and left-behind engine parts. Many of these castoffs have been parked here since John was a boy. For him, none of this stuff is considered junk, not at all; they're all the framework of jobs to be done, the raw clay that goes into a new work of art.

But the job of taking precious metals from the ground has never been a steady provider. When the mines closed, Campbell needed new work. For years, he built fire trucks that he sold to departments across the West.

Years back, he was running errands when he got a call that his shop was on fire. A longtime volunteer fire chief, he raced over to the station, borrowed a truck and raced home. "When I got there, the fire was roaring pretty good." His instincts kicked in. "When you've been doing something for 100 years, you just get on with it."

Later, he was flooded with calls and letters from friends and machine shop customers, wondering if he was safe and asking if he needed credit to stay on his feet. For Campbell, such gestures capture the perks of being a third-generation fixture in a small Western town.

Campbell's father died in 1999 at age 86, and the son looks to eventually retire as the last of a metal-bending breed. But he still goes down to Tonopah Station each day for coffee, jawboning and slapping his knee with a new generation of Emerson Titlows.

■ ■ ■

And there's a new generation of Campbell's family making a hand-forged mark in Tonopah. His stepson, Adam Skiles, became fascinated with the metal shop and soon created a figure Campbell keeps on his property: a surf-and-sand character with dreadlocks and sneakers.

Skiles created other figures now installed around town—statues representing area war veterans, a mining disaster hero and the brothers who helped found Tonopah.

Like his father before him, Campbell used a gentle hand to help carry on the metal-shaping trade in his family. "I just gave him some once-overs and showed him how to weld," he said of Skiles. "He took to it like a duck to water." Just like hammer-pounding John Campbell.

An Architectural Gem
Rises from the Ruins

■ **Belmont, March 2016.** Each time Donna Motis gazed out her kitchen window, through the leafless branches of her backyard cottonwood trees, she spied a rare slice of Nevada history: a three-story timepiece whose fabled architectural elegance was now tarnished by a sense of wretchedness and despair.

In its heyday, Belmont's old brick courthouse, with its square wooden cupola, was the moral compass of this once-thriving mining town, where for decades a no-nonsense brand of Old West justice was dispensed and lawbreakers met their fates with both bravery and tears. The imposing edifice was completed on July 4, 1876, when this silver boomtown was the Nye County seat. It saw its last case in 1905, long after the sliver was gone and the town had begun its cultural decline.

Like a crusty old lawyer whose career had fallen on hard times, the once-proud courthouse tumbled into a state of near-ruin. When it rained or snowed, Motis could see water pouring through the roof, staining the walls of a once-cherished building added to the National Register of Historic Places in 1972.

Weekend hikers on self-guided tours covered the walls with graffiti. Vandals carted off the building's priceless period furnishings. In the 1960s, the infamous Manson family even tried to make camp in the courthouse. Legend has it that feisty Belmont resident Rose Walters, rifle in hand, told the group to scram.

Then a few years back, this isolated high-desert burg with less than a dozen year-round residents decided to save its treasure. When the subject of the old courthouse came up at Dirty Dick's Belmont Saloon, locals cupped their beers and shot each other knowing looks. "We got to the point where we knew we either had to let it go to hell or put together a group of people to fix it," said Rick Motis, a sturdy 63-year-old former truck driver with sledgehammer hands.

Well, this old courthouse was not going to hell, not by a long shot. In 2011, residents formed Friends of the Belmont Courthouse, a nonprofit group whose mission was to rally the money, energy and expertise to stem the building's decline. They wanted to install a new roof and windows and, just maybe, bring the old courtroom back to life as a living snapshot of the past. The group includes Belmont residents Rick and Donna Motis, and lawyers and judges from across the state who want to preserve an important piece of Nevada history. "There was a time when the courthouse was the pulse of that town," said Nevada Supreme Court Justice Kristina Pickering, who sits on the group's board of directors. "It has endured so much neglect. For me, it symbolizes the pioneer spirit of the people who first settled here."

But there was a catch to this renovation job: The courthouse never had electricity or running water, and not much has changed. Belmont is off the grid; a collection of scattered buildings without electricity, running water or phone service. Generators and solar cells help heat and cool homes. Flashlights are kept on hand. "There's nothing out here," Donna Motis said. "When it gets dark, it gets dark. If you stand on a hill in the right spot, you might get a cell signal, but even that's iffy."

Rebuilding the courthouse without modern technology required contractors who ran their tools with generators and batteries, workers who didn't mind taking a few extra steps to get a job done. Rick Motis told of the day five men installed a 1,200-pound safe without a crane or winches. How did they do it? "Brute force and ignorance," Motis said with a laugh.

■ ■ ■

The Belmont courthouse came to be for a couple of reasons: One was that the community was booming in the frenzied search for the second Comstock mother lode.

The other was less savory: In the early 1870s, suspected horse thieves Jack Walker and Charles McIntyre were lynched at the jail and buried in unmarked graves beneath a pinion pine on the lower edge of town. The episode convinced officials that more formal justice was needed on the Nevada frontier.

In the treeless high desert, the $20,000 courthouse immediately became a modern wonder of its day—testimony to the true grit of the settlers. Rock for the foundation was quarried locally. Each brick was fired in the nearby Belmont kilns. Wood for the doors, joists and roof timbers came from trees felled in the Sierra and brought in by train and horse-pulled wagons.

With a population that ranged as high as 2,000, Belmont had

been the Nye County seat since 1867. It once featured an oyster house, bakery, two physicians, a drugstore, fruit store and watch repair shop. A newspaper wrote feisty editorials, including one in 1867 that read, "Here's to our governor. He came in with very little opposition; he goes out with none at all." The Cosmopolitan Music Hall hosted traveling vaudeville acts. A Chinatown and a mercantile store stocked everything from Paris perfume to hob-nailed boots.

From the beginning, the thriving community's new courthouse was more than a place for the sitting judge. It also housed the sheriff, district attorney and town treasurer, some of whom both worked and slept there. And even from those early days, the place was not without scandal. Once, a district attorney lost his re-election race but refused to leave. And in in 1894, County Treasurer Adam McLean was found dead in his bed on the first floor of the courthouse. He chose poison over being charged with embezzling more than $15,000.

The courthouse also saw its share of notable cases. One involved a Nye County sheep rancher named George Ernst, who was tried for tax evasion after trying to pay his grazing fees in nearby Elko County, were they were considerably cheaper. In a summation that went down in courthouse annals for its brevity, prosecutor Peter Breen stood before the jury and simply stated: "George Ernst has a flock of sheep / their fleece as white as snow. / He feeds them in Nye County / and taxes them in Elko." He won the case.

Then the roof fell in on the mining economy. In the election of 1900, fewer than 100 votes were cast in Belmont. After the county seat was moved 46 miles south to Tonopah in 1905, the courthouse was closed and the building fell on hard times. Over the years it was used to store hay and surveyor's equipment, and even accoutrements for a field hospital.

Tourists often left behind their signatures, which remain even today. "Barbara Swanson, June 9, 1940" decorates one wall. In another place, a soldier bound for France during World War II left a poem to his girl:

> When you and I our love must part
>   may it cause pain in both our hearts
> I to some foreign land will go
>   sleep cold in death as others do
> All this and more I have to say but
>   night calls and I mush away

With these lines
  you will a hidden question find.

Resident Terry Terras pondered over the lines before finally solving the riddle. Put together as a sentence, the first word of each line reads: "When may I sleep all night with you?"

In 1953, author Nell Murbarger wrote of the old mining town's decline for *Desert* magazine, observing that the courthouse still stood "as square and unadorned as a three-story bank vault, still as indomitable as the Bank of England."

Fifteen years later, the Manson family tried to take up residence there. The group left behind a piece of graffiti, written on the frame of a downstairs door that reads: "Charlie Manson + family 1969" with a peace symbol forming the O in Manson. Ghost hunters try to contact spirits that supposedly remain here. But most people, Terras said, come in search of the Manson Family. "Every time Manson comes up for parole, people flock to the courthouse to take pictures of that graffiti," he said. "That's got to be the most photographed door jamb in the entire country."

■ ■ ■

The Friends of the Belmont Courthouse initially decided to do things the grassroots way: They wanted all the money for the refurbishment to come from donations. The annual Fourth of July parade and art show raised $2,500 one year. They've had to get creative: The 30 new windows were financed by different donors. Nye County paid for a new roof. The cupola was also fixed and painted. So far, the group has raised about $130,000 and has spent $100,000, mostly on the windows. The group's board holds regular meetings to plan strategy, and members take them seriously: Kim Wanker, the 5th District judge in Pahrump, will drive 650 miles round trip to attend a planning session without staying the night.

When the work will be done—and even how much more they can do—remains up in the air. "That building is weather-tight," said Donna Motis. "Even if we didn't do another thing, it would stand for another 200 years. There's no way the elements are going to break down that building."

But many want to do more, including renovating the courtroom. There's talk of asking the state Supreme Court to hold a hearing there once the work is done. "We've never held a session in a ghost town or in a building without electricity or fire protection, but I'm open to anything," Justice Pickering said. "Personally, I think it would be cool."

Yet there's a stumbling block: Most of the photos taken at the time were exterior shots, so workers have no idea what the old courtroom looked like when in use. Faint lines on the floor suggest where the judge and jury sat, but what they really need—from some museum or home attic—is a historic photo of the old courthouse in action.

Until then, they are collecting period furniture for the project. Both Terras and Rick Motis offer tours of the courthouse, gladly accepting donations. "Any building that can stand that long deserves some loving care," Terras said.

Now, when Donna Motis looks out her kitchen window, she doesn't see a neglected relic of the past, but a symbol of Belmont's stubborn endurance.

Jim Marsh's Rural Dream

■ **Amargosa Valley, November 2018.** The big-city car dealer arrived at his own event here with a subtle sartorial touch befitting his character: a country gentleman's hat bought on a recent trip to his hometown in Nebraska. Like Jim Marsh himself, the fedora is equal parts city and country, expressing both the urban dealmaker and easygoing rural resident armed with a joke and a smile.

Because it is out here, well beyond the corralling city limits, that the 84-year-old owner of two Las Vegas car dealerships feels most comfortable, out where the population is scarce and the state's history was originally made, where the high desert gives way to the somber Funeral Mountains and Death Valley National Park beyond. "What's going on?" said Richard Heminger, a 76-year-old horseshoer from nearby Pahrump, shaking Marsh's hand. "You stayin' in trouble?"

On a recent Sunday morning, Marsh unveiled his latest creation to rural Nevadans: a replica of a chapel originally built in the mining town of Belmont in 1874. The 48-seat wooden shrine sits on the back lawn of Marsh's Longstreet Inn and Casino, an emporium built along the isolated border between Nevada and California and named after early settler Jack Longstreet, a historic touch that's vintage Marsh.

As Marsh spoke outside his new chapel at Longstreet, his voice as gravelly as an unpaved road, a woman stepped forward from the small crowd with tears in her eyes. Patty Brubaker and her husband, Bryan, had been the first couple married in the chapel just days before. Her last picture of her mother, Evelyn, was taken at the Longstreet casino duck pond. The mother's ashes are spread here. And now the daughter was married in the same place. "I want you to know," she wept, "that it meant the world to me, sir."

Marsh often evokes such emotions from rural residents. He's known by most Las Vegas Valley residents as the car salesman with the flashy two-toned shoes, whose offbeat television spots have featured him wearing only a barrel after a specious IRS audit that he claims compelled him to sell more cars. He's cavorted with burros, geese, chickens, mules, a water buffalo and, well, just about anything else to grab the attention of the car-buying public.

But Marsh has also embarked on another less well-known pursuit as a quiet rural benefactor. Over the years, through one unheralded purchase after another, the Nevada history buff has collected a rustic bevy of tiny motels and bars across the southern reaches of the Silver State, a place he has come to love.

There's the Santa Fe Saloon and Nixon Block and Mining Exchange building in Goldfield; the Tonopah Station casino, Banc Club and Humbug Flats bar in Tonopah; the Alamo Club in Pioche and the Manhattan bar and motel in tiny Manhattan, more than 250 miles away from the tarmac lots where Marsh makes his weekly car deals.

Through his car dealerships and Skyline Casino on Boulder Highway in Henderson, Marsh employs 250 people. But he has also hired another 100 workers in struggling small towns where steady jobs are hard to come by. "Jim keeps these little towns going; he takes on places that would otherwise be closed and breathes new life into them," said Kimberly Wanker, a 5th Judicial Court Judge based in Pahrump. "If it weren't for Jim, in little places like Belmont, Manhattan and the Amargosa Valley, there would be nothing."

When he's not selling cars, Marsh spends most of his time in Nevada's outback, attending auctions to buy antiques and historic mementos for his properties. He sponsors racing events and has been a regular at town fairs, playing emcee as he rides in the lead car at parades, always with that unique dash of Jim Marsh humor.

Because this urban car dealer is a bit of a rascal, a consummate prankster. Once, he dressed as Lady Godiva and rode a mule in the Belmont parade. In Las Vegas, he once unleashed a pack of goats to "mow" a friend's lawn; the animals also ate the neighbors' rose bushes. He prefers wearing ill-fitting Salvation Army tuxedos, tags still attached, to high-society events to draw stares and ruffle a few feathers. "He often looked like such a bozo, I'd get upset," said longtime friend Caralynne Rudin. "But I got used to it, so that when people at parties said, 'Can't you do something about this?' I'd say, 'No, I can't and neither can you, so don't even waste your time.' Jim just loves shocking people."

He became a teaser early in life. As a kid hanging around his father's Denver car dealership, Marsh got 86'd for a few days after he glued shut the mechanics' toolboxes so no work could get done. Years later, his favorite ruse is secretly positioning his Wyatt Earp lookalike mannequin—with handgun extended—in the offices of friends, in back car seats, even behind the smoked windows of his home shower, to get a rise out of the unsuspecting. He also tagged the manager of his Santa Fe Saloon, "the meanest bartender in Nevada," and even posted a sign to that effect outside the bar, causing endless ribbing among her customers. "I have to get him back on that," Laurel Arnold said.

But paybacks are hell, even for Marsh. Anthony "Buddy" Perchetti, a contractor who worked on Marsh's Tonopah Station casino, once bribed the front desk clerk to allow him in Marsh's regular room to pull a "short-sheet" gag, fixing the bed so Marsh could only get his legs in halfway. "I got even that day," Perchetti laughed.

Marsh will hear none of it. "The son of a bitch; he's rotten to the core," he joked of Perchetti. "Just because somebody once put a snake in his truck, he thinks it's me. I'm accused of it, but of course I deny it."

Rural Nevadans see the jokes as pure Jim Marsh. "He sees us for what we are out here," said Brubaker, a school bus driver whose husband works in a gold mine. "Sadly, most people see rural Nevada as just a bunch of brothels. But there's so much more. And Jim understands that."

■ ■ ■

Marsh landed in Las Vegas in 1971 after fleeing the rain and soured economy in Washington state. One day, he headed south in his 1948 DeSoto coupe and eventually rolled through rural Nevada's wide-open spaces. From that moment on, he was hooked. "I fell in love," he recalled. "I developed an instant attachment to the place."

He bought his first dealership near downtown, eventually developing his signature TV ads. "One day, one of the guys suggested I do something with my daughter Stacy. She was 17 at the time," Marsh recalled. "She was so nervous. She said, 'Dad, my hands are shaking.' We stumbled through and have been doing them ever since."

Many of the ads involve Stacy ribbing her hapless car-dealing dad. "Every time we did a commercial, I'd jab him about something," recalled Stacy Marsh, now a schoolteacher. "Eventually, I started getting letters from people about my behavior, that I should treat my father better. What they didn't know is that he wrote all the scripts. He loved the fact that people gave me grief."

Marsh sold a lot of cars, but he still couldn't keep his mind off the hinterlands. Back in the 1970s, he spotted a *National Geographic* photograph featuring a weathered-looking woman over the headline

"See the Other Nevada." Marsh eventually found the woman, named Rose Walter, who was considered the guardian of isolated Belmont and, as legend has it, once chased Charles Manson and his groupies out of town with a loaded shotgun.

He eventually bought some property from Walter and built a cabin he still uses today. But Marsh didn't stop there. He soon bought the Santa Fe Saloon after the previous owner had his liquor license taken away by the sheriff for, as Marsh tells it, "shooting the installations off telephone poles."

Marsh revels in telling such historic asides. For example, he says, a veteran miner in Goldfield, blinded by a shaft explosion, generations ago hooked up a line of piano wire from his rural shack outside town to the Santa Fe Saloon as a way to guide him to and from drinking bouts.

Kayla Correa, hotel manager at Marsh's Skyline property, regularly sees him walk in with some new artifact he has scrounged from the countryside and wants on display. In that way, he's more than just an owner, but also a curator. "Every antique and painting is purchased by him and placed by him," Correa said. "He'll say, 'This is something created 200 years ago, and I want it right here.'" Added Marsh: "And if they move it, all hell breaks loose."

Marsh said he buys the properties to make a profit. "There's a little greed in my soul," he said. "Mostly, I make sound business deals. I'm not going to buy something historic that becomes a big money pit; that's not my cup of tea. I'm not the great rural protector, but many deals have helped keep these communities afloat."

In fact, Marsh acknowledges, he's gotten a reputation as something of a skinflint. "There is some truth to that, I can't deny it," he said. "My grandmother back in Nebraska saved the stamps that didn't get postmarked. I learned frugality as a boy." Marsh's friends tease him about still living in the house he bought in 1971, with the same secondhand furniture purchased at some local pawnshop. "Everybody gives Jim hell in the bar," Perchetti said. "They're always telling him, 'It's your turn to buy.' And he is pretty tight, but if he decides to give you money, it's whatever you want. He's generous that way."

Over time, Marsh's downtown Las Vegas neighborhood has taken a turn for the worse and his car gets stolen now and then, but he stays put.

Because, as Stacy Marsh said, his priorities have been somewhere out there. "He feels like he was born 100 years too late," she said. "He loves those old towns, loves going back to the time frame when they were great. If he could, he'd stay up in Belmont all the time. At the end of a weekend, he'll say, 'Well, I have to get back to reality. It's time to get back to business.'"

At the christening of the new Amargosa Valley chapel, the minister blew an elk's horn, setting off braying by the grouchy old burro Marsh keeps nearby. The car salesman doesn't just use animals in his TV ads, he surrounds himself with rescue creatures—rabbits, tortoises, peacocks, horses, goats and mules—like his pet dog, Blue No. 2, a shelter hound he got after a hematoma on the animal's side made him unadoptable.

At the Longstreet Casino, Marsh also keeps one special resident. As the story goes, two geese flew onto the Wynn casino grounds. When their eggs hatched, most of the goslings were run over along Las Vegas Boulevard. Marsh got the lone survivor from Barn Buddies Rescue, which he calls Wynnie after the casino. Along with its mate, Happy, the silly goose now follows him around the property.

In the chapel, the ceremony was vintage Marsh. Worshippers perched on wooden pews, some distracted by sweeping views of the surrounding peaks outside the windows. The scene could have been an 1870s prairie service, complete with bothersome flies, as the minister walked the aisle banging on a small tambourine. At one point, someone produced a collection plate. And right there, Jim Marsh, the big-city car dealer who prefers the countryside, who wields a reputation of rarely parting with his money on good terms, was the first to reach for his wallet.

The East

Rural Nevada sheepherder Hank Vogler tends to his flock in eastern Nevada.
Photo by Randi Lynn Beach.

The Last Sheepherder

■ **White Pine County, July 2019.** The mid-April storm descends on the North Spring Valley at dusk, the snow sticking to the ground and to the backs of Hank Vogler's sheep. It's the height of harvest season, when the teams of itinerant, Spanish-speaking shearers move in to help the veteran rancher cull another year of wool from his flock of 10,000, and this sudden turn in the weather feels ominous.

The sheep are annoyed at their lot, especially the ones just relieved of their warm coats. They bleat and bawl, huddling in groups to conserve heat. A few older ones have already died of stress, their bodies stiffening in the snow, and a look of concern flashes across the old sheepherder's face.

The 70-year-old Vogler is behind the wheel of a pay-loader, dropping bales of hay that are distributed by workers, who keep the sheep moving in large circles in the open field. In the fading light, the animals resemble large armies forging across the landscape, as though positioning themselves for the battle ahead. Thousands have already been sheared; more will have their turn come morning. Right now, that seems a long time away. "The snow is stressing the sheep," Vogler shouts down from the machine. "You take your clothes off and get a shave in this kind of cold; it's a bit of a shock. You gotta get their bellies full after shearing, to keep their furnaces going."

A half-hour later, walking his isolated ranch headquarters an hour north of Ely, he spots the bodies of two older sheep that crawled beneath a trailer to die. Vogler shakes his head, his voice low with emotion. "That one old grandma looked good last year, but she had a bad winter and didn't make it," he said.

■ ■ ■

Vogler has herded sheep in central Nevada for 35 years, a stubborn adherent to an industry he knows is in great peril. He's an aging ambassador to a colorful 140-year old tradition that got its start in Nevada in the 1880s, when immigrant Basque families dominated the scene with their innate know-how and sprawling flocks. The trade has watched its sheep numbers plummet from one million a century ago to just

75,000 today, the vestiges of a once-thriving industry now propped up by a dozen remaining families, many of them Basque.

Reasons for the decline are numerous: Consumers have moved away from even the finer merino-blend wool toward synthetic-fiber clothing. Herders must also fight off predators such as coyotes and mountain lions, which can thin a flock by 15 percent or more in a year. There are regular droughts and wildfires, as well as bouts of loneliness and depression.

Vogler insists he also deals with two-legged threats—wildlife activists, for example, who claim that even healthy domestic sheep carry strains of a respiratory-tract bacteria that can cause fatal pneumonia in wild Bighorn sheep, whose numbers are also in decline. (Vogler says the connection is exaggerated.) And he laments the big-city water officials, who want to drain Nevada's rural aquifers to build more housing tracts around Las Vegas.

There are also the constant tensions of running herds on public lands managed by the Bureau of Land Management, whose officials don't always see things his way. Experience has taught him that some have personal agendas, like giving more credence to wildlife activists than they do ranchers. Still others assume he's just another disciple of Cliven Bundy, a rancher who has famously fought federal government overreach, and will thumb his nose at any regulation. (BLM officials, of course, say this is all nonsense.)

Sheep stockmen such as Vogler also struggle to hire herders from such South American nations as Peru and Chile, who tend to far-flung bands of sheep for months on end, often going weeks without encountering another human being. Tightening immigration laws mean it's harder to bring foreign workers into the U.S., and some bolt after arriving, leaving the bill for their visa and flight to the ranchers. The result: Remaining sheep ranchers say their children want nothing to do with the business, leaving them to fret about its future. "The commitment is huge," said Pete Paris, secretary of the Nevada Wool Growers Association. "This business has broken a lot of people who don't put in the requisite time, sweat and blood. You almost have to live with these sheep."

Vogler knows all too well about the round-the-clock commitment necessary to stay afloat. In 2018, he sold 100,000 pounds of wool, at an average of $3 a pound, but feeding sheep is expensive. Ever since he brought his Need More Sheep company here in 1985, the hard-luck business has many times broken his heart and nearly his pock-etbook. It also took one of his two sons, who died in a wreck doing ranch chores, making Vogler question much more than just his chosen pursuit. "I question my own mental health every single day," Vogler said. "Because if you like the same box of cereal for breakfast every morning, well, this job isn't for you. The phone rings too often in the middle of the night. You've got issues with predators like mountain lions and coyotes, or sheepherders losing sheep in difficult country. You're like a fireman putting out fresh fires every single day, and it's only crazy persistence that makes everything work."

■ ■ ■

For critics and friends alike, Vogler is an often-maddening collection of contradictions, a man of letters in a hands-on trade, a college-educated former ranch buckaroo who quotes Thomas Jefferson and can issue ranch commands in several Spanish dialects (as well as Basque, German and Mandarin Chinese). He's become an irascible industry spokes-man in magazine articles and news editorials, as a frequent radio talk show guest and as the author of a children's book about raising sheep.

Vogler says he writes for his fellow ranchers, "the people who live at the end of the road or the other side of nowhere" and doesn't much care what outsiders think. This take-no-prisoners approach applies more broadly, too, whether he's serving on the board of the Nevada Department of Wildlife or emceeing a celebration of sheepherding. As with many rural folks, his politics lean decidedly to the right, but Vogler doesn't consider himself to be a run-of-the-mill good ol' boy "I've been known to throw a skunk on the table at a garden party," he said.

Even within the tightly knit ranching business, Vogler insists on going his own way. With ranchers, he says, there's often a prevailing groupthink. "And if you don't advocate that groupthink at all times, you're in trouble," he said. "You're considered an outlaw." He might occasionally find himself at odds with others over predator control or somebody's herd spending too much time on a shared high-country trail, gobbling up all the vegetation. But the remaining families know the only way they're going to survive a diminishing market is to all get along.

Vogler doesn't even like the term "sheepherder," preferring to be called a stockman. "You can own 10,000 cows and no one calls you a cowboy, but own one sheep and you're a sheep man," he said.

Above his signature mud boots, blue jeans, flannel shirt and suspenders, his stockman's face is craggy, his eyebrows pronounced, graying hair slicked to the side. He has big shoulders and a ramrod posture, as if he's perpetually hung on a coat rack. If he often scowls around the toothpick in his mouth, the look is lightened by bursts of laughter; his is a deadpan, homespun wit. He likes to riff on country-western song titles, giving them a sheepherder's spin, such as, "I don't think my heart could stand another Ewe" or the Willie Nelson-infused, "Ewe were always on my mind." Just watch, and he'll imitate the accents of the old Basque sheepherders who taught him the trade, or describe with great relish such ranch chores as rubbing iodine on a ewe's umbilical cord or pulling out a juvenile sheep's testicles with his teeth. And he sizes up critics by saying, "If you added up all the people trying to put me out of business, the list would be longer than a polygamist's clothesline."

Recent years have tested Vogler's resolve. He survived a painful battle with pancreatic cancer, thanks to numerous operations. "Just about every doctor I've met tells me the same thing: You're gonna die," he said. "I've been given last rites so many times, the next time I'm in that position, I'll be able to administer them myself."

Vogler's unlikely joie de vivre despite hardship has endeared him to many in the business. "Hank finds humor in agony," said C. J. Hadley, the editor of *Range* magazine, which has printed Vogler's stories. "Despite massive setbacks—physical, mental and financial—he always comes back. He's tough. He's bright. He's raw and real."

■ ■ ■

He was born Henry Conrad Vogler IV, or just Hank, the grandson of an Oregon ranching scion, who grew up breaking colts, working on the fence and haying crews. Vogler's father was a drunk and gambler who discouraged his son from the cowboy way. From an early age, Vogler felt like a black sheep. While most members of his clan were blue-eyed Germans, he took after his Native American grandmother's roots—a mix of Chickasaw and Cherokee.

"My life was set at age 5," he recalls. "One stability I had was sitting at the chow table with my grandfather, the chore boys and buckaroos.

I knew what I wanted to do." He had mentors such as his Uncle Charlie, a veteran ranch hand with a sense of humor, and Robert Carlson, the old foreman who lost a leg and could still outwork three people.

After his grandfather sold the operation when Vogler was 15, he decided to go to school and learn how to run a ranch for somebody else. He later married his high school sweetheart and, as he likes to say, "my first daughter was 18 days old by the time I turned 18." The couple eventually had five children.

In 1971, Vogler graduated from the University of Nevada, Reno, with a degree in agriculture, laboring full-time to put himself through school. He worked at a Safeway, milked cows at the university dairy and punched the clock at a slaughterhouse. In his senior year, he managed a nearby ranch, facing a daily 100-mile commute to classes.

After graduation, Vogler returned to ranch life in Oregon, where, he says, in a card game against an opponent nicknamed Cowboy Bob, he won enough to buy seven sheep. That started it all: He eventually returned to Nevada in the mid-1980s and began taking over grazing permits from people who wanted out of the sheep business. "It's like buying a straw hat in the middle of winter—when other people get out, I get in," he explains. "Maybe it's my contrary nature. A lot of people in my family had a competition to see who could stay the drunkest. I went down another path."

In 1985, Vogler met a rancher who was behind with the bank and ventured out to the North Spring Valley to assess his operation. "When I dropped over that mountain, the hair on the back of my neck stood right up," he recalls. The feeling was neither good nor bad, maybe just a hunch—a sense of opportunity, or the dread of sensing all the work that lay ahead. He recalled seeing an old pink house, now gone, that was "a rat-infested piece of nothing. I had the heebie-jeebies from the moment I rolled into this yard." He took over the rancher's cattle and sheep permits to graze on public land and worked hard to pay off the six-figure debt in five years. He ran cattle for neighbors, refurbished barns, bought and sold an investment property in Ely.

He soon focused on running sheep. Nowadays, his two dozen herders and their dogs make sure the bands keep moving and don't overgraze areas across allotments that can be hundreds of miles away. Sheep also have a more varied diet than cattle, consuming weeds and leaves while cows eat only grass, Vogler says. Nevada's dry climate and cold winters, and the fact that the herds graze on the open range, he adds, produces a cleaner, better-quality, higher-yielding wool product.

He's up at 4 a.m. each day, driving the landscape in his white Ford pickup truck. "All I've got is these animals, and I'll do whatever I have to do to protect them," he said. No kidding: On the living room of his ranch house sits the stuffed remains of a mountain lion he caught ravaging his lambs. "Sheep are a needy little animal. They need tending. But I dunno. I like 'em," he said. "Some nights, when you're so tired you could fall asleep in a second, but too sore to move, you see those little lambs bucking and running around while their mothers are bleating, calling out as if to say, 'Goddamn it, come on home; we're about to have supper.' And to see those babies finally go back, all calling in unison for their moms, well, it's like a beautiful rural symphony."

■ ■ ■

Not long after taking over the North Spring Valley operation, Vogler's 17-year-old son, H. C., was killed after he hit a patch of ice and flipped his truck. Among other effects, the resulting trauma ended his marriage. "The only way I was going to survive was to stay busy. I thought about it day and night, trying to put it in perspective," he recalls. "My only reprieve was to hit the pillow at night and go to sleep. It took me six or seven years, and I'm still not really over it."

Not long afterward, Vogler was at a meeting where sheep ranchers were reviewing a new marketing campaign. He didn't like it, and told people so, saying, "You might as well be selling woman's brassieres. That's not our industry." That's when somebody spoke up: "If you know so much, why don't you write it." So Vogler did. He self-published a children's book he called *The Story of Rangelands*, channeling his late son and his love of the land. "My son had just died," he recalls. "I cried while writing much of that book."

In 2013, he literally ran into a woman in a grocery store in Elko, knocking her egg carton to the floor. He paid for the eggs and the rest of her groceries, and later he jump-started her stalled car. He married China-born Wei Chen not long afterward.

That year, following his health scare, Vogler began several upgrades on his ranch, building a new shop and bunkhouse. He also constructed a new house that sits on a bluff over his operation, with views of the valley and mountains beyond. "When doctors told me I was going to take a dirt nap, I decided to upgrade so the next rancher's wife would be more inclined to buy the place," he explains. "But much to the chagrin of my detractors, I'm still here. Either it's love of the job or plain stupidity."

Sometime in the late 1970s, he was out on the Oregon range, in a place with the name Whorehouse Meadows, when he spotted some words carved into a tree. It was a poem, dated 1930, and signed "Val Johnson 1934." He memorized it:

> You talk about your lamb chops and the woolen clothes you wear
> But never a word or never a care for the man who put 'em there.
>
> I've summered in the tropics, had the yellow fever chill
> I've wintered in the arctic, known every ache and ill.
>
> Been shanghaied on a whaler, and stranded in the deep
> But I didn't know what misery was until I started herding sheep.

■ ■ ■

It's the morning after the storm, and the shearers have waited until the sun has burned the last of the snow from the sheep's backs. The animals bawl as they're prodded from their pens, through a single-lane chute, and into the shearing shack. Inside, the workers lay the surprisingly docile animals onto their sides and back and, with a quick precision, cut away their woolen coats. Once sheared, the sheep exit a swinging door, jumping for freedom like inmates leaving the penitentiary. After being checked for contamination, the fleece is separated by the quality of the wool and pressed into 500-pound bales that are loaded onto semis.

Vogler walks the yard, speaking in serviceable Spanish to the men, who mostly understand his directions, occasionally glancing at one another for confirmation. The grounds are littered with small trailers that house the shearers as well as Vogler's sheepherders, who have come in from the surrounding countryside, along with their dogs. The grounds are abuzz with calling animals and chattering men.

In one large pen awaiting their turn are the pregnant ewes, whom Vogler refers to as "blushing brides," skittish because they've already been through the shearing ordeal. Next door are the yearlings that will get pregnant this year, a band the sheepherder calls his "ladies in waiting," new to the shear. "For them, it's like going to a party," Vogler said. "'Hey, there's my mom and aunt Betty. Let's go!' Once shorn, they'll know. They'll take two steps back."

His children, all college-educated, work such jobs as computer technician, probation officer, heavy-equipment operator, archeologist and Marine Corps officer. None want to take the reins of their father's lifelong investment. "I always ask myself, 'Can I continue to do this?' I worry about the future," Vogler said. "I guess my kids all made the right decision by getting the hell out of here. Still, they were good buckaroos, all of 'em."

Having someone assume the reins of the business he built is just one worry. There are fewer sheep and fewer resources—fewer shearers to harvest the fleece, fewer dedicated trucks to haul it to market. "I worry all the time about the future of sheepherding in Nevada," he said. "My son has one more year in the Marines, maybe he'll come back, maybe he won't. Maybe it'll skip a generation, and it'll be the grandkids who take over. I'm not the only one worrying about this. We all do."

He looks off toward another set of storm clouds. "In the end, when the bank finally comes for this place, I just want 'em to say that old Hank Vogler sure took care of it for them."

A City Girl with a Pickup, an Attitude and a Mission to Save Wild Horses

■ **Antelope Valley, March 2016.** Horse activist Laura Leigh drives a monster-sized truck, an imposing Ford F-250 4-by-4 with its chassis jacked up so high she often must tumble down from the driver's seat, the vehicle's battered white finish filthy and mud-caked from all of her bumpy, teeth-loosening, off-road escapades.

It's her fourth pickup truck in seven years—the cost of a controversial 100,000-mile annual journey across six Western states and a nomadic lifestyle that often means sleeping in her truck cab or in cheap motels, guzzling reheated gas-station coffee and downing peanut-butter sandwiches behind the wheel. She's always red-eyed, always on the road. Leigh tracks the people who track and corral America's wild mustangs.

She's a tough-talking New Jersey native with long red hair, cowboy boots and a tattered denim Carhartt jacket, a woman who slides into a *Sopranos*-like accent when she talks about her blue-collar childhood riding and caring for horses, telling tales of the city girl who went to school smelling like horse manure, who quickly fell in love with the animals' indomitable spirit.

In 2009, Leigh fled an abusive marriage in Washington state and moved to Nevada to become a high-desert loner. Four seasons a year, she documents the actions of conservative tight-lipped ranchers whose free-roaming cattle compete with mustangs for precious grass. And she challenges federal officials from the Bureau of Land Management, the government stewards of the public lands whose policy is often to remove the horses from the range.

Leigh chronicles the story of the mustangs, these symbols of the American West, watching intently as the wild-eyed, bucking and kicking animals are herded by helicopter into corrals and loaded onto tractor-trailers. Some have been adopted. Many have been sold later, only to end up in foreign slaughterhouses.

Her tools include the high-resolution cameras she uses to capture

Wild-horse advocate Laura Leigh out on the range, looking after Nevada's last wild mustangs. Photo by Randi Lynn Beach.

images of horses that are injured and killed during the frequent BLM roundups; her often-graphic photos and videos are posted on her website (https://wildhorseeducation.org), and used as evidence in court cases she files on behalf of the mustangs. Her lawsuits have helped to successfully open horse-gatherings and holding yards to public scrutiny and create safer conditions for the animals.

Rolling down the highway and off-roading among the sagebrush, her 9 mm handgun tucked away for protection, blasting Metallica and the Boss on her truck stereo, she's become a sassy Bruce Springsteen of the Nevada outback.

She has made enemies, using her camera to document ranchers who graze their cattle out of season. She's been the subject of unflattering coverage in cowboy-centric publications such as *Nevada Rancher Magazine* and *Range* magazine, which pointed out that her last name rhymes with "pee," a woman "Hollywood would have cast as a schoolmarm." Leigh, the magazine wrote in its most recent issue, "is a self-appointed wild-horse expert and, depending on the day, is either a venomous critic or a volunteer of and for the BLM. Her issue-driven-propaganda-producing fundraising website spins the ongoing plight of wild horses from an anti-ranching, anti-livestock point of view."

Leigh also has received ominous telephone calls: "I know you have a daughter, and I know where she is," a male voice threatened. But Leigh carries on. With her camera and video recorder, she jokes, she's like a hunter without a season.

In 2010, Doug Furtado, BLM's Battle Mountain District manager, invited Leigh to a meeting at a Reno hotel after hearing about this one-woman wrecking crew. "There wasn't a lot of trust there at first," he said. "She was upset with how the BLM was managing wild horses."

He now views Leigh as a sensible and formidable voice on the mustang issue. Furtado keeps a white grease board in his office to track the BLM roundups Leigh's advocacy has helped quash. He talks of her with a plainspoken deference. "Her favorite thing is having the conversation," Furtado said. "She's willing to do that with anyone willing to open that door. You can't say that about all horse advocates."

When it comes to the mustangs, though, Leigh sticks to her guns: She insists wild horses are scapegoats for range damage done by domestic cattle and sheep, and she disputes BLM claims that horses are dying of starvation and need to be removed.

Leigh fumes at officials she says believe anything said by a guy in a cowboy hat. She dislikes patronizing men who believe rural Nevada is no place for a single woman. "Any conversation that starts with 'Laura, you need to understand...' Well, we ain't havin' that conversation," she said. "I just tell 'em, 'We'll see ya in court.'"

The last years have tested her willpower and stamina. Since 2012, when Leigh was diagnosed with breast cancer, she has undergone eight surgeries and was severely injured as a passenger in a head-on car collision. Through it all, she has ignored the advice of friends and doctors, staying in bed just long enough to muster the energy to return to the range.

The battle for the wild horses sustains her, giving sharp focus to the life of a once-abused woman willing to fight for what she loves, she said. "Horses have the largest eyes of any land mammal," Leigh said. "They're windows to the soul. In the eyes of those free-running mustangs, we can see ourselves."

In 2010, Leigh's advocacy began in earnest when she documented a roundup in which an 8-month-old colt was pushed so hard by praying mantis-like helicopters over frozen volcanic rock that the animal's hooves literally began to fall off, she said. She would later take pictures and video of injured and dying horses. She filed numerous lawsuits, including one seeking access to BLM roundups closed off to the public. The 9th U.S. Circuit Court of Appeals eventually upheld that suit.

At first, she was timid, seeing her name listed against the U.S. government in legal papers. But she pressed on. She filed Freedom of Information Act requests and litigation that halted abusive tactics on the range. Horse gatherers contracted by the BLM can no longer gather mustangs if the weather is too hot or cold. They can't use whips or electrical hotshots or ram the fleeing animals with helicopters. "Contractors accused me of creating a drama storm," Leigh said. "The images I take aren't about the drama; they're about the continued welfare of wild horses."

Leigh's pickup eases down a rutted dirt road in the middle of Antelope Valley north of Ely. She's on the lookout for mustangs, making sure they aren't underfed or blocked from water sources by ranchers. In the back lies a scattering of hay. The cab resembles a cluttered ancient tomb before an excavation, or the domain of a horse activist always on the road. She points to a Canon camera with a long-range lens: "That one won all those court cases," she said, motioning to another on the dashboard. "This one shoots 11 frames per second."

She's on the scent of a herd of mustangs she's spotted on the horizon. She hops down from the truck, picking her way through the scrub brush. She bends to pick up a fistful of wild horse manure, breaking open one pod to show the animals' diet. "I love horse poop," she said. "But I wouldn't touch cow dung."

That's Leigh, who vows to keep "riding across the West, looking for a fight." "I've listened to people talk about how the horses are doing all the destruction, and then I tell them, 'Now, when can I slap the crap out of you?'"

She's joined by Jeanne Nations, a local property owner who sits on a BLM advisory board. Nations is a blond-haired woman who gets Leigh's mission. The two stand near Leigh's truck talking horses when Nations spots a band of mustangs on the run, coming their way.

The eight horses gallop across the landscape as though it were still 1870, their hair in the wind, the color of the lone colt matching Leigh's red hair. She grabs a camera and hustles in for a better angle, the other woman behind her.

Then Nations just watches the horse activist doing what she loves most. "Whoa!" she yells. "Go get 'em, Laura!"

Being a Gay Mayor in Nevada's Outback

■ **Ely, November 2019.** In January, on the advice of friends that included his seventh-grade English teacher and Cub Scout den mother, Nathan Robertson made up his mind: He was going to run for mayor in this year's June elections. He even had his campaign slogan, "More Planning. Fewer Potholes."

Robertson's roots date back five generations in this isolated rural town founded as a stagecoach station along the old Pony Express route. His ancestors, members of the Church of Jesus Christ of Latter-day Saints, worked in the mines and on nearby ranches. His father and grandfather have served as the town's optometrist.

At 35, Robertson has a personal stake here. And he disapproved of many older residents elected to public office merely because they were available, many wielding political axes. A businessman who'd returned to Ely after attending college and performing Mormon missionary work, Robertson wanted to bring the voice of a new generation to this mining community of 4,000 residents in the state's eastern reaches.

Still, close friends cautioned him, "Have you really thought about this?" The concern wasn't just possible age bias, that he'd be one of the youngest mayors ever elected in conservative White Pine County, which had voted for Donald Trump in 2016 with a whopping 72 percent.

There was something else.

He was gay.

And still, Robertson won, and by a wide margin—527 votes to 235—more than doubling the count of opponent Ed Spear, a self-described redneck cowboy.

With his unlikely victory, Robertson actually became Nevada's second openly gay mayor. The first didn't come from urban areas such as Las Vegas or Reno, but the tiny town of West Wendover, just 120 miles northeast of Ely, along the Utah border.

At age 28, Daniel Corona is also a fifth-generation resident who returned to rural Nevada after several years away. Like Robertson, he didn't flinch at being gay when it came to running for public office. Some suggest rural Nevada's two gay mayors represent a sea change in the cultural attitudes of small-town America, where a generation ago gay men and women fled to cosmopolitan Miami, Los Angeles and San Francisco, just to be themselves.

■ ■ ■

For both Robertson and Corona, their deep local roots may have played a role in their neighbors ignoring lifestyles they might otherwise find objectionable. The blood of a generations-old family presence in a community, experts believe, just might be thicker than the water of sexual preference. "These rural communities can be accepting of a local boy or girl made good," said Gregory Hinton, a historian and curator of "Out West," a national museum program series inspired by his own upbringing in small-town Cody, Wyoming. "They've seen them grow up as children and know their sexual preferences don't necessarily define them, that it's just one of their characteristics," said Hinton, who is gay. "The kid might now be a cross-dresser but he's our cross-dresser." Corona agrees. You can come home again, even if you're gay in rural America. "It depends on your family," he said.

For his part, Robertson didn't believe that being gay should disqualify him from public office. For three years, he and partner Shadrach Michaels, a local schoolteacher-turned newspaper reporter, had shared a home across the street from Robertson's grandparents. He'd neither flaunted nor hid his sexuality. Sure, the couple had occasionally held hands and even embraced in public, but no one had ever voiced disapproval, not even during his mayoral campaign.

During his candidacy, Robertson never mentioned he was gay. "It's not like people didn't know," he said over a bowl of soup at a restaurant. "But I think it counts for something if people around here know you, know your family. I'm a private person, and I did not want to defend my personal life in public."

Robertson insists he does not fit any stereotype, gay or otherwise. He works construction, collects old cars and can rebuild an old engine on his garage floor. He gets along with his parents and only came out when he was in his early 30s. He wouldn't attend a Pride parade even if he lived in West Hollywood, California. "That's not me, that's not who I am," he said. "You have a right to be who you are. Even if you're gay, you don't have to put on a feather boa, if that's not you."

While few Ely residents publicly brought up the issue of Robertson's sexual identity, some here say it remained right there beneath the surface. "There was definitely a lot of whispering," said Andy Bath, a school friend who co-owns a pharmacy in town. "For some people, it was a red flag. If anything, it was more with the LDS church. There was a lot of concern after the fact. And it looks like the majority of those people did not vote for him." Robertson's lifestyle has cost him a voice in his chosen faith. When he moved in with Michaels, he was ex-communicated, no longer allowed to take an active role in church life. He still attends weekly services.

But it just wasn't the churchgoers who resisted. After Robertson won an early mayoral primary race, the loser approached Bath, using a slur often applied to gays. "He said, 'I can't believe this f***** won.' It took me by surprise. And I told him, 'Well, you lost fair and square.' It just showed how much things need to change in Ely."

John Chachas says Robertson attended grade school with his daughters. Over the years, he's become paternal to the new mayor. "I love that kid," he said, his voice breaking. But Chachas, an insurance agent and former councilman, also knows the political slant that pervades his hometown. When told Robertson insists there were no cross burnings, he said jokingly, "Well, Nate was out of town that weekend."

Many others supported Robertson, he said. "Despite any criticism, he holds his head of high in this community. This is Ely, Nevada. It's home to hunters, rednecks and cowboys. How was Nathan even thinking that he was ever going to beat old-timer Eddy Spear? "But he spanked him good. And he sent a message."

Ely has demonstrated a narrow small-town mindset in other ways. Earlier this year, a city councilman questioned whether council candidate and mother Michelle Beecher could fulfill her public duties while raising a family. Beecher lost that initial seat to Spear but has since been appointed to another. She also hopes new blood will bring change. "I hope it says that Ely is forward thinking and that people can see past those things they may not like about a candidate." Spears says he doesn't care about any personal life: "I've known his family forever and I think we need to vote on people's merits, not their sexual orientation." Yet one official criticized Robertson for public displays of affection. "He went to an event, holding hands and flaunting with his husband, doing things even a heterosexual wouldn't do," said the person, who asked not to be named. "That leaves a sour taste."

■ ■ ■

In West Wendover, Daniel Corona did not campaign as a gay candidate in his 2016 mayoral run, yet he has been outspoken on so-called LGBTQ issues.

Corona came out when he was just 16. Today, the town of 5,000 has scores of gay residents, he says. He recently posted on his Facebook page: "In 2016 I became the first openly LGBTQ person in any city in Nevada to be elected to serve as mayor. This shouldn't matter, but it does," he wrote. "Until the day that kids are no longer thrown out of their homes & onto the streets because they want to live openly & authentically, until the day that trans people especially trans people of color no longer have to constantly look over their shoulders with the fear of being brutally murdered, until the day that we can no longer be fired from our jobs or evicted from our homes for living openly & authentically we will continue to celebrate LGBTQ+ representation."

Still, the issue of Corona's sexuality wasn't mentioned in the election, not even by his opponent. "It never occurred to me," Mayor Emily Carter said. "It's sad that it's even an issue in some places." Corona says his critics have singled him out in other ways. Some say he was elected in a town with a large Latino population because of his Hispanic surname. He's been dismissed as the "Marijuana Mayor" for efforts to bring the cannabis industry here.

Others snicker over the fact that he still lives with his mother and often rides with her to work when she reports to her job at the adjacent police department.

Gary Corona, a captain in the West Wendover Fire Department, insists most people don't judge his son harshly: "Our family has been in this town long enough that people know him. He's a person, and he's a good man. That's all that matters." Corona has received a few vulgar emails over his sexual preferences, but he takes them in stride. "If the only thing you can criticize is my sexuality, then I must be doing a good job," he said.

Corona's most telling encounter came while knocking on doors during his campaign, an experience he says shows how far rural Nevadans have come when it comes to cultural acceptance, and how much work still needs to be done.

"Let me ask you a question," one man asked. "I've heard a rumor around town. Are you one of those trans people?"

Corona said he wasn't.

Are you gay?" the man asked.

"Yes," Corona said.

"Well," the man answered. "That's OK, then."

■ ■ ■

In Ely, Nathan Robertson continues to fight the gay stereotype. When he came out a few years ago, a family member asked, "Does this mean you're going to start wearing pink and speaking with a lisp?" His grandmother, who lives across the street, still sends he and his partner separate Christmas cards.

Michaels, who has lived in Los Angeles and San Francisco, is more attuned to any anti-gay current in town. When he worked as a middle school teacher, parents told him they didn't want their children in his classroom because he was gay. He had doubts about moving to such a small rural place, but Robertson assured him that Ely had a gay population: "He said there was an interracial lesbian couple," he laughs, "but I've lived here three years now, and I've never seen them."

Months into his job, Robertson goes about his work, walking the town in his baseball cap, jeans and flannel shirt, working on his cars, driving the old beater he bought in Salt Lake City for $500, the one he jokingly calls the "meth-mobile."

He refuses to recognize anti-gay conspiracies, saying he "doesn't lose any sleep" over people who won't approach him with issues they might have with his sexuality.

Michaels is proud of his partner. "Nathan wants to be the best mayor he can be," he said. "We warned him people here were going to insist on giving this gay guy a run for his money. But he threw caution to the wind and did it anyway, because he loves this town."

But he still ribs Robertson about his subtle approach to his sexuality. The other night, he gestured to his partner and laughed.

"He's terrible at being gay."

Robertson blushed. "Yeah," he said. "I guess I am."

When Death Calls, Jay Gunter Answers the Phone

■ **Hawthorne, April 2016.** When the telephone rings in the middle of the night, as it often does, Jay T. Gunter knows that some desperate family is in trouble. They might be his neighbors. Perhaps someone landed in jail or, worse, suffered a fatal accident. Either way, the lanky 65-year-old is the man to call.

People wear many hats in Nevada's sparsely settled desert, doubling up on their responsibilities because there just aren't enough working professionals to go around. Take Gunter: The veteran funeral director is also the elected justice of the peace, ready to preside over late-night arraignments or last-minute search warrant applications. But that's not all: He's a volunteer firefighter's assistant and the deputy registrar in rural Nye, Esmeralda and Mineral Counties. And he's Esmeralda County's deputy coroner, responding to deaths at all hours. So when that phone rings, there are no groggy-eyed excuses about the lateness of the hour. He's on the road, few questions asked. "When people call and say they want me to come get mom or dad, I don't say, 'Sorry, that's not my territory,'" he said. "I tell them that I'll be there as soon as I can.'"

In large cities, consumers have their pick of ubiquitous funeral homes. Not so in rural areas, where professionals such as Gunter cover wide swaths of real estate: His turf comprises 50,000 square miles across central Nevada, an area the size of Arkansas. Silver State funeral directors have the nation's third-largest client base, according to the National Funeral Directors Association—a factor of the small number of mortuaries amid the state's wide-open spaces. For each of 50 funeral homes statewide, there are 54,000 potential clients. Gunter is the only undertaker between Pahrump and Fallon—268 highway miles. He's driven 600 miles round trip, clear across the state to Ely and beyond, just to retrieve one body, and he has ranged 150 miles to consult with an isolated ranch family on funeral arrangements.

Make no mistake, he doesn't complain. He knows all-day excursions are part of the job. Around these parts, the long-striding nearly

Undertaker Jay Gunter leans on his hearse, ready to take a call into Nevada's wilds. Photo by Randi Lynn Beach.

6-foot-5-inch figure is a well-known commodity to people who know him as "Judge" from his time on the bench, or simply "Jay-T," a neighbor for decades.

So when a family member dies, they call Gunter, their voices heavy with grief, knowing they'll receive a few kind and thoughtful words from someone they've known for years as a hunting partner or community volunteer. In rural areas, funeral directors such as Gunter are more than just undertakers. They're community leaders whom people often seek out for emotional guidance. "In small-town America, the funeral director is someone who knows the family, the person from whom they seek healing when death comes," said Arbie Goings, who trains rural funeral directors in handling mass fatalities. "Families trust the bodies of diseased loved ones to their care. These people have high standing in the community."

Half of Gunter's 44 years as a funeral director have been spent in Hawthorne, where he has handled 2,400 funerals, even burying three generations of one family.

He bears the gentle mannerisms of a country doctor. But there's something edgy about the way he tools along the state's byways and back roads in his vintage white Cadillac Masterpiece Hearse, following a trail of death across the high-desert plains. It's almost as though David Lynch should be riding shotgun.

■ ■ ■

Born in Sacramento, Gunter worked in Idaho and in Carson City before moving to Hawthorne two decades ago. He liked the area for its fishing and hunting and soon became accepted. When he ran for justice of the peace in 2006, the married father of one got 57 percent of the vote.

He turns heads when he enters a room. His face ruddy from time spent outdoors, he wears an oversize belt buckle and a ring bearing an ivory elk's tooth, a touch of country style to his somber suit-wearing profession. And he keeps his sense of humor, joking his middle initial stands for "trouble."

People know Gunter is honest and fair. There's no pressure to buy a casket that's out of a family's financial reach. "It's easier to talk a family up from a $5,000 to an $8,000 casket than it is to convince one with little money to go for one that costs $1,200 and not $5,000," he said.

Each year, Gunter and a part-time employee drive 50,000 miles to conduct business, sometimes doubling up on body pickups in their marked industrial van.

He's retrieved bodies from roadway shoulders following traffic accidents and picked them up in hospitals, hospice care centers and ranch bedrooms. He has driven four-wheel-drive vehicles through the snow and mud to reach other spots—once walking two miles into the woods with a stretcher—where hunters, farmers, ranchers, off-road enthusiasts and hot-springs bathers have died from accidents, or when someone walked far into the outback to commit suicide. One body he recovered had been missing eight years. In all kinds of weather, he's responded to the top of Mount Grant just outside Hawthorne to recover the bodies of a half-dozen people killed in several different single-engine airplane crashes.

If Gunter is ever going to get a speeding ticket, it will be on the way to retrieve a body. On the return trip, he drives slowly out of respect for the dead. Once, on his way to Tonopah to pick up the body of an old friend, a state patrolman who didn't recognize Gunter's new vehicle stopped him for speeding. "Where'd you get this van, Jay?" he asked after pulling over the undertaker. Gunter said he was going to pick up the body of an elderly woman they both knew. "Oh, you don't have to hurry with her; she doesn't have any family," the officer said, pausing. "And, by the way, you were going 83 miles an hour." He drove away with a warning.

Gunter has done his homework. He knows the average American family will suffer a death every eight years. And when that time comes, he'll be there for them.

Tony Hughes, whose family once ran the newspaper here, said Gunter arranged the funerals of his two brothers, including one who couldn't afford a headstone. "So Jay went out and got a real nice rock, had it engraved and placed at the gravesite," Hughes said. "He didn't have to do that, but that's the kind of man he is. I've seen big tears in his eyes at funerals. He chokes up. Not many funeral directors do that."

Hawthorne resident Patty Thyne has another Gunter story: When her son, Kenneth Bostic, was killed in 2006 while serving in Iraq, Gunter arranged for the body to be transported all the way back to Hawthorne with military honors. "They brought Ken home in a C-130," she recalled. "It was all Jay; he knows how to work with people. He's got a big heart. He always has, and he always will."

Gunter looks out for his country clients. In the funeral parlor, he doesn't use much makeup, even with women, because ranch women don't wear much in life. Sometimes, he'll do their hair himself, or bring in a trusted hairdresser so they can look like they did when they laughed and told jokes in the stylist's shop.

He has a minor in psychology, which comes in handy. Once, when a man looked to him for solace after losing his elderly mother, Gunter gave him a plainspoken answer. "Look, I don't have any magic words," he said. "But I lost my own mother a few years ago, so I know how bad you're hurting."

Friends often ask Gunter who's going to handle his funeral. He scratches his head over that one, but his answer has a ring of rural wisdom. "When it comes to death," he tells them, "we all take our turn."

A Small-Town Police Blotter Tells Tall Tales

■ **White Pine County, April 2016.** Sheriff Dan Watts is a muscular man with a shaved head and salt-and-pepper goatee. Three decades in law enforcement have taught him this about places such as Ely—the biggest small town in his mammoth patrol area: Some residents don't have a heck of lot to do. And nearly everyone loves a juicy piece of gossip, scandal, buzz or scuttlebutt—as long as it doesn't involve them, of course.

Luckily, in Ely, like towns and cities across Nevada, there's a regular chronicle of the human condition that's become a must-read among residents. It's the daily police blotter—a haiku-like compilation of bite-size bits of salaciousness and dirty laundry. Consider it the public stockade of American culture, particularly in small towns and rural areas, a circumstance most people avoid like a court summons or a too-tight set of handcuffs. "Yeah," Watts laughs. "The blotter gives people something to talk about."

The White Pine County Sheriff's Department has published a blotter for decades. Years ago, Watts explained, the brass decided to block reporters from snooping through the department's incident reports, recording reams of personal information officers just didn't want to go public. So officials created the blotter's spoon-fed news nuggets written by deputies. In the late 1980s, the practice was discontinued for unknown reasons.

When Watts became sheriff nine years ago, he heard the rumblings. Residents cornered him at meetings and on the street. And they weren't happy. "They wanted the blotter back," he said. "I hate to say this, but they looked forward to reading it. People said they didn't know what was going on without their daily blotter."

■ ■ ■

Officers received a report of a fight that had taken place at a local bar. When officers arrived, the individuals involved reported that nothing had happened. The incident was documented.

Reporting party stated that the lights were on in her home and she was unable to turn them off. Officer turned the lights off for her.

Reporting party stated that someone had painted an alien message on the ground in a local parking lot. Officer patrolled the area and reported that it was only a shadow from a vehicle.

■ ■ ■

In Ely, blotter items range from the just plain weird to the serious—the names of residents arrested on charges including public intoxication, indecent exposure, spousal abuse, not to mention embarrassing drug and alcohol arrests. White Pine County spreads for 9,000 square miles. Of its 10,000 residents, 7,000 live in Ely, and the rest in smaller towns including McGill, Baker, Lund, Black Horse and Pony Springs. Watts' small staff of deputies patrols it all.

The sheriff is a Boulder City native who once worked as a Vegas sign hanger before moving north to an area marked by drug use and transient mine workers. He's amazed by the reasons people call on law enforcement here—like the lady who couldn't get her window to close or the man who got drunk and lost his shoe. "One guy said his TV reception wasn't good," he said. "You just have to shake your head, be patient and explain we don't have the manpower to handle such things."

The blotter is published by a handful of area newspapers and on Facebook. That has boosted readership, with people reading from as far away as Las Vegas. Gary Cook, publisher of *The Ely Times*, a weekly newspaper, called the blotter insanely popular, the place people check first to see if a relative has been arrested, and for what. "One resident complained his neighbor was piling snow too close to his fence," he said. "These items say a lot about a community, but mostly that people have too much time on their hands."

■ ■ ■

Reporting party stated she was using a gambling machine at a local casino, but left the machine to do other business. When she returned to the machine, someone else was using it. She was advised no crime had occurred.

Reporting party stated that her gun came up missing around four years ago, and now she believes it was stolen. A report was completed.

Reporting party claimed her ex-husband piled all of her belongings on the sidewalk outside her house. A report was completed.

■ ■ ■

Sergeant Jaime Swetich began writing the blotter five years ago. Now 41, the Ely native knew the kinds of things that got in people's craw here. He said deputies respond to any kind of call—from an alarm at a credit union to a report of a barking dog, each documented in a written report.

But Swetich began to see a pattern: the same barking dog and same complainant. To relieve the monotony, the 19-year veteran took a new tack: He became the satirical Shakespeare of the department's police blotter. He peppered the blotter with words such as "cacophony," "temerarious" and "conflagration"—the more flowery and outrageous, the better. "I try to find big words so people have to look them up," he said. Locals said they had to consult their dictionary to negotiate the blotter. A high school teacher thanked him for raising awareness of the language.

One item read: "The reporting party claimed another male subject had been beleaguering him. Both subjects were advised to abstain from all superfluous confabulation." And: "Found to be due to a malfunction, the alarm was." And another: "The subject was intoxicated, but was enervated from his protracted wayfaring."

The blotter is so popular suspects ask that their arrests not be included—like the well-known resident collared for propositioning a stranger in a hotel men's room. "I had to inform him that we don't do favors," Swetich said,

But Swetich sometimes softens. Like the time he and a partner answered a 2 a.m. call from an elderly dementia sufferer who swore that "little people" were invading her home. She said they were coming from a crack in the ceiling over her bed. The officers taped the crack and pretended to arrest an invisible suspect. "I told her, 'We got 'em,' and she was thrilled," Swetich said. "Often this job isn't crazy crime fighting. In any big city, nobody would have even gone out to talk to her."

■ ■ ■

Reporting party states that his neighbor was pumping metal into his apartment causing physical ailments. The incident was documented.

Officer received report of a person sleeping on the floor of a local casino. Officer contacted person to advise him he needed to leave the establishment.

Reporting party stated her husband who was intoxicated left their home and had taken their TV. The area was patrolled, but the husband was not located.

■ ■ ■

Jim Jones has been a lifelong fan of the police blotter. The Santa Cruz, California, resident eventually became an unofficial expert on the perverse rationale behind the items: "Most blotters report not crime but perception—what people are afraid is going to happen." He was also so captivated by blotters' often lyrical style that he published a 2014 book, *Police Blotter Haiku*, featuring blotter excerpts from around the country "boiled down into seventeen syllables of raw humanity." One reads: "They argued, he left. She smeared pasta on his car. He shouldn't have left." And, "'This is not a bomb.' Scrawled on a box that wasn't. So they checked."

Most blotter items fall into categories: mistaken identity, people getting on each other's nerves and, "Is the guy standing outside my door actually a bear?" Many incidents pose two opposing realities. "One guy says, 'I think it's OK if my dog poops on your lawn.' And the neighbor responds, 'No, it's not, but it is OK for me to take out my machete and chase you down the street.'"

Residents of wealthy communities with high tax rates feel free to call police on the slightest whim, while those in blue-collar communities deal with the poor impulse control that comes with drug and alcohol abuse.

Jones is compiling a book of blotter items involving men without shirts. "If you see a shirtless man someplace where he should be wearing his shirt, he's going to be a loose cannon," he said. "A lot of this takes place in towns not in good shape, where meth is used, where there's not a lot of jobs."

He paused: "And then there's Florida."

■ ■ ■

Reporting party stated two individuals stayed at his home and now he wants them out. Officer contacted the individuals and advised them to leave.

Officer responded to report of man who was intoxicated and

throwing a fit. He had banged his head through a window and was hitting himself with a hammer. The individual advised that he was fine and requested no assistance.

The reporting party claimed a family member took her photo without permission. A report was completed.

■ ■ ■

The sheriff knows wacky calls are part of the job. So he has advice for his deputies. "I tell them 'Guys, if they call us, it's important to them—even if it's not to us or anybody else,'" Watts said. "So, go out there and calm them down and advise them how to fix the problem."

Then they write a report, which goes into the police blotter.

The Last Straw:
A Rural Home Built from Hay

■ **Big Smoky Valley, February 2016.** Kim Bozarth arrived here a cultural outlier among rough-edged, do-it-yourself men: an outspoken woman espousing liberal politics in a high-desert landscape where conservative thought is king.

The year was 2012, and the divorced mother of four grown children had come to reinvent herself—to abandon her urban life in Reno and build an all-natural house in this sweeping valley surrounded by majestic 11,000-foot mountain peaks. Locals scratched their heads at this city tumbleweed and her half-crazed notion to—now get this— build a home from bales of straw. Originating in Nebraska, straw-bale homes are known for their natural integrity and insulation.

For Bozarth, 55, the idea fit her philosophy to live more simply: "I wanted to haul my own water, grow and make my own food. I wanted to work at living." Bozarth comes from self-determined roots: Her mother rode wild mules as a girl and became one of Reno's first female blackjack dealers. Bozarth is a retired Army sergeant who served as a Russian transcriber in Europe. She knew all about handling recalcitrant men and getting back to the land. She taught courses in the new field of permaculture—agricultural designs based on natural ecosystems—and had supervised the building of several other straw-bale structures. In the end, Bozarth's central Nevada adventure tested her resolve to adapt to harsh natural conditions. It also led to a complete and welcome surprise: romance.

The first building disaster was quick in coming. On Labor Day weekend in 2012, two dozen friends pitched tents among the sagebrush to wage an old-fashioned Amish-style barn raising—helping erect the frameless load-bearing structure and cutting and assembling the 450 bales of straw Bozarth had shipped in for $1,300. Work done, they placed tarps around the unfinished house and went home; Bozarth returned to Reno. Weeks later, she was on the phone with a crusty rancher named Chuck.

Kim Bozarth and her dog stand outside the rural Nevada home she built from straw. Photo by Randi Lynn Beach.

"You know, the cows ate your home," he said matter of factly.

"Excuse me?" she gasped.

She hung up the phone: Old Chuck was not the kind who engaged in hyperbole. She hurried to the site to find two local men standing there, beers in hand, watching as a dozen range cattle munched on her dream home. She was living the child's fable *The Three Little Pigs*.

Bozarth already knew one of the men, Jesse Johnson, a slow-speaking neighbor with a gray beard and bib overalls who had used his yellow backhoe to lay her home's rock foundation. She had called for weeks before she got him on the phone to explain his role in her vision. "Yup," he said in his gravelly voice. "I can do that."

But when Bozarth later arrived with several workers, Johnson admitted he had left his backhoe parked 10 miles away. "That's great," Bozarth fumed. "I'm here, just like I said I'd be, with a crew I'm paying by the hour. And now I'm waiting on you." Jesse quickly got his back-hoe and was soon doing other heavy-construction jobs—working for an hourly rate and 12-packs of Budweiser, which were hard to attain in the isolated Big Smoky Valley.

Now, after the call from rancher Chuck, here was Johnson, calmly watching the cattle eat Bozarth's beloved home. She wanted to cry. Instead she barked, "Ya think you might run those cows off?" Once again, Johnson fetched his backhoe and dug trenches for postholes for a fence to keep out the animal invaders. Meanwhile, Bozarth drove to a bar in nearby Carvers and announced, "I need men who can build a fence, and I need them now. I'll pay $15 an hour." A few raised their hands.

Weeks later, 130-mile winds severely tilted the straw-bale home, nearly toppling the roof. "My house looked like a parallelogram," Bozarth said. Well, you guessed it, Johnson and his backhoe came to the rescue, setting the house plumb again. Among locals, he's known as a "peach skinner": His dexterity with his machine could peel the skin off a piece of fruit.

Johnson was impressed with this newcomer. "I'm like her," the 57-year-old Minnesota native said. "I've been known to take leaps into the wilderness."

Bozarth soon began stopping by Johnson's shop for a cold beer after a day's work. She played pool near the sign that said, "Danger: Men Drinking," ignoring the girlie posters on the wall. It was a respite from her life with no running water. She began calling the valley "the hood," and the shop boys, after laughing at her, soon adopted the phrase. She had avoided her nightmare of being dismissed as a "ridiculous joke."

One night, Bozarth awoke to hear Johnson's croak: "You in there?" The two pulled up chairs to watch a storm light up the night sky. He was a longtime bachelor who cared for his elderly mother. She hadn't even had a cup of coffee with an eligible man in 11 years. "Can I ask you a favor?" Johnson eventually said. "Can I go into your container and just hold you?" Bozarth's inner voice screamed, "No!" But she relented. "It was the most human thing anyone had ever said to me."

The next day Bozarth worried the innocent episode would ruin their budding friendship. After a week away, she went to check on him. That's when Johnson asked her to tour his nearby mining claim. Later they stood together on a hillside, watching the sunset. Johnson, of course, had another question: "Can I put my arm around you?" "He was like an eighth-grader, so I said, 'Sure,'" Bozarth said.

Johnson confessed he had fallen for the strong-willed woman who would not let her dream die, no matter what nature threw at her. All those months, as he worked atop his backhoe, he said, "I was sittin' there, eye-ballin' you." Then he added, "I'm sorry, but with your head there on my shoulder, I forgot what I was gonna say." Said Bozarth: "We were two cooked gooses." The pair soon got married.

And so life intervened on Bozarth's straw-bale dream: She helped care for Johnson's mother, who later died. She and Johnson staked a claim at a nearby gold mine and have poured their energies into striking it rich together. They took her Jeep to roam trails with a cooler full of beer. But the groom also took time to build his new bride an underground greenhouse near the straw-bale house, where the couple sleeps. Bozarth has vowed to complete her project in the next year, finishing the inside floor and walls with natural mud. "I needed this time to fall madly in love."

Nowadays, Bozarth blogs about her Big Smoky Valley adventures at https://www.kimbozarth.com. She also has a new project: a book, *The Cows Ate My House.* Johnson is a main character.

Keeping a Dying Native American Language Alive

■ **Ely, May 2016.** Boyd Graham rises at 4:30 a.m. each day, leaving the Duckwater Shoshone reservation in the vast Railroad Valley to embark on a 150-mile round trip journey: He's an unofficial emissary for his tribe, its cultural and linguistic interpreter.

At age 77, when most men his age have significantly slowed, this slender retiree with thick, overarching eyebrows teaches a Shoshone language class at White Pine High School—offering lessons not only to Native American youth but also anyone curious about the habits and sounds of his ancient culture.

"E hakanni," (pronounced Uh ah gah neh) he tells four teenagers each afternoon when they meet in a corner of the school's busy library. And when the class bell rings and they rise to leave, he bids them goodbye.

"Abishai." (Ah bee shy.)

This semester, the students are all boys, a pair with Native American heritage and two non-Indians who work just as hard to get their pronunciations right.

Chris Hill, a husky 17-year-old who wants to play college football, took the class as an elective: "I didn't want to take Spanish. I wanted to stick with a language from the American territory." Prompted to say a few words in Shoshone, he freezes. "Help get me started here, Boyd," he says before launching into a sentence with a translation that starts with "Your father's hat. . ."

In walks Tavix Robertson, a sun-bronzed teen, his long hair pulled into a tight ponytail. The back of his jacket bears an image of a skeleton in a feather headdress riding a horse over the saying "Ride Free." He is one-third Native American—half of that lineage Shoshone, the other Paiute. "I just thought it'd be cool to learn about our culture," he said softly.

They have come to the right place. Like many Native Americans from his generation, Graham worries that his language is dying. When he was young, tribal elders gathered to tell stories and interpret

Shoshone elder Boyd Graham teaches his native language at a White Pine County high school. Photo by Randi Lynn Beach.

legends, but radio and television and the invasion of English put a stop to most of that. Some tribes have battled to keep their language relevant in a modern world: In 2014, Navajo elders in Arizona blocked a candidate for tribal presidency because he could not speak the native tongue fluently.

Graham is trying to school the young before they reach adulthood. "We want to get them interested in our language and way of living," he said. "For our own youth, it's a way to instill pride and get them away from drugs and alcohol."

Born in Tonopah, Graham is one of nine children. His father, Raymond Graham, was a miner and tribal leader who was instrumental in founding the Duckwater Shoshone reservation about 220 miles north of Las Vegas.

For generations, the Shoshone were landless, working on privately owned ranches and mines to earn a living. In 1940, Raymond Graham negotiated the tribe's move to an isolated expanse where more than 150 Shoshone still live.

Like most of his generation, Graham left the reservation as a young man. He spent time in the U.S. Navy and lived in San Francisco. But he kept his language alive, speaking with his parents, grandmother and great-grandmother, who knew almost no English. He returned to Duckwater to allow his father to retire from cattle ranching.

Then, in 2000, he became a language instructor at the Shoshone tribal center in Ely, working with members who had married outside the tribe and forgotten their tongue. In 2010, Graham approached the high school about teaching a class. Principal Adam Young immediately liked his organic teaching methods. "Boyd takes students on walks, teaches them little by little," he said. "Some take the class multiple years because they like him so much."

Tribal member Virginia Sanchez also likes what she sees. "Boyd is almost 80," she said. "For him to have the stamina to teach young people at his age is incredible." She said Graham carries on a vital Shoshone tradition. "Our creation story says if you take care of your region, it will take care of you," she said. "Part of that means passing on the language of our elders. Boyd carries that with him."

Graham's wife, Lillian, said the couple can't go anywhere without running into one of his students. "These kids will wave at him, and I'll say, 'Who's that?' He'll just say, 'One of my kids,'" she said. "He's known all over Ely. He's respected because of what he does with the language."

Lillian, a Shoshone from Reno, doesn't speak the language—which gives her husband ammunition to tease her. "He thinks it's funny," she said. "I learned a little Japanese, so I speak Shoshone with an accent. He gets a kick out of the way I pronounce things. So I tell him, 'If you don't like it, teach me.'"

One day, Graham showed up for class in blue jeans and a blue-checkered short-sleeve shirt, an outfit topped off by a hat with an eagle adorned by a war feather and inscribed "Native Pride." As he waited for his flock, he told about the dangers of driving Nevada's outback before dawn. Antelopes ram and dent his car. Deer smash his headlights. Jackrabbits skitter under his tires. Once, two deer struck him at once. He knew the animals were dead, but didn't stop to salvage the meat; he didn't want to be late for school.

He knows learning spoken Shoshone is not easy. It requires restricting air in what's known as a glottal stop. T is pronounced as D, and P is spoken as B. As a result, the dropout rate is often high. But he's been amazed by some non-Indian students, such as the Chinese-American teen with a gift for pronunciation. "Perhaps Shoshone is close to his native language," Graham said. "He was amazing."

This semester, his students are rowdy teens. The class first met in a classroom equipped with gurneys and wheelchairs. But the teens raced around on the equipment, so he moved the students to the library to keep their attention. The gambit worked. Graham hasn't taught students any Shoshone cuss words, but they know some anyway.

Left-handed, he writes the alphabet onto a white grease board as other students using the library look on in curiosity. One of Graham's students fiddles with his cellphone but then puts it away. "Are we gonna have a quiz on the animals next week?" another asks. They pay attention, taking notes, repeating each word out loud. The instructor smiles. He knows that somehow, somewhere, his long-gone elders are happy.

Oddly Named Towns Recall Nevada's Colorful Past

■ **Jiggs, January 2016.** This is what it's like to live in a town named after a century-old cartoon character, an isolated high-desert speck with a one-room schoolhouse and lots of Wild West history, a place populated by cougars and mustangs if not the ghosts of long-gone cowboys.

The other day, 76-year-old rancher Simone Zaga, who runs cattle and sheep here, called an out-of-state mail-order company to buy grape seeds. When she gave her address as Jiggs, Nevada, the operator paused:

"Huh?"

"Just put down Spring Creek," the white-haired Zaga replied, pronouncing the word "crick." "I don't really live there, but it's close."

"So, where exactly is Jiggs?" the operator asked.

"About forty miles from Elko," Zaga said. "Not really forty miles, but it's easier to say."

In the end, Zaga got her seeds, but such are the challenges in a town whose unlikely name fails to conjure up its colorful past: a rich mining, ranching and rabble-rousing history that produced two governors (Edward "Ted" Carville and Lewis Rice "Old Broadhorns" Bradley), kindled countless years of heartache and toil and was the stomping grounds for Western author Zane Grey's fictional outlaw, King Fisher.

No, Jiggs is named after a portly top hat-wearing cartoon character in the popular comic strip *Bringing Up Father*. Children of a World War I-era saloon owner who followed the fictional exploits of the diminutive henpecked husband suggested the name.

When it comes to whimsical names, Jiggs has some pretty outside-the-lines company across rural Nevada: a passel of towns, mountains, rivers and canyons whose names make many outsiders—and residents—shake their heads in wonder. Consider Weed Heights, named not for the pesky plant but after mining executive Clyde E. Weed. And Tobar, a now-defunct railroad camp where workers mistook a crude sign reading "to bar," pointing the way to a tent saloon,

A lonely phone booth sits in the oddly named town of Jiggs in eastern Nevada. Photo by Randi Lynn Beach.

for the name of the settlement. An area on topographical maps of central Nevada is named "Goblin Knobs," not necessarily because it's haunted but because a surveyor once noted that "local tuff weathers into hoodoos and weird knobs."

Historians attribute such far-fetched names to Nevada's history of mining and railroad development, where harried, hard-working men pounded wooden signs with speculative place-names that somehow stuck, even though those locales have rusted into ghost towns and the stories behind the names have sometimes become more fiction than fact. Drive across Nevada and you'll pass through towns named Puckerbrush, Gabbs, Scotty's Junction, Blackjack, Carp, Duckwater, Fatty Martin Lake or Toe Jam Mountain. There's Stagecoach, Steamboat, Lovelock, Deeth (rhymes with teeth), Tunnel, Sulphur, Pinenut, Slim Creek and Adverse. And don't forget the old mining town known as Dinner Table, or Adaven, which is Nevada spelled backward.

Jeff Kintop knows some doozies as chairman of the Nevada State Board on Geographic Names. Like Beer Bottle Pass and Parachute Canyon. And Owyhee, where settlers wanted to name the town after a river in Hawaii, but couldn't spell very well. And Beowawe, where a railroad speculator once scouted out future towns. "He supposedly weighed over 300 pounds," Kintop said. After watching the outsider hammer in spikes, the Paiute Indians coined the name Beowawe. "It means 'Great Posterior,'" Kintop said.

Such tales make the story behind Jiggs seem a bit more likely. Over generations, the town was named Cottonwood, Dry Creek, Mound Valley, Skelton and Hylton.

Today, Jiggs is the only town in the expansive Mound Valley, framed by the rugged Ruby Mountains and Pinion Range. In 1846, the infamous Donner Party allegedly passed through here. In 1965, a Volkswagen ad campaign was shot in Jiggs, where the town's entire population fit in one Beetle bus. Now nobody officially lives in Jiggs, but the little outpost is the social center for some two dozen ranch families.

When Albert Hankins bought the hotel and saloon in 1918, his children begged him to use the name Jiggs. After learning that the character in the cartoon *Bringing Up Father* was harassed by his wife, Maggie, women in town even started the Maggie Club.

Sitting in the kitchen of her converted log cabin with Quaking aspen wooden beams, Zaga ticked off the name of every Mound Valley ranch by memory, using her fingers to keep track, her mind moving north to south. Folks here use only the last four digits when giving their telephone numbers; the prefix and area code are understood. The directions to Zaga's ranch are just as plainspoken: Take the first dirt road after the cattle guard a few miles south of town.

Jiggs isn't much to look at. There's a volunteer fire department, school and country hall. The soul of the place is Jiggs Bar, which features a menacing steer skull and a sign reading, "Cowboys Welcome." Inside, holiday lights adorn the antlers of a mounted elk head.

For years, Zaga and her husband, Fred, frequented the saloon "to BS people," preferring Tuesdays when Pete tended bar and Fridays when Jessica was there. Fred's gone now, but Zaga still uses the "royal we" out of old-country habit.

She attended the one-room schoolhouse in the late-1940s, where Mrs. Reed played piano and the boys danced with the boys and the girls with the girls—until the teacher forced them to match up nice and proper.

Life in Jiggs has always been simple. People dressed up only to run errands in nearby Elko. "Ranchers aren't rich like people think," Zaga said. "They might wear nice things to town, but they're the only nice clothes they have. They take them off the moment they get home."

In her sunroom, she pointed out the 20 animal trophies she and Fred have collected. There's the cougar rug on the wall ("I shot that one with a shotgun") and the bull elk ("Used a bow-and-arrow on him").

But along with its frontier spareness, Jiggs has allowed for some culture, too. Zaga motioned toward the piano. "I used to play some," she said. Mrs. Reed taught her well.

Lessons of a One-Room Schoolhouse

■ **Gabbs, August 2018.** The two teens have struck up an odd-couple friendship that could likely take place in only a few schools across the American West. Dave Jim is a strapping 15-year-old, a barrel-chested, soon-to-be 11th-grader who weighs 220 pounds. His best buddy, Devin Gaither, is a plucky 13-year-old who barely tips the scales at 110 pounds. Both the products of ranch families, the boys sit next to each other in this tiny rural school, in the far northern reaches of Nye County, along a desolate stretch of state Route 361. Gaither, for one, is amazed by their closeness. "It's nice to have a friend like Dave," he said. "If we went to a regular school, he'd probably be one of the kids who'd be mean to me."

But the Gabbs School is not regular, not by a long shot. It's one of a handful of classrooms across Nevada with an unusual teaching method: Jim and Gaither are among a dozen students between the seventh and 12th grades with a single instructor, in this case retired Air Force veteran and insurance agent-turned educator Tom Lyman. Down the hall, another teacher guides kindergarten through sixth-grade students.

The new school year starts August 13, and buying new clothes and supplies is typically a challenge for Gabbs residents. For Crystal Howell, who has three children here, it means putting the rubber to the road: She and her family must make the 320-mile round trip to Reno—not just to find the latest styles, but anything at all. "It's a lot of traveling," she said. "So we make a day out of it." And the road trips don't stop there. "Once basketball season starts, we've got to drive a long way just to find sneakers," Jim said.

Spending summers in an isolated town in central Nevada's hinterlands, without malls or swimming pools, means boredom is a constant. For Timothy Howell, a 14-year-old entering the 10th grade, August couldn't come fast enough. "You get tired of just riding your bike," he said. That's OK with his mother. "The one plus is that there's not a lot of girls in town, so I don't have to worry about that," Crystal Howell said.

The educational arrangement in Gabbs is a close cousin to the one-room schoolhouses where generations of Nevada pioneers received their educations. Falling populations in rural Nevada's mining and agricultural-based communities mean there aren't always enough students to fill out each grade. That has given rise to what are known as remote rural schools.

"Even though populations drop in rural towns, we have to evolve and keep pace," said Humboldt County School Superintendent Dave Jensen, who oversees a handful of such schools in the state. "We have to make sure our kids, even in the most remote locations, are exposed to a 21st-century education." For students, that means taking courses via the internet, spending their days peering at a computer screen. Their classroom resembles a collection of homeschooled students who have gathered in one place. Nye County School Superintendent Dale Norton said the Gabbs School is doing its job. "Parents wanted their kids to graduate in town," he said. "They didn't want them on a bus for an hour and 40 minutes to another high school."

There are drawbacks to no-frills education: no prom, no hallways teeming with teenagers, no Friday night football games and no art or music classes. But that suits some rural students just fine. "I'm not really good with strangers. I'm not exactly talkative," said 16-year-old J. J. Thompson, who is taking some college-level courses. "In regular school, you have to be outgoing. What I like about my school is that I know everybody. I can be myself. We're more than classmates. We're family."

His father, Jim McKinnon, graduated from Gabbs High as part of a class of 10 in 1997 and now works as the school's custodian. (His wife, Crystal Howell, is Lyman's aide.) McKinnon attended a regular high school with all the major sports. Now he and his wife must fill in the gaps to make sure J. J., the eldest of three children, has a normal teenager's life. They take him to dances at the high school in Tonopah. "As parents, you have to step in," he said.

He likes the setup in Gabbs. "This school is what you make of it," he said. "If you want to succeed, it's the perfect setup. Kids who aren't self-motivated get lost in big schools. But not here. In Gabbs, the teachers are here to push you."

The classroom can be chaotic. Each day, the shirt-and-tie-wearing

Lyman fields a barrage of questions. "I've got a dozen students, each taking a different course, so I'm dealing with seventh-grade math, eighth-grade grammar and 12th-grade government," he said. "Geometry isn't my strong suit, so I end up taking courses like that right along with many students."

Gabbs, named after paleontologist William Gabb, was founded in the early 1940s as mines competed to meet World War II demand for metals to make fuel. In 1943, Gabbs became a township with a population of 426 and featured a library, a city hall, several parks and a newspaper. It incorporated as a city in 1955. In the 1980s, the population reached its peak of nearly 1,600, thanks to an influx of mine workers. At the time, the elementary, middle and high schools drew 175 students, and some classes featured nearly two dozen graduates. Then the mining economy collapsed. In 2001, the population of Gabbs fell below the level necessary to keep its incorporated status. As people moved away, the grade and middle schools were shuttered, and sections of the high school were closed.

Today, 150 people hang on in Gabbs, which offers a bar, a convenience store, a gas station and a motel. The school's 2015 graduating class featured four students. The 2016 class had two, and in 2017 and 2018, each graduating class had just one. When Lyman started at the school in 2011, fresh after earning his teaching degree, the high school had four teachers and the elementary school three. Now they're down to one apiece, with an aide to assist. "This classroom might overwhelm a 23-year-old teacher fresh out of college," Lyman said. "But I'm an old fart who's seen a bit of the world. Still, I don't do much teaching per se. I just help them understand what's on the computer screens."

■ ■ ■

One day last spring, the K-6 group met the older students in the hallway in front of the office to recite the Pledge of Allegiance. As an aide helped roll up the flag, the students sang the state song, "Home Means Nevada," which begins, "Way out in the land of the setting sun / Where the wind blows wild and free / There's a lovely spot, just the only one / That means home sweet home to me." Then the high schoolers filed back into their classroom, past a sign that harks back to earlier days: "No Cellphones: Any Device that is Visible is Considered in Use."

But times have changed. "I just never took it down," Lyman said of the sign. New rules ban texting but allow students to listen to music through earbuds once their lessons are done.

Lyman walks a fine line with his disciplinary strategy. With an average GPA of 3.1, most kids perform at levels beyond their statewide peers. Each must complete several lessons a day, goals divided between morning and afternoon sessions. If they don't earn a C, they must repeat the class. Because they work independently, some finish lessons early. "I'm trying to teach them independence," he said. "And I know if there were too many rules they would rebel. Students will say, 'I've done my work. Why can't I talk?' And I'll say, 'Fine, but keep it down.' It's working well. The kids are doing great. So I just let things go, as long as it's not crazy."

With district money, Lyman bought such incentives as a telescope for after-hours stargazing and an Xbox video game system for students with free time. He's paid for many games out of his own pocket. Twice a day, students break for a half-hour gym session to play basketball and blow off steam.

In this class, there are no hall passes. Students move about freely. If they have to use the restroom, they just get up and go. But Lyman has to lay down the law. "Hey guys, no chips!" he says this day in response to the sound of rattling snack wrappers. "Put 'em away, and I don't mean just stuffing 'em in your mouth."

After a gym break, freshman Louis Afraid-of-Hawk, a 15-year-old American Indian, took a seat at a study computer in the Xbox gaming room.

"C'mon back," Lyman told him.

"Nah, I'm gonna work over here."

"No," the teacher said patiently. "You need to come back to the classroom."

Back in the room, 16-year-old Christa Gentry raised her hand.

"Mr. Lyman?" she said. "I've changed my mind. I need help."

Gentry is one of two girls in the class. A year ago, she played on the junior varsity co-ed basketball team, the Gabbs Tarantulas. She's self-assured: "I wasn't much of a scorer. I was more like a wall for them." Lyman leaned over her computer and coached her through a few science questions.

Later, Gentry told him, "I hate biology."

"You got it done, though," he answered.

Gaither is the youngest here. Cowboy hat set aside, he props his boots on a desk and listens to music on his phone, dressed in his Carhartt work jacket. Behind him hang posters of a human skeleton and phases of the moon.

He's done his schoolwork. Now it's time to be a teenager. When class finishes, he'll ride his minibike a mile home to his nearby ranch. Maybe he'll hang out with his friend, Jim, theirs an unlikely bond that might not happen anywhere else but in a rural school in a remote Nevada town like Gabbs.

The West

Innkeeper Walt Kremin relaxes in a barber chair in Gold Point. Photo by David Becker.

The Reluctant Innkeeper

■ **Gold Point, August 2019.** You know those roads out in the middle of nowhere that veer off the main highway and jettison straight out to a pinpoint on the horizon, past bullet-riddled signs and desert buttes? Well, that's where you'll find old Walt Kremin and his little bed-and-breakfast, right where the worn tarmac of State Route 774 turns to dirt.

For decades, the 73-year-old Bronx-born cowboy has staked his claim in this forgotten mining town, which in the last century has seen its population dwindle from 1,000 to just six, including Kremin. The place is so lost the county sheriff rolls in just once a month and locals swear the ghosts of prospectors past sometimes let out eerie hee-haws in the dead of night.

Before cellphones arrived, the nearest public call box featured a party line, outside the defunct Cotton Tail brothel some 20 miles down U.S. Route 95. But for some oddball reason, strangers keep showing up to nose around this high-desert outpost 180 miles north of Las Vegas, oohing and aahing at all the mining history and hulks of old vehicles left to bake in the sun, such as the 1916 Dodge flatbed with the suicide doors somebody hauled down from the hills. Some need a bed for the night and so Kremin, well, he guesses he'll oblige them. He'll ready up one of a half-dozen old mining shacks he's converted into comfortable lodging. Pressed hard, he might even cook them a meal.

Kremin, you see, is something of a reluctant innkeeper. "I don't like making beds," he said. "I also know that I wouldn't sleep on sheets somebody else slept on. So the beds get made." Since his two business partners left him years ago, Kremin has eased around on his cramped-up leg, doing what he can, putting off what he can't.

A lifelong bachelor, he likes being his own boss up here in this hideaway in the hills with its sweeping God-given vistas. Being something of a curmudgeon, he says he doesn't need any woman "who wants the luxury of a Walmart," or society at-large poking a nose over his shoulder. People call Kremin's rustic operation one of rural Nevada's best-kept secrets. And that's the way he wants to keep it. But to keep the doors swinging, he agreed to a little publicity, knowing that if too many people show up, he'll just tell them to skedaddle.

Still, travelers keep coming—motorcyclists, desert roustabouts, lost families. In an average month, Kremin hosts more than 100 guests, a burden that gets him out of bed before first light hits the Lida Valley and flat-topped Jackson Mountain just beyond. Sometimes, he'll call in help, but stubborn Kremin prefers to handle things alone, declaring, "I don't like to be anybody's hall monitor."

Recently, Kremin tends bar at a saloon he refurbished from the original real estate office. He spent years running around the mountains and antique shops looking for old knickknacks to make it look just right, like an authentic relic of the Old West.

He wears a straw cowboy hat, sky-blue shirt and work boots, a pair of red suspenders barely holding up his blue jeans. And this being rural Nevada, he's also got his 9 mm Smith & Wesson strapped to his hip. He's never shot another man, just the pesky bobcats that prey on his domestic cats.

Kremin is known to enjoy a little coffee in his morning whiskey. He pours himself another shot of Usher's Green Stripe and in his clipped New York accent tells the unlikely story of how he ended up here.

■ ■ ■

He arrived here in 1973, when there weren't many more folks around than there are now. He fell for the morning fog banks and how the hills glowed pink at dusk. He soon joined up with his brother, Chuck Kremin, and house painter Herb Robbins, to buy buildings in the old silver-mining town, which was established in the 1880s and first called Lime Point and then Horn Silver before folks decided on Gold Point.

In 1997, after Robbins won $223,000 on a Vegas slot machine, the partners got to work creating a bed-and-breakfast. But time scatters like desert dust. Chuck Kremin left because of his diabetes and the fact that his wife was afraid of ghosts. Robbins quit after the pain from a scaffolding accident became too much. He still lives in town.

That leaves Walt Kremin, who knows he can't be everywhere at once, so he rigged up a sensor that trips when visitors arrive, bringing him down in his utility cart to open for business. "I don't know how to mix drinks," he said. "If they're complicated, I tell people to make it themselves. Or tell me what's in 'em, because my memory is terrible."

But get him going, and Kremin emerges from his shell. He'll spring up on those wobbly legs for a walk around town, maybe offer a tour of the vintage post office, explaining how the settlers carved a life here

140 years ago. Deep down, Kremin's not so irascible after all. "I enjoy people. That's why I don't quit."

Visitors respond. "It's well off the beaten path but well worth the trip," one wrote on Kremin's website. "Have fun! I always do!"

Another reviewer wrote: "While we were looking around, up drives a man that opened the bar and told us some great stories. I think his name was Walt. I'm already making plans to return."

And another: "It took me about a year of hearing 'Ya gotta go to Gold Point' before I actually went. Now it is hard to keep me away."

Kremin only accepts cash, but the nearest ATM is 100 miles away, so guests often leave with a handshake and a promise to send a check. He's never been stiffed.

So come on out, if you must, but don't expect Kremin to leave the light on for ya.

Wild Horse Auctions

▨ **Fallon, June 2013.** The gate swings open, and the mustang rushes into the auction pen. Yearling by its side, the mare paces the muddy floor, neck craning, nostrils flaring—a graceful creature that has never known saddle or rider now turned biddable commodity. The unluckiest of America's wild horses end up in places like this: a livestock yard in rural Nevada, where potential buyers coolly assess each animal's physique, looking for a deal. On this day, some 23 mustangs state officials removed from public rangeland outside Reno will have their fates determined in the crescent-shaped bidding theater.

A showdown looms. In the crowd are so-called kill buyers scouting product to ship to a foreign slaughterhouse. Also on hand are animal activists who, checkbook in hand, plan to outbid the kill buyers. The mood is prison-yard tense, with armed state Department of Agriculture officers looking on. Sally Summers, an activist in Wrangler jeans and hiking boots, suspiciously eyes a well-known kill buyer named Zena Quinlan. Then the auctioneer begins his racing beat.

▪ ▪ ▪

The federal Bureau of Land Management says the mustang population is out of control. Activists say the BLM has scapegoated an animal whose poise and dignity make it a symbol of the West. The two sides disagree on just about everything: on how to stem the growth of mustang herds, whether domestic cattle or wild horses do more damage to rangeland, whether mustangs are a native or invasive species.

Critics say the bureau bends to the interests of ranchers, who for generations have grazed their livestock on public lands leased for below-market cost. "The agency removes horses, but you don't see them taking cattle off the range," said Bob Edwards, a former BLM Wild Horse and Burro Program official. Officials counter that it's the animal activists who are inflexible. When the BLM proposed gelding more males, activists sued, saying it robbed stallions of their spirit.

Each year the BLM rounds up thousands of mustangs—pintos and bays, roans and grays—and trucks them off to be readied for adoption or sent to fenced-in Midwestern tracts, where ranchers are paid by the government to house the horses for the rest of their lives. About 31,500 remain on the range. On June 5, a panel from the National Academy of Sciences' National Research Council blasted the bureau's emphasis on roundups as "expensive and unproductive." The report called for more birth control—a vaccine for mares, chemical vasectomies for males—and urged the BLM to show greater transparency in how it operates.

■ ■ ■

In the bidding theater, the auctioneer continues his rat-a-tat patter. The animal advocates sit nervously amid a dozen men in blue jeans, boots and sweat-stained cowboy hats. Summers, who founded Horse Power, a Reno nonprofit whose mission is to protect the wild horses, looks across the stands to see whether Quinlan, the kill buyer, joins the action. Quinlan's arms are crossed. She's not bidding.

A stocky cowboy sipping a beer in the top row takes control of the action. With a flip of a finger, Jack Payne signals a bid and raises the price on a mare and foal. Usually, such a pair might fetch $300. But the price is already higher. As Laura Bell, representing the horse activists, raises the stakes by $25, the cowboy ups it $100. Finally the bidding ends. Bell takes the pair for $600.

Activists are stunned. At this rate, they won't be able to save all these horses. Led from the ring by a wrangler, the mare calls out, an entreaty answered by another mustang waiting in a corral just outside the auction floor.

■ ■ ■

The fight for America's mustangs dates back to 1950, when a Reno secretary named Velma Johnston spotted blood dripping from a truck loaded with wild horses bound for slaughter. Eventually known as Wild Horse Annie, Johnston spearheaded a movement to protect wild horses and burros. Soon even Hollywood got involved: The 1961 film The Misfits, with Clark Gable and Marilyn Monroe, portrayed a Nevada cowboy who becomes disgusted with brutal wild horse roundups. A decade later, the Wild Free-Roaming Horse and Burro Act directed the BLM to maintain a "natural ecological balance" among horses, wildlife and cattle. While signing the measure, President Richard Nixon cited the "indomitable spirit and sheer energy of a mustang running free."

In 2004, Conrad Burns, a Republican senator from Montana,

inserted a rider into an appropriations bill that permitted the sale of older or unadoptable horses. President George W. Bush signed the bill into law, opening the doors for mustang slaughter. In a corrective measure, Congress has passed appropriations language every year since 2005 to prohibit the BLM from selling horses to anyone who intends to have them killed. But wild horses taken from Native American reservations or state-managed lands—like the 23 up for auction in Fallon—receive no such protection.

■ ■ ■

At the auction house, Bell and Payne continue their bidding war. Another pair, a gray mare and her foal, go for $1,050. With another flip of his finger, Payne raises the price on a horse by $200.

"This is crazy," Bell says. She claims one mustang after another, but at a steep price.

"We're getting smoked," Summers says. She's gotten a tip that the aggressive bidder is the auction house owner. She runs down the stairs toward the auctioneer.

"He doesn't want these horses!" she yells. "He's driving up prices! That's illegal!"

The auctioneer looks up. After an awkward silence, he allows the bidding to continue and another horse is led into the ring.

■ ■ ■

A dozen mustang activists silently file out of the auction house. The evening's take: nineteen adult horses and four foals. No mustangs will go to slaughter. But the price astounds them.

Shannon Windle, president of the Hidden Valley Wild Horse Protection Fund, signs a check for $11,997.40, which includes taxes. In coming weeks, the activists will return to save scores of other mustangs, at a cost of $50,000.

Windle later complained to the state that auction owner Payne illegally drove up prices on the mustangs, animals that activists call the wild ones. Officials replied that, as a licensed bidder, Payne could buy horses at his own auction house. "If those horses weren't worth it, those ladies shouldn't have bid that high," Payne said. "But if they don't get 'em, I do. And I've got a home for 'em—a slaughterhouse in Mexico."

Summers and her colleagues load up horses that whinny and huff into the night air. She'll deliver three to an activist's ranch outside

Reno. As she drives her trailer west, toward the same stretch of highway where Wild Horse Annie first saw the bloody trailer, she's tired but philosophical. Sometimes, she laments, it feels like the activists have made little progress. "But tonight, we saved 23 horses that aren't going to slaughter. And that's a victory."

A sign welcomes travelers to the town of Eureka along "The Loneliest Road in America." Photo by David Becker.

Nevada's U.S. Highway 50:
A Road Less Traveled

Baker, September 2016. In 1977, when U.S. Highway 50 was still the road less traveled, just another anonymous stretch of asphalt traversing the American West, Denys Koyle's life took an unpredictable turn.

At age 28, she moved her young family from Huntington Beach, California, to this windblown frontier town on the state line between Nevada and Utah. She founded the Border Inn and scratched out a living tending to the occasional motorist who passed her ramshackle spread that baked under a relentless sun amid skittering lizards and prickly desert scrub brush. To squeeze out the day's last dollar, she would stand on the empty roadway well after dark, gazing up a 19-mile grade east into Utah: If she saw headlights descending, she'd stay open. Most times she closed. That was before Highway 50 became famous.

It was an unlikely stroke of luck for Koyle and countless merchants along this meandering two-lane road that bisects Nevada's midsection like an unadorned cowboy belt: In 1986—three decades ago this year— the old highway became known as "The Loneliest Road in America." That July, a single photograph and caption in *Life* magazine assured readers that Highway 50 wasn't just isolated, but downright lonely— something unpeopled and desolate, even apocalyptic. "It's totally empty," one American Automobile Association (AAA) official said of a 287-mile stretch between Fernley and Ely. "There are no points of interest. We don't recommend it. We warn all motorists not to drive there unless they're confident of their survival skills."

The stark image angered many Nevadans trying to promote the historic wilds of the Silver State as a national tourist destination. Many wanted to sue *Life*. State tourism officials turned a tin-horned, would-be insult into pure gold: a campaign featuring state-issued passports along with a dare to try to survive a ramble down this lonesome highway. Motorists soon flocked here from the United States, Europe and Asia, helping to revive the fortunes of struggling merchants such as Koyle. "The '90s were good," said the 68-year-old, her hair now a flash of white. "It's fun to go pay cash for a Lincoln Town Car."

Still, decades later, many locals ask: Is Highway 50 really all that lonely? The road became part of the Lincoln Highway, one of the first transcontinental routes for automobiles in the U.S. The U.S. 50 designation came in 1926. Today, the artery crosses a dozen mountain ranges—with summits called Pancake, Pinto and Little Antelope—descending into vast desolate valleys where the asphalt runs ramrod straight for 25 miles, passing the bombed-out shells of old mines and the weed-strewn cemeteries where Nevada's pioneers are buried. Now, lawless drivers often shoot game from the highway. On dirt roads that spiral off this way and that, cars kick up long, lazy trails of dust. One leads to the Hamilton ghost town, where enough silver was mined to help pay off some Civil War debt.

Along the way, scattered towns stand as testimonies to the past, as well as the early culture that was carved out here. In Eureka, there's an 1880 opera house that hosted plays, masquerade balls, dances and concerts. Ely's Hotel Nevada was once the state's tallest structure at six stories. The road features lead-footed travelers on the highway marking the shortest distance from Denver to San Francisco and locals in beater trucks hopscotching between towns at well under the speed limit. Government biologists are counting sage grouse, and two cross-country cyclists from Norway are greeted in one town with the offer of a free guest house and a refrigerator full of beer.

But Highway 50 is a fickle host.

■ ■ ■

Decades ago, before its "loneliest road" designation, bored wintertime drinkers at roadside bars wagered for drinks on how many vehicles would pass in an hour. Those who guessed one or none usually won.

Now, summer brings streams of tourists, whose stamped Highway 50 passports can earn them a certificate that proclaims, "I survived America's loneliest road." In just two hours, Koyle recently stamped a dozen passports brandished by tough-looking bikers and carloads of suburban families. "People stop in every little town and spend some money with their passports," she said. "And rural Nevada needs all the help it can get."

Ely resident Ferrel Hansen recalls a day when the powerful local casino owner stormed into his office. Norm Goeringer was a spark plug of a man. And he was spitting mad. He'd seen the magazine blurb about this loneliest road business, which he considered a slap in the face. "Norm was a volatile but reasonable man," recalled Hansen, then a local tourism official. "He wanted something done about it. And he wasn't the only one."

Hansen called state tourism officials. Rich Moreno, then a tourism public affairs officer, chased down the story. Turns out the *Life* writer never even drove the road, but dialed up some unnamed AAA adviser in Denver or someplace, who said he'd heard of some road up in Nevada that was pretty darned lonely. The AAA later sent a letter to businesses along Highway 50, apologizing that it had done them a disservice. But the damage had been done. "Ferrel wanted to sue *Life*, or at least demand a retraction," Moreno said. "And I'm thinking, 'Yeah, right.' But then my boss said, 'Well, what are we going to do?'"

Moreno's solution was to goof on the whole episode. He helped create a program that used a mock Western tone to challenge motorists to try their luck on Highway 50. Starting with a few hundred, the number of passports reached tens of thousands. Ely area tourism director Ed Spear still shakes his head at the irony: "I guess if you throw enough crap at the wall, some of it's going to stick."

Spear, 67, is an Ely resident whose conversations often meander like those of Hank Kimball, the county agriculture agent on the 1960s *Green Acres* TV show. Under Spear's direction, the community where "nobody lives inside the box" hosts such wacky events as chariot competitions and bathtub races at Cave Lake. Before that, folks set fires in the tubs—salvaged from a local hotel—and shot cannons at them. There are also fireworks shot from moving trains, an event Spear calls "the most fun you can have with your pants on."

But the loneliest highway campaign isn't without glitches. State tourism officials recently warned merchants to slow down handing out passports because there wasn't enough funding to print more of them. At the White Pine County tourism office, manager Wayne Cameron hands out a list of businesses where motorists could get their passports stamped. The problem: The word "loneliest" was spelled wrong. Cameron sighed. "The state did that."

Leslie Oliver is serving lunch at Pony Express Meats and Deli in Eureka, the place that bills itself as "the friendliest town on the loneliest road in America." She walks with a cast to help heal leg ligaments she tore in a hay-baling mishap. "I've never been lonely, and I've lived here all my life," she said.

That's probably because of characters such as Tony Rowley. At 64,

Rowley features a wiry gray beard, greasy cap and bib overalls. He's known as the mayor of this unincorporated town. There's even a rib-eye steak sandwich named after him at the deli because he spends so much time jawboning there. Rowley's grandparents delivered mail to ranches all along Highway 50, in the beginning by horse-drawn carriage. His mother ran the general store, selling old rocks and bottles, until she died a few years back. "Lonely? Rowley huffed. "We all moved out here to get away from people."

■ ■ ■

Down the road at Middlegate Station, a rustic bar and gas station on the site of an old Pony Express relay point, the sentiments are much the same. Serving up drinks behind the bar, co-owner Russ Stevenson schools tourists on the curiosities along his stretch of Highway 50. There are the petroglyphs that marked ancient Native American deer kills, the quirky roadside volcanic-rock graffiti fashioned by passersby, and the mysterious grave in the nearby salt flats that supposedly holds the bodies of two young girls who died of diphtheria on an 1850s wagon train; still dutifully kept up by an unknown benefactor.

But most people want to know about the shoe tree. On a pair of nearby cottonwoods hang hundreds of pairs of ballet shoes, red sneakers and screaming pink stilettos—an oddity that got its start in 1989 with a fight between newlyweds en route from Reno to Utah. As Russ' wife, Fredda Stevenson, tells it, the couple spent all their money gambling and pitched a tent under the tree. The bride threatened to walk home. That's when the groom threw her sandals on a branch. He then drove to Middlegate Station and told Fredda the story over a beer.

"If you want to stay married, you've got to apologize," she told him.

"But it was all her fault," he protested.

"If you learn to say you're sorry, you'll be happy the rest of your life," she said.

The couple later returned to throw their baby's shoes into the tree. Hundreds followed. But in 2011, a liquor-fueled local cut down the tree to spite his soon-to-be ex wife, who had shoes hanging there. Fredda and Russ hosted a memorial service attended by hundreds. Now more shoes have blossomed in a pair of nearby cottonwoods.

It's just the latest tale along America's loneliest road. "You're not going to see Nevada history driving Interstate 80," Fredda said. "On Highway 50, you can't miss it."

But, when it comes to sheer forlornness, Stevenson and others point to forsaken U.S. Route 6 that runs 167 miles between Tonopah and Ely, where you can drive for hours and spot maybe a cow, or maybe not. Now that, they say, is a lonely road.

Lethal Letha, the Big Cat Hunter

■ **Big Smoky Valley, February 2017.** The men arrived at Letha Roberson's house early, with crackers and beef jerky for the job of skinning and harvesting the downed mountain lion. But the one with the knife and the know-how provided a profound twist to this gritty ritual of the hunt: A woman was showing them how it was done.

The day before, Roberson guided Glen Stoner to a spot where he'd felled the big cat from its tree perch 300 yards away with a powerful shot from a high-powered rifle. Later, Stoner, his father and his grandfather joined Roberson to celebrate at a nearby bar as the regular drinkers marveled at the snarling carcass of a predator so stealthy many people here have yet to see one, let alone kill it.

In Western states such as Nevada, Utah, Idaho and Arizona, where mountain lion hunting is legal, many hunters go years without bagging a big cat. So the occasion called for countless shots of whiskey and gin. At midnight, Roberson had dragged the body of the big cat into the kitchen to keep it from freezing. Now it was time to skin the animal right there on her kitchen floor.

Roberson, a 43-year-old with short, brown hair, had skinned countless wild animals and could finish this 7-foot, 110-pound cat in a half-hour. She began expertly slicing away at the back leg with a scalping blade, equal parts butcher and surgeon. Hung over from the night before, she steadied her hand with a shot of rum in her coffee. The men watched in silent awe, as though witnessing an autopsy. "Well, that's it," said Donnie Stoner, Glen's father, gazing down at the body. "Cleaning fish is about as far as my wife would let me go in her kitchen."

■ ■ ■

For Roberson, a 140-pound Idaho-bred former tomboy, college rugby player, Army National Guard helicopter mechanic, mineworker and backwoods guide, the hunting, killing and skinning are all just part of an independent, rough-hewn rural lifestyle she has carved out for more than 20 years in this sweeping valley 250 miles north of Las Vegas.

The once-divorced daughter of a milkman works at the Round Mountain gold mine, the only woman to operate a 35-foot, 230,000-pound Caterpillar D-11 bulldozer that rumbles over crushed boulders with such shuttering vibration it often sends drivers to the chiropractor.

When she's not working, Roberson gathers up her yowling hunting dogs; the hounds are named Jesse, Walker and Tucker Two (Tucker One was killed by a mountain lion). She hops into her 2009 Dodge Power Wagon with the camouflage interior and vanity-plate acronym OMFR that suggests scaling "one more fucking ridge" and heads out in search of big cats.

Across the rustic American West, many women pride themselves as being as tough and self-sustaining as their fathers, husbands and sons. Yet even among this no-nonsense tribe, Roberson stands apart, staking her claim in a traditionally male-dominated domain. Corey Kemp, who drives a haul truck at the mine, is amazed by Roberson's pluck. "She's a wrecking ball," he said. "Letha doesn't ask you for help; you ask her for help." Kemp has seen Roberson maneuver her bulldozer up mining pit walls at impossible angles, performing dangerous jobs many male operators refuse to chance. "You see her and you say, 'Are you supposed to be doing that?'" Kemp said. "She's a real rarity."

Fellow hunter and mine worker Billy Berg describes Roberson by saying, "That's just Letha." Roberson was married 20 years when Berg noticed her lack of feminine ways. "I asked my dad, 'That's a girl?' But once you get to know her, you see that soft side. She's tough; she can hunt and drink with you, but she's got feelings and you have to remember that."

Roberson often feels like a misfit born 150 years too late, someone more at home in the Wild West than the new West. She avoids cities, doesn't like stoplights and wears a hard hat to work each day to reach her seat in a bulldozer cab that looms 15 feet off the ground. She speaks in a country twang and swears like a drill sergeant, often with a strong accent on the first syllable of words, like DEE-vorce and JU-ly. Her home is a gallery of animal trophies, with elk, mountain lions and raccoons hung on her walls.

On one table, several animal skulls surround a bottle of Wild Turkey, like some offering to the gods. Roberson has bagged bighorn sheep, coyotes, mule deer, antelope, badgers, foxes and bobcats and has climbed trees to face off with a cornered mountain lion. The only thing that scares her are snakes. On her wall hangs a photo of a mountain lion perched in a tree. "I liked that cat; it was pretty, so I took its picture." Asked if she then killed the animal, she nodded.

Roberson established her killer instincts early: When she played college rugby, teammates called her not Letha, but Lethal. She hasn't combed her hair in 15 years and has worn makeup just once—for her wedding. She's changed just one diaper in her life, as a 10-year-old babysitter. Roberson avoids the kitchen, surviving on instant ramen. She owns an arsenal of knives, pistols and shotguns, and carries a .44-caliber Magnum mini-rifle in her backpack. Her jeans pocket has a small worn circle from a round canister of chewing tobacco. "I have OCHD," she said, dressed in hunting gear and a camouflage cap, drinking from a camouflage coffee cup. "That's obsessive-compulsive hunting disorder."

Roberson no longer keeps a professional guide license in Nevada so only takes friends out on trips, folks like the bar owner whom she traded a guided hunt for an offer of "free drinks for life." She met the hunting Stoner family the previous week after Glen Stoner found her friend Connie Kendall's wallet in a grocery store parking lot and refused a reward. "Want to hunt a cat?" the women asked.

The big cat on the floor hadn't wanted to die. Berg's 14-year-old daughter shot it twice the previous day, and her father shot it once more. But the lion ran off, and Berg tracked it until sunset. The next day, he returned with Roberson to help finish the job. In the kitchen, the men marveled at the cat's will to survive. They noticed it was missing several toes, which they figured were lost in a trap.

They took turns skinning, asking, "What am I doing wrong here, Letha?" Connie Kendall arrived with her husband, Stan, and watched Roberson finally roll up the pelt, head still attached, like a blanket. Later, Roberson fried the meat in garlic and salt, and the group washed it down with gin-and-tonics and beers.

Before taking the pelt to a taxidermist, the hunters were required to present state game wardens with a premolar tooth and a small slice of tongue or muscle to help determine the cat's age. Most years, hunters are limited to two cats apiece, but harvested mountain lions remain a rarity in Nevada. In 2014-15, for example, the state issued 5,709 hunting tags but only 99 mountain lions were taken, for an average of 2 percent. That morning, there was no malice or bravado to Roberson's actions, just the necessary steps to get the job done.

Neighbors have called her to put down animals they are resistant to dispatching themselves. "She's real cold-blooded," Stan said, watching Roberson work. Answered Connie: "It helps."

■ ■ ■

Roberson got her first hunting license when she was 12. She killed her first deer with a single shot, and her grandmother taught her how to skin the animal. "I was hooked," she said.

She considered a career as a criminal investigator, but found herself drinking too much, until she "had a breakup with Jack" Daniel's and left college. She attended guide school in Montana and worked in Idaho and Colorado before taking a job in central Nevada in 1997. She married a fellow guide and helped run a farm in Oregon for eight years until she filed for divorce and returned to the Silver State. She related the breakup with the nonchalance of a snake shedding its skin. She doesn't think she'll marry again, saying she has no time to hold hands or go to movies. "I want to go where I go," she said. "With a husband, you've got to discuss things." Though she just might settle for a man who cooks, cleans and has a fire going when she gets home from work. Most importantly, he can't be a hunter; that's Roberson's role. For now, her policy toward men is "catch and release."

One winter afternoon, as she drove down Highway 376, Roberson discussed the thrill of the hunt. "It's the challenge of getting close enough to take the biggest, baddest, most-horned creature you can," she said. "It's facing an animal in its own element, knowing that I'm smart enough and stealthy enough to get there." With mountain lions, Roberson's real rush is running her dogs, hearing their yelps when trailing a big cat. But she doesn't always kill; she trails many elk or wildcats only to let them go. Most of all, Roberson relishes exploring the backcountry; canyons with names like Hell's Kitchen, Last Chance and Devil's Hole. She believes if you wear out one pair of boots in Nevada, you'll never leave. So she keeps old, not-quite-worn-out boots on fence posts around her property to remind her of adventures she's yet to have.

The change came after she was kicked in the head by a horse and nearly died. That's when I realized how short life is," she said. "I decided I just had to be me."

On a snowy morning, Roberson's pickup crept through the tiny hillside town of Manhattan, where residents had reported seeing a lingering mountain lion. Her eyes scanned the tree line. She let loose four dogs with their radio and GPS collars to give them some exercise, but could not locate the cat. At noon, Roberson pulled over to the roadside and snapped open a bottle of home-brewed beer provided by a friend. "Well," she said. "It's 5 p.m. someplace."

An hour before, she had barged up a narrow track through two feet of snow, the branches of pinion pines scraping the sides of her rig. She finally got stuck on a large boulder that stubbornly wedged beneath the truck chassis. Roberson never panicked. She swore once, and then sorted through her tool chest for a jack and a pair of tow straps. She wrapped her front-end winch cable around two pine trees for leverage and slowly dragged the asteroid-sized boulder out sideways. Roberson had done it again—dealt with just another roadblock wild Nevada placed in her path. "See," she said, "we didn't have to call no boys."

A Small-Town Museum
Struggles for Survival

■ **Beatty, December 2016.** Amina Anderson is the hardworking manager of this former mining boomtown's museum. She's so busy, in fact, that she can't always answer the telephone. As she worked on the ceiling of the new display wing in August, the phone rang way down below, her cue that an impatient outside world had once again come calling. "When you're alone up on a ladder holding a hammer and nails, it's hard to get there in time," she said. "I don't always make it." Such is the challenge of running a cash-strapped private museum where projects large and small are most often accomplished by the locals themselves—with volunteer time, know-how and, in many cases, even funding.

Across Nevada are tiny art, history and cultural outposts in rural areas whose survival depends on their ability to devise new and better ways to raise money. With county funds perpetually in jeopardy and national grants hit-and-miss, members of museum boards like the one in Beatty know that the only people they can really count on are museum visitors—from within the community and out of town alike.

In nearby Goldfield, for example, residents are taking donations to help establish a nonprofit museum in the town's long-abandoned high school. And in Winnemucca, the locally run Humboldt Museum used gift store receipts as well as public and private funding to create a mobile platform for its popular self-guided walking tours of the downtown area. "You have to think outside the box every single day," said Dana Toth, Humboldt Museum's executive director. "You can't be complacent because things are always changing." At 33, Anderson knows how to rally her community to get any job done.

Her schooling began in 2010 when she took over as museum manager, working in a converted Catholic church in this isolated town 120 miles north of Las Vegas. It quickly became clear that she needed more space. "There was no more room for new displays," Anderson said. "We had stuff stored behind stuff, stuff stored on top of stuff." She told the museum board that building a new wing would require

Amina Anderson struggles to keep her tiny museum afloat in the town of Beatty. Photo by David Becker.

an extraordinary think-on-our-feet effort. While the museum's operating costs were largely covered by a motel room tax, Nye County was enduring a cash shortage and could not be counted on for funding. That left local history buffs who had fallen in love with the little museum.

To solicit help, Anderson used both new and old methods. She scoured the internet for public and private grants as well as family endowments. She also posted notices on the museum's Facebook site and hung fliers at the post office. And people responded. A quarry owner donated truckloads of dirt to help level the once-hilly construction ground.

Eventually, in a stroke of luck, Anderson learned that the University of Nevada, Reno, had purchased a prefabricated 1,200-square-foot building it later found was too small for its purposes. The Beatty museum project bought it for a steal and had the dismantled structure delivered by truck.

One Saturday last June, after Anderson and scores of locals showed up at the site to do what they could, the water department donated a forklift that the fire chief delivered atop one of his trucks. "It was like an old-fashioned barn-raising," recalled Anderson, dressed in sneakers, a purple T-shirt and cargo shorts. "With a little community museum like ours, that's exactly how you do it." That was just the beginning.

That museum telephone? Anderson used it a lot. "I'd call the fire department and say, 'Hey, guys, I need some help with framing or drywall,' and they'd come," she said. She also harnessed the labors of community service workers and reached out to traditional funding sources. The town advisory board paid for the cost of electricity and split charges with the museum for a mammoth air-conditioning unit. Valley Electric, the local energy cooperative, connected the building to its lines free of charge.

Family precedent guides Anderson's insight and drive. Twenty years before, her grandmother, Claudia Reidhead had co-founded Beatty's original history museum in a cottage on her property. The facility later moved to another building in town and finally to the old church. During lean times, Reidhead paid the museum's electricity bill, later with the help of the town board. To raise money, local women sponsored town festivals where they held white elephant sales and auctioned handmade crafts such as crocheted doilies and pot warmers. One year, they threw a fashion show in the community center, attracting young men around town by advertising a swimsuit contest. The suits were vintage 1890s swimwear, worn by young models covered from head to toe. While no doubt disappointed, the young men all donated anyway. "My grandmother knew this about her town: History vanishes; it just disappears," Anderson said. "She knew that all the items used to settle this area are so easily lost, along with the old stories that make it all interesting. So they had to be collected." Her source of success, Reidhead said, was BST—"blood, sweat and tears."

Dennis McBride, director of the Nevada State Museum, knows how hard it is to keep a small private institution afloat: He's seen some efforts flourish and others fail. While working at the Boulder City Museum, McBride recalled, a woman asked his advice on how to start a small history museum in nearby Searchlight. "They were having problems raising money," he said. "They became a satellite of the Clark County Museum, establishing themselves with a more stable institution. It gave them the freedom of regular funding they knew was not going to go away."

But not all small facilities can pull off such a feat. When Toth wanted to create a mobile online system to update the self-guided tours of downtown Winnemucca's historic buildings, she knew that government handouts would not pay for the $2,200 system and $300 monthly maintenance. Her solution: She went to the visitor's authority, added a few grants and private donations and topped it all off with proceeds from the Humboldt Museum gift shop. Now Winnemucca's downtown walking tour has replaced the old paper pamphlets with a state-of-the-art cyber guide. "We want to keep things fresh and new," Toth said. "But finding the funds to accomplish that is usually the hard part."

In Beatty, residents unveiled the new museum space they built themselves. Anderson said community involvement slashed the $85,000 construction cost in half. And the volunteering goes on. Beatty resident Jim Weeks, who resembles Milburn Stone, who played "Doc" in the old *Gunsmoke* television show, used his own time to create a computer program detailing the folks who are buried in the town cemetery.

Anderson and her crew of volunteers keep their sense of humor. She shows a visitor a 100-year-old can of "jackrabbit's milk," its label advertising a "fast-action diet for lagging dragging salesmen, truck drivers, fishermen, hunters, miners, ranchers and talkative females. Keep away from stenos, office girls, beauty operators and waitresses." Anderson smirked and said, "I'm not sure I'd buy this." She gestures at a mannequin dressed up as one of the region's early miners. "He's not much of a conversationalist," she quipped, "but he's a great listener."

And so Beatty's tiny labor of love presses on. Sometimes, no one walks through the door. Other days, a busload of tourists might show up. Through it all, Anderson carries on her grandmother's vision. "I'm working on it," she said. "They're big shoes to fill."

Nevada's Starry Nights:
The Ultimate Cool

■ **Tonopah, December 2019.** The sun has just now set, casting the western horizon of this old mining town in a rich, glowing crimson as Russ Gartz strides out of a convenience store, prepared for yet another dark sky mission. "Look!" he calls out, like a boy in the back seat on a family vacation. It's a cry of pure astonishment, like he's spotted something he's never before seen. "The moon!" He points to a crescent disc that appears over the left shoulder of nearby Brock Mountain. "Hah!" Gartz says. "Hello, there!"

Far from the big city, where chronic light pollution drowns out the night skies above—those silent luminaries of mythology, wonder and surprise—the 58-year-old Gartz is one of Nevada's rural stargazers. On an early-winter evening, he's at it again—dressed in a red cap, two pairs of socks (two of everything, actually), ready for temperatures to dip into the high 20s.

Gartz likes to arrive early, so he can position his telescopes and binoculars just so, welcoming each new point of light as it appears in the darkening sky. He's like a dutiful social host, extending a hand to greet each arriving celestial guest at his regular evening star party. He starts up his old truck, hurrying to take his observational post just outside town. From there, he gazes up into the distant realm he calls "the heavens," suggesting that Gartz regards any communion with these night skies as a near-religious experience.

Usually, Gartz is on the lookout for such otherworldly celebrities as the Orion and Cassiopeia constellations or the seven sisters of the Pleiades, a nearby star cluster that appears even to the unaided eye. But he says he also likes the moon for its mysterious cultural references, reciting the poetry of Maleva the Gypsy from the 1941 film *The Wolf Man*:

Even a man who is pure of heart and says his prayers by night,

May become a wolf when the wolf bane blooms
* and the autumn moon is bright!*

In a state well known for the shimmering lights of the Las Vegas Strip, Nevada is getting some international recognition for something decidedly darker. It's the state's night skies. Because rural Nevada has some of the blackest nighttime skies on the planet.

■ ■ ■

Earlier this year, the isolated Massacre Rim Wilderness Study Area, in the state's far northwest reaches, was named as an International Dark Sky Sanctuary, only the seventh place on Earth to receive such a designation. Out there, the night skies are so dark, astronomers say, you can see your shadow by the light of the Milky Way.

But amateur stargazers such as Gartz say southern Nevadans don't have to travel that far to appreciate the nighttime darkness. From tiny Ely and Gerlach to the Great Basin National Park and even Tonopah, the heavens shine just as brightly. Friends of Nevada Wilderness, to help many forsaken high-desert communities use those dark skies to attract tourism, is developing brochures and advertising campaigns that each could use to promote themselves.

For five years, since it started its summertime Star Train, Ely has drawn tourists from as far away from Australia and China. At $41 per adult, the rides, which run 60 miles to the Great Basin National Park, bring business to local hotels and restaurants. Kyle Horvath, director of tourism for White Pine County, estimates that the economic boost from all of the Nevada Northern Railway's specialty theme rides is $3 million annually, a figure he says will rise "significantly" in the next few years. Leading the way are the nighttime stargazing rides, whose success has convinced the county to invest in other after-dark activities. They include nighttime photography seminars, sponsored hikes and family events at night-viewing parks. "New construction is required to use lighting that does not pollute our night skies, which bring a unique niche to our area," Horvath said.

Gartz is a guide at the Tonopah Star Trails and Star Park, which hosts summer events known as Star Parties. He sees the money and wonder stars bring into town. Once, a French couple asked him to hold their baby daughter as they looked through his telescope. On another night, a British tourist found the Andromeda galaxy without even using a star map. In winter, when visitors leave and temperatures plummet, Gartz sets up his telescope in his front yard for a one-man star party. "Stargazing is like fishing," he said. "You can plan all you want, but you never know what the weather will bring." Yet star-gawking is like fishing in another way. Said Gartz: "You've got to be patient."

A retired government worker, Gartz moved from California to Carson City and then again to Tonopah for the wide-open spaces his spirit craved. He has ruddy features and a gray-haired ponytail. In his spare time, he writes comic book fantasy novels about vampires and witches. But it's out here beneath the stars that his imagination really runs wild.

■ ■ ■

Look at any map that plots the United States at night and you'll see that most of the nation is dominated by light, so much so that an estimated 80 percent of Americans can no longer see the Milky Way.

The West is different, a place where the night is filled with delicious darkness. And Nevada skies are some of the darkest out there. In 2017, travel writer Oliver Roeder designated Gerlach, Nevada, in the Black Rock Desert as "The darkest town in America" in his search for the nation's least-lighted places. "On NASA maps, you can see the lights from Las Vegas, Reno and Salt Lake City. Then there's central Nevada," said Nichole Andler, chief of interpretation for the Great Basin National Park. "It's like a big hole in the middle of things, just really dark. It's wonderful and something Nevadans should be really proud of."

The reason? The lack of a human footprint. Most of rural Nevada is undeveloped, with ranchers and farmers clustered around water, always in short supply. The Silver State is also dominated by mountains and an array of higher, clearer altitudes—almost Martian in its unpeopled loneliness.

Melodi Rodrique, a physicist at the University of Nevada, Reno, uses remote access to the Great Basin Observatory in her astronomy class. She relishes her occasional drives to the Great Basin and its high-altitude observatory. "There's really nothing out there," she said. "You drive and you drive and you drive, and you don't see anybody or anything. There's nothing but beautiful desert."

But it's not just scientists who are drawn to Nevada's rural darkness. Great Basin National Park attracts 10,000 night sky visitors each year, many of them attending its annual astronomy festival.

Yet some believe the state can take better advantage of its natural wonders. "There are people worldwide who care about dark skies," said Shaaron Netherton, executive director of the nonprofit Friends of Nevada Wilderness. "And we've got them right here. They could provide an economic boost to a lot of small towns."

Netherton is producing brochures with new night sky tourism slogans, such as designating Nevada's isolated stretch of U.S. Route 6 as "The starriest road in America," a play on the old Highway 50 campaign, which boasted the road's loneliness. Then there's a tour she said could be called "Park to Park in the Dark." A joint application by Netherton's group and the Bureau of Land Management led to Massacre Rim's selection as an elite night sky sanctuary. The site now joins similar sanctuaries in New Mexico, Texas, Utah, New Zealand and Chile. But the area, 150 miles north of Reno near the Oregon and California borders, is so isolated, with so few roads, that most stargazers must hike in to find their viewing spots.

All across the outback, rural Nevadans get a kick out of introducing their city cousins to real darkness. "I like to take people out to the Black Rock Desert, set up chairs for the sunset and then lay down on blankets and just watch the stars," Netherton said. "Out there, you have a 360-degree view of the heavens."

Andler said the number of tourists who visit the park just to see the night stars increases every year. On those trips, she's often asked, "What's that fuzzy thing in the sky? They've never seen the Milky Way before. They're spellbound by the dark bands and dust clouds and the fact that there's so many stars."

Yet some rural Nevada old-timers have been enjoying the view for decades. James Heidman helped organize the Tonopah Astronomical Society, which once boasted 15 members until people moved away. Now 73, he's lived in Tonopah for 26 years and likes to search for what he calls "deep sky objects." "One night, it was so dark out there, the air was as still and crystal clear as can be," he recalled. "Jupiter has 50 or 60 moons, but only four of them are good-sized. On most nights, you can see them as mere points of light. But that night, we could see them as actual discs. It was pure wonder."

Some night sky watchers have explored deep space from within big-city limits. In 1997, Las Vegas lawyer and amateur astronomer John Mowbray photographed the Hale-Bopp comet as it hurtled over Red Rock Canyon at a brisk 43,000 miles per hour. Mowbray's story of capturing the elusive comet shows how mystical such nighttime

encounters can be. His father had recently died, and he felt philosophical as he ventured to Red Rock Canyon at dusk to set up his
tripod and camera. The evening was both cloudy and windy, and he
decided to call it a night. "Then the clouds parted, and I went crazy,"
he recalled. "I shot five rolls of film and drove to the Walmart, where
a nice lady and I worked together to develop the images."

Mowbray will always remember that night, and others like it, being
out there, alone, just him and the stars. "You stare up at the Orion
Nebula, where stars are formed, knowing that the light hitting your
retinas was generated 650 years ago," he said. "And you have to ask,
'Does it even exist anymore as I'm seeing it now?' It's like a time cap-
sule. And it puts a whole lot of things in your life into perspective."

■ ■ ■

On a recent October night, Gartz is finally in position, at a viewing
spot on the old Mizpah Mine site, overlooking downtown Tonopah.
The lights of the high school football complex suddenly drowned out
his usual post at the star park on the southern edge of town, so he has
moved on. The night is cold and his hands burn as he adjusts his telescopes, casting around in his orange tackle box for lenses and screws.

At long last, as a nearby dog barks, he's ready. "It's showtime!" Gartz
says. "Let's look into the skies!" He points out the Cassiopeia constellation, which he likens to "a bent question mark." Along with the
setting moon, he directs his telescopes toward Jupiter, where its four
visible moons can be seen lining up like planes preparing to land at
McCarran International Airport. Saturn—even its glorious rings—is
also clearly visible. By 8 p.m., it's so dark, even this close to town, that
Gartz negotiates by flashlight. "That fuzzy stuff is the Milky Way," he
observes. He points out a shooting star.

To answer questions from tourists, Gartz carries a trusty amateur astronomy guide. He also has an iPad on which the Star Walk
app breaks down the complex map of stars into mythological figures
as the ancients might have imagined them. "Each night, the heavens
expose just how little I know about them," he said. "But the views are
endless, and there's always time to learn."

As the night wears on, he continues his search of those Seven Sisters. But his quarry seems lost amid the endless pinpricks of glim-
mering light. The Ursa Major constellation, home of the Big Dipper,
sits on the northern horizon like a huge starry ladle. "Where are my

Pleiades?" he said. "I just saw you two nights ago." Finally, success. "The Pleiades!" he cries out. "Ah! There you are!"

After a few hours, Gartz packs up his telescopes. He could stay out here all night, a rural stargazer content to be out under Nevada's dark skies. But he has to work in the morning. "Nature," he says softly, "is the ultimate cool."

Nevada's Brothel Lobbyist: Promoting the World's Oldest Profession

■ **Carson City, May 2015.** Most lawmakers in this state capital simply call him "Georgie," a soft-spoken old opinion-swayer with a cane who revels in his political incorrectness. For half a century, George Flint held court in the hallways of the Legislature here, most lately in the first-floor coffee shop, at the round table nearest the elevators, so he didn't have to walk too far on his gimpy left leg and two replaced hips. Flint is Carson City's oldest political advocate, toiling on behalf of the world's oldest profession—a lone brothel lobbyist in the only state to sanction legal prostitution. Even at 81, he had intended to keep working, but a heart attack hit him last month. So now he's calling it quits to a career of using a folksy, lean-over-the-fence style to advocate the legal pleasures of the flesh.

The subject makes some lawmakers queasy, so he was surprised when the Speaker of the Assembly visited Flint's hospital bed with some news. Forty-one of 53 legislators had signed a proclamation declaring April 12 as "George Flint Day" at the capital, marking his "outstanding and valuable contributions as Nevada's longest-standing senior lobbyist." Flint keeps the document by his convalescent hospital bed, where he can continue to absorb the power of the gesture. "George should be a scholar on how to be a lobbyist," said state Senator Mark Manendo, who helped organize the decree. "People just love him, especially the old-timers."

Most admit that Flint isn't what you'd expect. He's a doting great-grandfather who—unlike cigar-chomping Joe Conforte, one of his brothel-owner bosses—never sashayed around town in a $2,000 suit with several slinky women hanging on his arm. Flint is savvier than that. He collects art, is an amateur expert on Napoleon and has traveled much of the world. But for decades he represented the interests of the more than 300 legal prostitutes working in the state's 17 brothels, shady hideaways with names like the Love Ranch, Angel's Ladies and the Cherry Patch II.

Oh, and there's another thing: Flint is also the son of two preachers, an ordained Pentecostal minister who runs Chapel of the Bells, a quickie wedding salon in downtown Reno. He can lecture on the history of adultery and paraphrases scripture discussing politicians who avoid him: "In the latter days, men's hearts will fail them for fear."

He's also a keeper of secrets: In the old days, lawmakers who fought him in public later discreetly sought freebie coupons at a brothel just 10 minutes from the Legislature. Flint has also challenged the Holy Rollers, insisting Jesus' best friend was a so-called fallen woman—Mary Magdalene. If a prostitute was good enough for Christ, he reasons, she ought to be good enough for the fine people of Nevada. It's also been good enough for Flint: Decades ago, he visited brothels—not as a lobbyist, but as a client: "I've never hidden the fact I've tasted that merchandise."

Mostly, however, Flint was just a good lobbyist. With a well-timed slap on the back, he put a friendly face on an industry many found repulsive. Years ago, the famed Mustang Ranch threw a steak-and-lobster party for legislators. Three showed up. He's also cagey, jokingly advocating a tax on all bedroom sex because, of course, everyone would overreport.

Born in San Pedro, California, Flint spent his youth in Wyoming, where brothels were illegal but accepted. A sportswriter in high school, he later studied theology in Des Moines, Iowa. In 1963, he was a married father of four running a wedding chapel in Reno when he heard about proposed legislation against the wedding industry. He drove to Carson City and persuaded lawmakers to retract the bill. "I made a note: Georgie, you better get involved," he said. "It was my baptism into lobbying."

In 1985, some 14 years after prostitution became legal here, he began representing an industry threatened by AIDS, speaking out in support of laws designed to protect sex workers and their clients. Many members of the Nevada Brothel Association attribute their longevity to Flint. "George would challenge commissioners who often didn't know what they were talking about," said Joe Richards, who once owned three brothels. "When George is gone, the industry's going to be history."

For years, Flint chased a desert mirage: Ten of Nevada's 16 counties allow brothels; he wants them welcomed statewide. That means bringing brothels to Las Vegas, supplying legalized sin to Sin City. Now, the 30,000 to 50,000 illegal sex workers in southern Nevada bring crime and drug use. Making brothels legal, he insists, would put that shadow economy out of business.

Not everyone agrees. In 2010, when Flint approached Barbara Buckley, then Speaker of the Assembly, "She said, 'George, get the hell out of my office,'" he said. "I told her, 'I get the hint; I'll come back later.'" Later, when he made his case to former Clark County Sheriff Doug Gillespie, the lawman cut him off. The lobbyist recalled: "He said: 'Flint, you don't need to explain anything to me. But let me tell you something: Keep your [butt] out of Clark County.'"

Buckley recalls that she liked Flint far more than his industry. "He's a character. He cared about his work," she said. In a meeting to discuss a proposed state tax on brothels, Flint went on the offensive. "Oh, the puns," Buckley recalled. "He said, 'What would you tax—this or that?' I never want to relive that again."

These days, Flint knows that troubled times lie ahead: Thanks to Craigslist and burgeoning sex-for-sale websites, legal prostitution is imperiled in Nevada. Of the state's remaining brothels, only a handful make a profit, he said. His budget for political contributions has dropped from $100,000 annually to $20,000. He senses a political shift. This year, freshman lawmakers bring modern ideas. Sighed Flint: "Another anti-brothel movement can't be far off."

But the one-man brothel lobbyist has a successor in mind: his own daughter, Margaret, who currently advocates for animal rights. Trouble is, she doesn't want the job. "I don't have a passion for brothel workers," she said. "That's my dad."

Flint will miss the fine art of brothel opinion-swaying. "My heart is there. It's hard to give up."

One Man's Hard-Luck Castle

■ Goldfield, January 2016. Randy Johnston's crowning achievement sits upon a dusty mountaintop in desolate Esmeralda County, looking more like a castle than one man's desire to poke a stick in the eye of every construction inspector who ever cramped his builder's style.

It is a citadel of sorts—built to last 1,000 years, with block walls 16 inches thick, seven tons of steel rebar on the same concrete foundation used in bomb shelters and not a stick of wood in the framework: all to outlast the worst vicissitudes the bone-dry high desert can dish out. Johnston spent $3 million on his stylish, 8,000-square-foot mountain redoubt, well, because he could.

The consummate tinkerer spent three decades in Lake Tahoe, constantly harassed by local government inspectors who poked their noses into his every pet project, right down to a side-yard toolshed. Then, on a weekend off-roading adventure in the Nevada desert near Goldfield, 150 miles north of Las Vegas, he stumbled onto a place where a man with a little money, imagination and a two-by-four-strong sense of pluck can build whatever he damn well pleases. "No fees, no inspections, no permits, no nothing," he says. "Nobody to come out and say, 'You can't do that. Color's not right. Dimensions are wrong.' It was enough to drive a man crazy."

And so in 1998, after receiving a sizable inheritance, Johnston chucked his overregulated California life and began work on his circular mountain masterpiece—with its 22 rooms, winding staircase, ornate tile work, two mammoth pipe organs and a rooftop observatory affording views of mountains and valleys that stretch into forever. It's one man's quirky vision, a thumb-your-nose project built without blueprints, one brick at a time, mostly with his own hands, (with the occasional help of local fellas named Denny, Doc and Kenny), heeding only to the dictates of his own imagination.

He calls it the Hard Luck Castle, named after the abandoned 19th-century mine at the end of a dirt road nine miles from the nearest pavement. For years, Johnston has offered tours to fellow desert wanderers and Death Valley tourists who want an inside look at the place that runs on a few generators, but mostly on solar and wind power.

Now, at age 69 with his passion project nearing completion, Johnston is throwing in the trowel. The place has been for sale for years, but now he feels the clock ticking. His health is beginning to teeter, he says, and doctors are scarce among the Joshua trees and howling coyotes in the Nevada outback. He's also weary of the 250-mile round trip to Pahrump for groceries and supplies.

The final insult came when a flood closed Highway 267, stopping the flow of visitors whose $10 tour donations helped keep him going after his inheritance ran out. In the past two months, not one traveler has crossed the flatlands into the Gold Mountains to see Johnston's attraction, which includes 40 deeded acres and the old mine.

"The entire Hard Luck Mine and Castle estate is for sale," his website reads. "Everything—and we mean everything—comes with the sale. All the owner wants to leave with is his truck, his trailer, and his dogs." He recently slashed the asking price from $3.2 million to $1.5 million. Still, no one with a checkbook has ventured to look at the place. "I've had a few calls, but nothing more than that," Johnston says. "And most of those people were asking about the mine." It's enough to make a man think no one appreciates his personal vision.

Now he sits out in the desert, putting the last touches on his dreamscape, with his two dogs, Hunk and Molly, as his only company. But Johnston isn't feeling sorry for himself. He likes telling how his castle came to be—about the 1986 off-roading trip in a souped-up Volkswagen bus when he and his son discovered a cabin at the site, where they took shelter in a snowstorm. He fell in love with the place and returned year after year. Finally, after countless lunches courting the reluctant owner, he bought the property for $17,000.

Disaster struck with the first load of gravel he hauled up the winding dirt road. A broken axle forced him to abandon his old trailer among the rocks and scrub brush, decorating it with Buddhist, Christian and hedonist figures to resemble a wacky altar to some mad new religion. For Johnston, that religion is building whatever the hell you want.

He keeps tinkering, waiting to install the last bit of circuit board for his pair of 3,000-pipe organs. He wants to build a campground with a pyramid-shaped carport. He's also putting the finishing touches on an obelisk that defines his unique vision: On various sides he has listed the names and election dates of all the U.S. presidents. He plans to add historical footnotes, Egyptian hieroglyphics, words of wisdom and his personal collection of slang words. "You know," he says, "like 'bitchin', and 'far out.'"

For now, the long winter months have become kind of lonely as he waits for a visitor, a would-be buyer, anyone really, to maybe venture out to appreciate his handiwork. He has no regrets. "Hell, no, I love this place," he says. "But trying to sell it is a pain. Eventually, I'll find someone who wants to come out here and keep the place going." When that happens, Johnston plans to pursue another dream that involves registering a 50-foot sailboat in Panama and disappearing on a new adventure.

And what if his sturdy mountain castle does stand for a millennium? How would he want future desert-dwellers to remember its creator? "Oh, I don't know," he says, scratching his head. "Maybe just as some idiot who built his dream house out in the middle of nowhere."

The Keeper of the Keys
at a Ghost Hotel

■ **Goldfield, January 2016.** For three decades, Virginia Ridgway has been the keeper of the keys to an inn known worldwide for its posh history and guests who so enjoyed the accommodations they refused to leave—the ghosts of the Goldfield Hotel. The long-shuttered building celebrated its last paying customer in 1945. It sits forlornly empty at the center of a mining boomtown three hours northwest of Las Vegas.

But still the curious come: fans of the paranormal and history buffs who want a glimpse of the place once considered one of the most elegant overnight stays in America's West. They park along U.S. Highway 95 to peer through the windows, scanning a classic revival-style lobby trimmed with mahogany that features the original black-leather couches, guided columns and guest niceties now covered with dust.

They take pictures and flag down locals for questions. But there's only one way to actually get inside and that's to call the 82-year-old Ridgway, who lives just a block away. Some try to shove cash at her, others wave press credentials, but as Ridgway says in her smooth west Texas drawl, "I can't let anybody in unless I'm with them."

She's always been partial to those who share her penchant for the paranormal. Since the early 1980s, under two owners, she's led countless tours, visiting her favorite haunted rooms, conversing with their eternal inhabitants But the aging gatekeeper is handing over her ring of keys. Two bad hips mean that the watchful one will soon step aside as the 24-hour caretaker. "I just can't do it anymore," says Ridgway, who sits in a wheelchair. "I got two broke hips. I can't even get myself up the front three steps to walk into that hotel."

Carrying on will be Malek Davarpanah, an antique-shop owner who, like Ridgway, carries a torch for the four-story hotel christened in 1907 in an opening ceremony where champagne reportedly poured down the ornate front steps.

The Goldfield was the definition of luxury, featuring running water and private baths, an on-call doctor, crystal chandeliers, an elevator and telephone service to every room—its U-shaped design ensuring that every guest room enjoyed an outside view. The hotel shut its doors at the end of World War II; its last guests were officers and their families stationed at the Tonopah Army Air Field. In 1982, it was included on the National Register of Historic Places.

Davarpanah, 50, who volunteers with Goldfield's Chamber of Commerce, gets hundreds of calls a year from those seeking entry into the hotel, but always passes them on to the hotel's longtime guardian. "Most are persistent," he says. "They say they're willing to pay. They just want to get in there."

Ridgway's affinity for the Goldfield began in the 1960s. A fan of murder mysteries and a believer in the otherworldly, she insists there were people inside to greet her. "There were people everywhere, in the lobby and in the hall," she says. "Other people couldn't see them, but I could."

A decade later, she opened an antique and curio shop called the Glory Hole, just across the street from the Goldfield. Whenever she saw outsiders peering into the hotel's windows, she walked over to fill them in on its history. Eventually, its owner gave her keys to conduct free tours. "You never charge for the things you love doing," she says.

The Goldfield has enjoyed some Hollywood-style exposure such as appearing in the 1971 film *Vanishing Point* as the site of a radio station. It has also hosted numerous cable TV paranormal investigation shows such as *Ghost Hunters*. Still, nothing frightens Ridgway about the Goldfield. "To me this is a happy hotel," she says. "The entities there choose to exist there."

Over the years, Ridgway's tours have made believers out of doubters. "I didn't believe any of that stuff before I visited the hotel with Virginia," said Yvonne Roberts, whose father, Red Roberts of Carson City, is the hotel's out-of-town owner. "My dad has always brushed these things off. But now I feel differently." Ridgway tells a tale of the spirit who lives on the first floor: a woman named Elizabeth who she says was impregnated generations ago by the then-hotel owner.

Janice Oberding, who has known Ridgway for 15 years, says the key keeper has become a cult figure in the paranormal community. "People who want to get in good with her always bring flowers for Elizabeth," she says. "The last time I was there, Elizabeth's room was just full of flowers and toys, which pleases Virginia to no end."

Yet now months have passed since Ridgway has set foot in the hotel. On a recent day, she hands over the keys so Davarpanah can show a visitor around. He stands outside in the winter cold, fiddling with the lock. "Don't be surprised if we get some unwanted visitors," he says. "Once this door is open, people will be here. Everyone has stories. They see the open door and they flock like vultures."

He quickly slides inside, showing off a hotel check-in desk with the ancient mail slots and telephone switchboard sitting silent. The Goldfield's soon-to-be guardian says he likes the feel of the place, but prefers not to discuss whether he believes in ghosts.

But Ridgway believes. She's even got a second-floor room picked out to inhabit after she dies. "I'm kind of excited; it's gonna be fun," she says. "When visitors come, I'm going to spray them with gardenia cologne. That's how they'll know I'm there."

Epilogue:
An Old Fox Named Lamb

■ **Clark County, May 2021.** I've profiled a lot of characters for this book, but probably the one who best represents the stubborn grit that comes in such great supply across rural Nevada is an old wrangler named Ralph Lamb. He's gone now, but don't fool yourself; Ralph was no lamb. More like a fox or a coyote or maybe even a wolf.

He was one of 11 kids born on a ranch in Alamo. Both his grandfather and father, William Grainger Lamb, died in horse accidents. Lamb's granddad was thrown at night during a cattle drive, and his father was crushed while trying to save a 12-year-old boy whose horse had bolted during a rodeo. Ralph and his siblings took odd jobs to help make ends meet during the Great Depression.

Ralph was country come to town—with a vengeance. In the 1960s and '70s, he was considered one of the most powerful men in Nevada, a kid from the sticks who served as the Cowboy Sheriff of Clark County—the closest thing America had to the Old West, with gangsters substituting for gunslinging cowboys.

In those days, Vegas was a pretty rough place, barely urban; more like Elko but with more casinos. Ralph's job was "keepin' things cleaned up" with a blunt my-way-or-the-highway rule of law unparalleled in today's policing world, a mix of shrewd country wisdom and what critics called the capriciousness of a conniving big-city politician.

Ralph's brother Floyd was a Nevada senator and before Ralph was voted out of office in 1978, word was that you didn't do nuthin' in Clark County—open a strip club, build a casino or even pass gas—without consulting the Lamb boys first.

In the '60s, Ralph arrested a few dozen Hells Angels, gave them haircuts and dismantled their sacrosanct motorcycles. He demanded that the Beatles show up personally in his office to apply for an entertainment license to perform on the Strip.

In his day, Ralph broke noses and rearranged dental work, "monkeying up" wanna-be mobsters with "the language those boys understood." My favorite story was how he once grabbed John "Handsome

Johnny" Roselli by the tie and worked him over in the lobby of a crowded casino. A reporter said the sheriff "slapped the cologne" from the tough guy's face.

■ ■ ■

When I interviewed Ralph for the Los Angeles Times in 2012, he had long ago stepped away from the public limelight, but he still carried weight around town. That year, CBS premiered a series titled Vegas, starring Dennis Quaid, who took on the persona of a 1960s-era sheriff named—what else?—Ralph Lamb. Ralph was pleased by the portrayal. Even then, he laughed about his tough-guy image. "A lot of guys could have whipped me," he says. "They just never came along." He continued riding rodeos until failing eyesight sidelined him at age 83.

I met him in a diner in North Las Vegas, not far from the boulevard that bears his family name, and the waitress brought him to his regular table, served him coffee and his usual dish without asking. With a whiskered face peeking out from beneath a cowboy hat, Ralph still had the aura of an old-school lawman. He spoke with a gravelly twang, as down to earth as dirt, whether he was ordering a second slice of apple pie or saying things like. "Well, hell, John, why don't you come up to the house and we'll talk about it?"

Ralph made his share of enemies over decades in law enforcement. One was a young lawyer named Oscar Goodman, who in 1999 became the mayor of Las Vegas. In the 1970s, Goodman represented "a lot of folks whose last names ended in vowels that Lamb didn't want around town. Goodman always insisted that Ralph was on the take. "He always wore suits way beyond his salary," he said. "I can't put it any other way."

Ralph's eyes narrowed that day eating apple pie when I told him what Goodman had said. "I always stayed clean, I just dressed up," he said. "I knew where I belonged."

While Ralph was eventually investigated for federal income tax fraud, he was acquitted. Years later, he still felt shame over the episode. He said he never took a dime that wasn't his. "It hurt me," he said of the investigation.

I left my interview convinced that Ralph was the real deal. And I was sure-as-hell glad I'd decided to forgo the cologne that day.

■ ■ ■

Weeks passed after our interview, and I stayed busy as a journalist covering the American West. One weekday morning, I woke up in Madison, South Dakota, where I was reporting a story on vengeance long delayed.

Not long before my arrival, Norm Johnson, a high school sports coach, answered a knock on his door to come face-to-face with a man from his distant past. The man twice asked Johnson's name. When he was finally sure of his identity, the intruder shot the 72-year-old Johnson twice in the face, leaving him to die on the doorstep of his tidy brown-clapboard home. Carl Ericsson later told police that he killed Johnson to avenge a long-ago locker room prank: In high school, Johnson, then the star football quarterback, had put an athletic supporter over Ericsson's head for laughs. He stewed over the slight for decades before finally deciding to strike back. Now he faced first-degree murder charges.

A phone call woke me at my hotel while I was still in the middle of my reporting. It was an editor in Los Angeles, and she was breathless. The night before, during a midnight screening of the film *The Dark Knight Rises*, James Holmes had walked into a Century 16 movie theater in Aurora, Colorado, and opened fire, killing a dozen people and injuring scores of others. I needed to get on a plane for Colorado.

As I packed for the airport, I checked my Blackberry to find more than a hundred messages, all of them critical. I was a jerk, a fraud, someone who had besmirched the reputation of a great American. Pretty quickly, I was able to figure out what was happening. And it wasn't good.

My Ralph Lamb profile had run that morning on the newspaper's front page. The night before, during a spell-check by the copy desk, a computer glitch had altered a single word of my story, but it was enough to set my world on fire. Toward the end of the story, I used a simple transition to describe how the once-popular Sheriff Lamb had finally been voted out of office in 1978. My paragraph read as follows: "But cracks eventually appeared in Lamb's public persona. Critics believed that as both sheriff and chairman of the county's regulatory Liquor and Gaming Control Board, Lamb had opportunities for malfeasance." But the computer added a second letter t to the word but, making it butt. The new sentence: Butt cracks eventually appeared in Lamb's public persona.

I checked my voicemail. There were 30 messages. Along with irate readers were reporters from a Los Angeles television station and a weekly culture magazine. Apparently, butt cracks in the *Los Angeles Times* was news. But before I began any damage control—not to mention catch my plane to Colorado—I had one call to make. I needed to call Ralph. To apologize. He was a proud man who didn't deserve any ridicule. He picked up the line and spoke in that gravelly country voice. When I explained what had happened, there was a pause.

"Well, hell, John," Ralph said. "I thought you meant that line." Then the kicker. "I kinda liked it."

All was well with Ralph, and that was important to me.

"Well, sheriff," I said. "If it's OK with you, then it's certainly OK with me."

I headed off into my reporter's day from hell.

Ralph died three years later, at age 88. Rural Nevada had lost one of its own.

ABOUT THE AUTHOR

John M. Glionna was a Seoul-based *Los Angeles Times* foreign correspondent from 2008-2012 and covered South Korea, North Korea, Japan, Australia, New Zealand, the Philippines, Indonesia, Malaysia, Singapore and the Pacific Islands. Later, as the paper's Las Vegas bureau chief, he covered the American West, writing about everything from people to politics. He has written extensively about California and co-taught a journalism course at the University of Nevada, Las Vegas. Currently a freelance writer, he divides his time between Las Vegas, San Francisco and Los Angeles.

PERMISSIONS AND SOURCE ACKNOWLEDGMENTS

The author gratefully acknowledges the following publications for permission to reprint stories originally published in their pages. All stories remain under copyright by the original publisher:

Las Vegas Review-Journal

"The Rural Nevada Football Team That Rarely Scores," originally published as "Rural Nevada football team scores on the field of life," October 14, 2018.

"Coach 17: Preserving Nevada's Railroad History," originally published as "Historic railroad car finds new life in Northern Nevada," July 29, 2018.

"Frank Van Zant's Feverish Rural Dream," originally published as "Northern Nevada monument pays tribute to Native American culture," July 7, 2018.

"A New Vintage for Nevada Farming," originally published as "Fifth-generation farmers put own stamp on land in Nevada," January 4, 2016.

"The Denim Hunters," originally published as "Prospectors search for denim gold in old Nevada mine shafts," January 3, 2019.

"Queens of the Mexican Rodeo," originally published as "Escaramuza riders preserve piece of rural Latino culture," June 21, 2020.

"Former Addict Helps Keep Rural Addicts Clean," originally published as "Sarge, an ex-user, helps coordinate Nye County drug program," June 13, 2016.

"The Beard of Knowledge," originally published as "End of the line for Mark Hall-Patton," March 4, 2021.

"The Coffee Cup: Tending to Hearts and Stomachs," originally published as "Boulder City's Coffee Cup earns place in hearts of diners," February 10, 2018.

"Death Squad: Sorting Out the Remains of the Rural Dead," originally published as "Macabre duties all in a day's work for Nye County official," May 6, 2018.

"Outback Nevada's Women Pioneer Pals," originally published as "Pioneer women reflect on life, friendship in Nevada outback," April 30, 2016.

"Where the Drinkers—and the Chickens—Come Home to Roost," originally published as "Manhattan saloon recalls bygone era in rural Nevada," July 24, 2016.

"The Circuit Judge Upholds an Old-Time Tradition," originally published as "Traveling circuit judge in Nevada a throwback to bygone era," March 20, 2016.

"At This Joint, You Swallow Your Politics with Your Food," originally published as "At Austin's International Cafe and Bar, prepare to swallow politics with your food," July 10, 2016.

"A California Family Breathes New Life into a Historic Nevada Town," originally published as "Family plans to bring new life into Tonopah," February 6, 2016.

"Dodging a Virus in Esmeralda County," originally published as "Inside the Nevada county that the coronavirus has skipped—so far," August 16, 2020.

"Steel and Sweat: Forging Yesterday's Tools," originally published as "Third-generation machinist keeps wheels turning for Tonopah mining-centric economy," December 18, 2016.

"An Architectural Gem Rises from the Ruins," originally published as "An architectural gem from Nevada's past is returning from ruin," March 6, 2016.

"Jim Marsh's Rural Dream," originally published as "Las Vegas car dealer Jim Marsh built replica 19th century chapel," November 26, 2018.

"A City Girl with a Pickup, an Attitude and a Mission to Save Wild Horses," originally published as "Activist chronicles wild horse round-ups to guard against mistreatment," March 14, 2016.

"Being a Gay Mayor in Nevada's Outback," originally published as "Nevada's first gay mayors have deep roots in Silver State," November 25, 2019.

"When Death Calls, Jay Gunter Answers the Phone," originally published as "When death calls in rural Nevada, Jay Gunter picks up the phone," April 23, 2016.

"A Small-Town Police Blotter Tells Tall Tales," originally published as "Who's in trouble in Ely? Check the police blotter," April 17, 2016.

"The Last Straw: A Rural Home Built from Hay," originally published as "Reno woman realizing dream of simple, rural life in straw-bale home," February 21, 2016.

"Keeping a Dying Native American Language Alive," originally published as "Shoshone tribal member passes on native language," May 1, 2016.

"Oddly Named Towns Recall Nevada's Colorful Past," originally published as "Oddly named towns hark back to Nevada's colorful past," January 3, 2016.

"Lessons of a One-Room Schoolhouse," originally published as "Rural school a throwback to era of one-room schoolhouse," August 5, 2018.

"Nevada's U.S. Highway 50: A Road Less Traveled," originally published as "Loneliest road in America suits Nevada residents just fine," September 17, 2016.

"Lethal Letha, the Big Cat Hunter," originally published as "Mountain lion hunter tracks big cats in Nevada outback," February 11, 2017.

"A Small-Town Museum Struggles for Survival," originally published as "Museum operators find resourceful ways to keep the doors open at rural Nevada cultural outposts," December 16, 2016.

"Nevada's Starry Nights: The Ultimate Cool," originally published as "Nevada's dark skies draw tourists, locals to view natural wonders," November 27, 2019.

"One Man's Hard-Luck Castle," originally published as "Tinkerer wants to sell dream castle in Goldfield for $1.5 million," January 16, 2016.

"The Keeper of the Keys at a Ghost Hotel," originally published as "Ghost Guardian: Keeper of keys at Goldfield hotel soon to turn over responsibilities," January 17, 2016.

Los Angeles Times

"Flash and Mr. Cool," originally published as "He was 'goofy and innocent and often annoying,' but he inspired a tough town to celebrate eccentricities," September 24, 2019

"The Priest Who Conducts Mass in a Casino," originally published as "This Catholic priest celebrates Mass in a casino. He calls prayer a 'sure bet,'" December 25, 2016.

"The Cowboy Commissioner," originally published as "In Nevada, cowboy commissioner rides a career as political maverick," March 1, 2015.

"The Reluctant Innkeeper," originally published as "Gold Point, Nev., has a population of six. One of them runs the inn. It's not exactly his calling," August 5, 2019.

"Wild Horse Auctions," originally published as "Auction sends wild horses to sanctuary—or slaughter," June 13, 2013.

"Nevada's Brothel Lobbyist: Promoting the World's Oldest Profession" originally published as "Nevada brothel lobbyist put a friendly face on often-reviled industry," May 5, 2015.

Desert Companion

"Cowboy Ministers," originally published as "The Gospel of Bo: Cowboy Preacher Ministers the Nevada Range," Fall 2021.

"Jack Malotte: A Rural Native Artist Gets Political," originally published as "Self-Drawn Man," Fall 2021.

"The Coyote Hunters," originally published as "Dogs," December 2018.

"The Last Sheepherder," originally published under same headline, October 2019.